DATE DUE

American Civil War
Biographies

American Civil War Biographies

Kevin Hillstrom
and
Laurie Collier
Hillstrom

Lawrence W. Baker, Editor

AN IMPRINT OF THE GALE GROUP

DETROIT · SAN FRANCISCO · LONDON
BOSTON · WOODBRIDGE, CT

American Civil War: Biographies

Kevin Hillstrom and Laurie Collier Hillstrom

Staff

Lawrence W. Baker, *U•X•L Senior Editor*
Carol DeKane Nagel, *U•X•L Managing Editor*
Tom Romig, *U•X•L Publisher*

Rita Wimberley, *Senior Buyer*
Evi Seoud, *Assistant Production Manager*
Dorothy Maki, *Manufacturing Manager*
Mary Beth Trimper, *Production Director*

Michelle DiMercurio, *Art Director*
Cynthia Baldwin, *Product Design Manager*

Shalice Shah-Caldwell, *Permissions Specialist*
Pamela Reed, *Imaging Coordinator*
Leitha Etheridge-Sims, *Cataloger*
Robert Duncan, *Senior Imaging Specialist*
Michael Logusz, *Imaging Specialist*
Randy A. Bassett, *Image Database Supervisor*
Barbara J. Yarrow, *Imaging and Multimedia Content Manager*

Marco Di Vita, Graphix Group, *Typesetting*

Library of Congress Cataloging-in-Publication Data

Hillstrom, Kevin, 1963–
    American Civil War. Biographies / Kevin Hillstrom and Laurie Collier
Hillstrom ; Lawrence W. Baker, editor.
        p. cm.
    ISBN 0-7876-3820-X — ISBN 0-7876-3821-8 (v. 1) — ISBN 0-7876-3822-6 (v. 2)
        1. United States—History—Civil War, 1861–1865—Biography. 2. United
States—History—Civil War, 1861–1865—Biography—Miscellanea. I. Hillstrom,
Laurie Collier, 1965– II. Baker, Lawrence W. III. Title.

E467.H656 1999
973.7'092'2—dc21
[B]
                                                                99-046920

Contents

v

Advisory Board

Special thanks are due to U•X•L's Civil War Reference Library advisors for their invaluable comments and suggestions:

- Deborah Hammer, Former Librarian, Queens Borough Public Library, Jamaica, New York

- Ann Marie LaPrise, Librarian, Detroit Public Library, Elmwood Park Branch, Detroit, Michigan

- Susan Richards, Media Specialist, Northwest Junior High School, Coralville, Iowa

Reader's Guide

American Civil War: Biographies presents biographies of sixty men and women who participated in or were affected by the Civil War. These two volumes profile a diverse mix of personalities from both the North and the South, including military leaders, politicians, abolitionists, artists, spies, and escaped slaves. Detailed biographies of major Civil War figures (such as Abraham Lincoln, Jefferson Davis, Ulysses S. Grant, Frederick Douglass, Robert E. Lee, Stonewall Jackson) are included. But American Civil War: Biographies also provides biographical information on lesser-known but nonetheless important and fascinating men and women of that era. Examples include Thaddeus Lowe, the daring commander of the Union's manned balloon corps; Mathew Brady, the famed Civil War photographer; and Rose O'Neal Greenhow, a Confederate spy who drowned during an attempt to smuggle gold into the South in the hoops of her dress.

American Civil War: Biographies also features sidebars containing interesting facts, excerpts from diaries and speeches, and short biographies of people who are in some way connected with the leading figures of the era. Within each full-length biography, boldfaced cross-references direct readers to other individuals profiled in the two-volume set. Finally, each volume includes photographs and illustrations, an "American Civil War Timeline" that lists significant dates and events of the Civil War era, and a cumulative subject index.

American Civil War Reference Library

American Civil War: Biographies is only one component of a three-part American Civil War Reference Library. The other two titles in this multivolume set are:

- *American Civil War: Almanac:* This work presents a comprehensive overview of the Civil War. The volume's fourteen chapters cover all aspects of the conflict, from the prewar issues and events that divided the nation to the war itself—an epic struggle from 1861 to 1865 that changed the political and social landscape of America forever. The chapters are arranged chronologically and explore such topics as the events leading up to the war, slavery, Europe's view of the war, the secession of Southern states, various Civil War battles, and Reconstruction. Also included are two chapters that cover two unique groups during the Civil War: women and blacks. The *Almanac* also contains over ninety photographs and maps, "Words to Know" and "People to Know" sections, a timeline, and an index.

- *American Civil War: Primary Sources:* This title presents fourteen full or excerpted speeches and written works from the Civil War. The volume includes an excerpt from Harriet Beecher Stowe's *Uncle Tom's Cabin,* President Abraham Lincoln's Emancipation Proclamation and Gettysburg Address, and the letters between Union general William T. Sherman and Atlanta, Georgia, city leaders. Each entry includes an introduction, things to remember while reading the excerpt, information on what happened after the work was published or event took place, and other interesting facts. Photographs, source information, and an index supplement the work.

- A cumulative index of all three titles in the American Civil War Reference Library is also available.

Acknowledgments

The authors extend thanks to Larry Baker and Tom Romig at U•X•L for their assistance throughout the production of this series. Thanks, too, to Christine Alexanian for her quick and thorough copyediting and Amy Marcaccio Keyzer for lending her considerable editorial talents in the form of proofreading. The editor wishes to thank Marco Di Vita at Graphix Group for always working with common sense, flexibility, speed, and, above all, quality. Admiration, love, and a warm hug go to Beth Baker for her year of bravery. And, finally, a very special hello goes to Charlie and Dane, whose decision to move up their pub date made the Summer of '99 so very interesting.

Comments and suggestions

We welcome your comments on *American Civil War: Biographies* and suggestions for other topics in history to consider. Please write: Editors, *American Civil War: Biographies,* U•X•L, 27500 Drake Rd., Farmington Hills, Michigan 48331-3535; call toll-free: 800-877-4253; fax to 248-414-5043; or send e-mail via http://www.galegroup.com.

American Civil War Timeline

1775   Philadelphia Quakers organize America's first antislavery society.

1776–83 English colonies' War for Independence against Great Britain ends with the formation of the United States.

1788   The U.S. Constitution is ratified, providing legal protection to slaveowners.

1793   Eli Whitney invents the cotton gin, which will dramatically increase Southern cotton production.

1803   President Thomas Jefferson purchases the Louisiana Territory from France.

1775
"Yankee Doodle"
is written.

1789
George Washington
takes office as the first
U.S. president.

1800
The Library of
Congress is
established.

| 1775 | 1789 | 1800 |

1816   The American Colonization Society is formed with the idea of settling free blacks back in Africa.

1820   Congress passes the Missouri Compromise, which maintains the balance between slave and free states in the Union.

1828   Congress passes the so-called "Tariff of Abominations" over the objections of Southern states.

1831   Slave Nat Turner leads a violent slave rebellion in Virginia.

1832–33 The "Nullification Crisis" in South Carolina ends after tariffs on foreign goods are lowered.

1833   The Female Anti-Slavery Society and the American Anti-Slavery Society are founded.

1837   Abolitionist Elijah P. Lovejoy is murdered by a proslavery mob in Illinois.

1838   **Frederick Douglass** escapes from slavery and joins the abolitionist movement.

1839   New York governor **William Henry Seward** refuses to return three escaped slaves to Virginia.

1839   Abolitionist **Theodore Dwight Weld** publishes *American Slavery as It Is.*

1841   **Horace Greeley** launches the *New York Tribune,* which becomes a leading abolitionist newspaper.

1845   Texas is annexed by the United States over the objections of Mexico, which regards it as part of its country.

1846   **Dred Scott** files his famous lawsuit in an effort to win his freedom.

1825
The New York
Stock Exchange
opens.

1844
Samuel F. B. Morse
transmits the first
telegraph message.

1818
Congress adopts
a U.S. flag.

1818   1825   1844

1848   The Mexican War ends with the United States acquiring five hundred thousand square miles of additional land in western North America.

1849   **Harriet Tubman** escapes from slavery.

1850   *The Narrative of **Sojourner Truth*** is published.

1850   **Harriet Tubman** makes the first of her nineteen trips to the South to lead slaves to freedom via the Underground Railroad.

1850   The Compromise of 1850, including the controversial Fugitive Slave Act, becomes law.

1852   **Harriet Beecher Stowe**'s novel *Uncle Tom's Cabin* is published, increasing support for the abolitionist movement in the North.

1854   The Kansas-Nebraska Act is passed, returning decisions about allowing slavery back to individual states.

1856   South Carolina congressman Preston Brooks attacks Massachusetts senator **Charles Sumner** in the Senate chambers over an abolitionist speech.

1856   **John Brown** and his followers attack and kill five proslavery men in Kansas.

1857   The U.S. Supreme Court issues its famous ***Dred Scott*** decision, which increases Northern fears about the spread of slavery.

1858   New York senator **William Henry Seward** warns of an approaching "irrepressible conflict" between the South and the North.

1858   Illinois senate candidates **Abraham Lincoln** and Stephen Douglas meet in their famous debates over slavery and its future place in America.

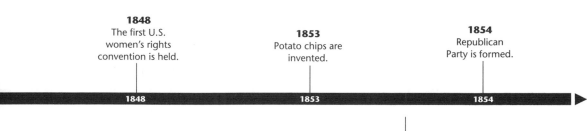

1848
The first U.S. women's rights convention is held.

1853
Potato chips are invented.

1854
Republican Party is formed.

1848   1853   1854

1859 Abolitionist **John Brown** leads a raid on Harpers Ferry, Virginia, in an unsuccessful effort to start a slave revolt across the South.

5/18/1860 The Republican Party nominates **Abraham Lincoln** as its candidate for president.

11/6/1860 **Abraham Lincoln** is elected president of the United States.

12/20/1860 South Carolina secedes from the Union.

1/9/1861 Mississippi secedes from the Union.

1/10/1861 Florida secedes from the Union.

1/11/1861 Alabama secedes from the Union.

1/19/1861 Georgia secedes from the Union.

1/26/1861 Louisiana secedes from the Union.

1/28/61 **Pierre G. T. Beauregard** is fired as superintendent of the U.S. Military Academy at West Point for supporting secession.

1/29/1861 Kansas is admitted into the Union as the thirty-fourth state.

2/1/1861 Texas secedes from the Union.

2/8/1861 The Confederate Constitution is adopted in Montgomery, Alabama.

2/9/1861 **Jefferson Davis** is elected provisional president of the Confederacy.

2/18/1861 **Jefferson Davis** is inaugurated as the president of the Confederacy.

3/4/1861 **Abraham Lincoln** is inaugurated as the sixteenth president of the United States.

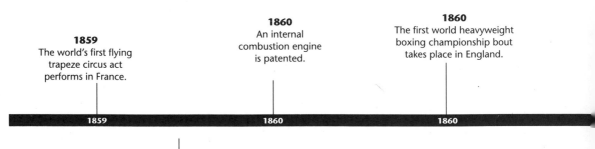

1859
The world's first flying trapeze circus act performs in France.

1860
An internal combustion engine is patented.

1860
The first world heavyweight boxing championship bout takes place in England.

1859   1860   1860

3/6/1861 The Confederacy calls for one hundred thousand volunteers to join its military.

4/1861 **Edward Pollard** publishes *Letters of a Southern Spy,* harshly criticizing **Abraham Lincoln** and all Northerners.

4/12/1861 South Carolina troops open fire on Fort Sumter, marking the beginning of the American Civil War.

4/13/1861 Major Robert Anderson surrenders Fort Sumter to the Confederates.

4/15/1861 President **Abraham Lincoln** calls for seventy-five thousand volunteers to join the Union army.

4/19/1861 President **Abraham Lincoln** orders a blockade of Southern ports.

4/20/1861 **Thaddeus Lowe** makes a successful balloon flight from Cincinnati, Ohio, to Unionville, South Carolina.

5/1861 **Winfield Scott** develops his "Anaconda Plan."

5/6/1861 Arkansas secedes from the Union.

5/7/1861 Tennessee forms an alliance with the Confederacy that makes it a Confederate state for all practical purposes.

5/13/1861 Queen Victoria proclaims British neutrality in the conflict between America's Northern and Southern sections.

5/14/1861 **Emma Edmonds** disguises herself as a man and joins the Union army.

5/20/1861 North Carolina secedes from the Union.

5/23/1861 Virginia secedes from the Union.

1861
American inventor Elisha G. Otis patents a steam-powered elevator.

1861
American Civil War begins.

1861

1861

6/3/1861 Stephen A. Douglas dies in Chicago, Illinois.

6/10/1861 Napoleon III declares French neutrality in the American Civil War.

6/11/1861 Counties in western Virginia resist Virginia's vote to secede and set up their own government, which is loyal to the Union.

7/20/1861 Confederate Congress convenes at the Confederate capital of Richmond, Virginia.

7/21/1861 Confederate forces win the First Battle of Bull Run, the war's first major battle.

7/22/1861 **Julia Ward Howe** writes the words to "Battle Hymn of the Republic" in her hotel room.

7/25/1861 U.S. Congress passes the Crittenden Resolution, which states that the North's war aim is to preserve the Union, not end slavery.

7/27/1861 General **George B. McClellan** assumes command of Federal forces in Washington.

8/30/1861 Union general **John C. Frémont** proclaims martial law in Missouri, which is torn by violence between pro-Union and pro-Confederate forces.

11/1861 **John Bell Hood**'s Texas Brigade is organized.

11/6/1861 **Jefferson Davis** is elected to a six-year term as president of the Confederacy.

11/8/1861 Union Captain Charles Wilkes seizes two Confederate officials traveling on the *Trent,* a British vessel. The incident triggers deep outrage in England.

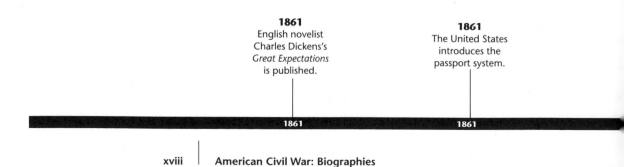

1861
English novelist
Charles Dickens's
Great Expectations
is published.

1861
The United States
introduces the
passport system.

1861

1861

11/20/1861 The Union organizes the Joint Committee on the Conduct of the War in order to review the actions and qualifications of the North's military leadership.

11/27/1861 Confederate officials seized from the *Trent* are released from custody with apologies.

2/6/1862 Union general **Ulysses S. Grant** captures Fort Henry on the Tennessee River.

2/16/1862 **Ulysses S. Grant** captures Fort Donelson on the Cumberland River.

2/22/1862 **Jefferson Davis** is inaugurated as president of the Confederacy.

2/25/1862 Confederates abandon Nashville, Tennessee, to oncoming Union forces.

3/1862 **Emma Edmonds** makes her first trip behind Confederate lines as a Union spy.

3/9/1862 The Union ship *Monitor* battles the Confederate ship *Virginia* to a draw at Hampton Roads, Virginia.

4/6–7/1862 Union and Confederate forces fight in the inconclusive Battle of Shiloh in Tennessee.

4/16/1862 The Confederate Congress passes a conscription act requiring most able-bodied men between the ages of eighteen and thirty-five to sign up for military service.

4/25/1862 The Union fleet under the command of Admiral **David R. Farragut** captures New Orleans.

5/13/1862 Slave **Robert Smalls** leads a group of slaves who steal the Confederate ship *Planter* and turn it over to the Union Navy.

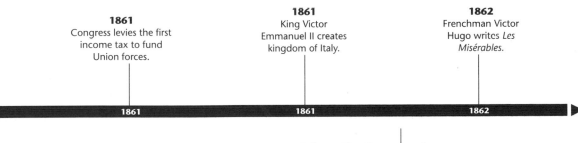

1861
Congress levies the first income tax to fund Union forces.

1861
King Victor Emmanuel II creates kingdom of Italy.

1862
Frenchman Victor Hugo writes *Les Misérables.*

1861

1861

1862

6/1/1862 General **Robert E. Lee** assumes command of Confederate forces defending Richmond, Virginia.

6/6/1862 Union forces take control of Memphis, Tennessee.

6/17/1862 Confederate forces led by **Thomas "Stonewall" Jackson** leave the Shenandoah Valley after a successful military campaign.

6/25/1862 The Seven Days' Battles begin between **George B. McClellan**'s Army of the Potomac and **Robert E. Lee**'s Army of Northern Virginia.

7/2/1862 President **Abraham Lincoln** calls for three hundred thousand enlistments for three-year periods in order to further strengthen the Union army.

7/17/1862 U.S. Congress passes laws allowing blacks to serve as soldiers in Union army.

7/29/1862 Confederate commerce raider *Alabama* leaves England and starts attacking Northern trading vessels.

8/29–30/1862 The Second Battle of Bull Run ends in a disastrous defeat for the Union.

9/5/1862 General **Robert E. Lee** leads the Army of Northern Virginia into Northern territory for the first time, as his force enters Maryland.

9/15/1862 **Thomas "Stonewall" Jackson**'s army captures twelve thousand Union troops at Harpers Ferry, Virginia.

9/17/1862 **George B. McClellan**'s Army of the Potomac and **Robert E. Lee**'s Army of Northern Virginia fight at Antietam in the bloodiest single day of the war. Neither side registers a conclusive victory, but the draw convinces Lee to return to Virginia.

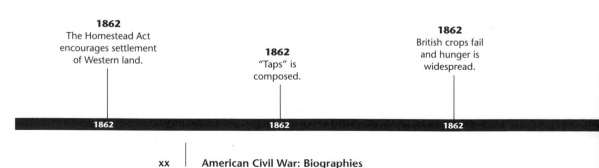

1862
The Homestead Act encourages settlement of Western land.

1862
"Taps" is composed.

1862
British crops fail and hunger is widespread.

1862   1862   1862

9/22/1862 President Abraham Lincoln issues his preliminary Emancipation Proclamation, which will free slaves in Confederate territory.

10/8/1862 Confederate invasion of Kentucky ends after the Battle of Perryville.

10/12/1862 Jeb Stuart's Confederate cavalry completes ride around George B. McClellan's Union army after raid on Chambersburg, Pennsylvania.

11/7/1862 President Abraham Lincoln removes General George B. McClellan from command of the Army of the Potomac, replacing him with General Ambrose Burnside.

12/13/1862 General Robert E. Lee's Confederate forces hand the Union a decisive defeat at the Battle of Fredericksburg.

1/1/1863 President Abraham Lincoln issues the Emancipation Proclamation, which frees all slaves in Confederate territory.

1/1/1863 John Singleton Mosby is named captain of the Confederate guerrilla rangers.

1/2/1863 Union victory at the Battle of Stones River stops Confederate plans to invade middle Tennessee.

1/23/1863 General Ambrose Burnside's new offensive against Robert E. Lee's Army of Northern Virginia sputters to a halt in bad weather. Burnside's "Mud March" convinces President Abraham Lincoln to replace him with General Joseph Hooker.

3/3/1863 U.S. Congress passes a conscription act requiring most able-bodied Northern men to sign up for military service.

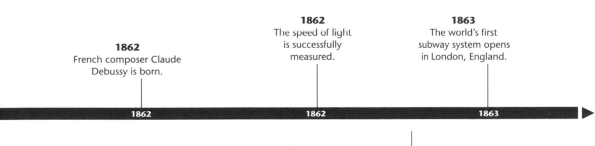

1862
French composer Claude Debussy is born.

1862
The speed of light is successfully measured.

1863
The world's first subway system opens in London, England.

1862   1862   1863

4/2/1863 Bread riots erupt in Richmond, Virginia, as hungry civilians resort to violence to feed their families.

5/1863 Union spy **Pauline Cushman** is captured and sentenced to death by Confederate general **Braxton Bragg**, but she is rescued near Shelbyville, Tennessee.

5/2/1863 General **Robert E. Lee** and the Confederates claim a big victory at Chancellorsville, but **Thomas "Stonewall" Jackson** is killed during the battle.

5/22/1863 General **Ulysses S. Grant** begins the siege of Vicksburg, Mississippi, after attempts to take the Confederate stronghold by force are turned back.

5/26/1863 Ohio congressman **Clement L. Vallandigham** is exiled to Confederate territory for criticizing President **Abraham Lincoln** and encouraging Union soldiers to desert.

6/9/1863 The largest cavalry battle of the Civil War ends in a draw at Brandy Station, Virginia.

6/20/1863 West Virginia is admitted into the Union as the thirty-fifth state.

7/1–3/1863 The famous Battle of Gettysburg takes place in Pennsylvania. Union general **George G. Meade** and the Army of the Potomac successfully turn back General **Robert E. Lee**'s attempted invasion of the North, doing terrible damage to Lee's Army of Northern Virginia in the process.

7/4/1863 Vicksburg surrenders to General **Ulysses S. Grant** and his Union force after a six-week siege of the city.

7/9/1863 Union troops take control of Port Hudson, Louisiana. The victory gives the North control of the Mississippi River.

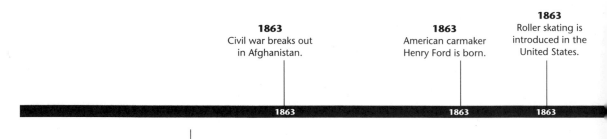

1863
Civil war breaks out in Afghanistan.

1863
American carmaker Henry Ford is born.

1863
Roller skating is introduced in the United States.

1863   1863   1863

7/13/1863 Antidraft mobs begin four days of rioting in New York City.

7/18/1863 Black troops of the Fifty-Fourth Massachusetts regiment make a valiant but unsuccessful attempt to seize Fort Wagner in South Carolina from the Confederates.

8/21/1863 Confederate raiders led by William C. Quantrill murder 150 antislavery settlers and burn large sections of Lawrence, Kansas.

9/2/1863 Union troops take control of Knoxville, Tennessee.

9/9/1863 Union forces take control of Chattanooga, Tennessee, after the city is abandoned by General **Braxton Bragg**'s army.

9/20/1863 The two-day Battle of Chickamauga ends in a major defeat for the Union.

9/23/1863 General **Braxton Bragg** begins the Confederate siege of Chattanooga.

10/17/1863 General **Ulysses S. Grant** is named supreme commander of Union forces in the west.

11/19/1863 President **Abraham Lincoln** delivers his famous Gettysburg Address at a ceremony dedicating a cemetery for soldiers who died at the Battle of Gettysburg in Pennsylvania.

11/25/1863 The three-day Battle of Chattanooga results in a major victory for the North, as Union troops led by General **George Henry Thomas** scatter General **Braxton Bragg**'s Confederate army.

12/8/1863 President **Abraham Lincoln** proposes his Ten Percent Plan, which says that seceded states can return to the Union provided that one-tenth of the

1863
President Abraham Lincoln proclaims the first national Thanksgiving Day.

1863
The Capitol dome in Washington, D.C., is capped.

1863

1863

1860 voters agree to form a state government that is loyal to the Union.

12/27/1863 General **Joseph E. Johnston** takes command of the Confederate Army of Tennessee.

3/12/1864 General **Ulysses S. Grant** is promoted to leadership of all of the Union armies.

3/18/1864 General **William T. Sherman** is named to lead Union armies in the west.

4/12/1864 Confederate troops led by **Nathan Bedford Forrest** capture Fort Pillow, Tennessee, and are accused of murdering black Union soldiers stationed there.

4/17/1864 General **Ulysses S. Grant** calls a halt to prisoner exchanges between North and South, further increasing the Confederacy's manpower problems.

5/5/1864 General **Robert E. Lee**'s Army of Northern Virginia and General **Ulysses S. Grant**'s Army of the Potomac battle in the Wilderness campaign.

5/9–12/1864 General **Robert E. Lee** stops the Union advance on Richmond at the brutal Battle of Spotsylvania.

5/11/1864 **Jeb Stuart** is mortally wounded in a battle with **Philip H. Sheridan**'s cavalry at Brandy Station, Virginia.

6/1864 U.S. Congress passes a law providing for equal pay for black and white soldiers.

6/3/1864 The Union's Army of the Potomac suffers heavy losses in a failed assault on **Robert E. Lee**'s army at Cold Harbor, Virginia.

6/18/1864 General **Ulysses S. Grant** begins the Union siege of Petersburg, which is defended by **Robert E. Lee**'s Army of Northern Virginia.

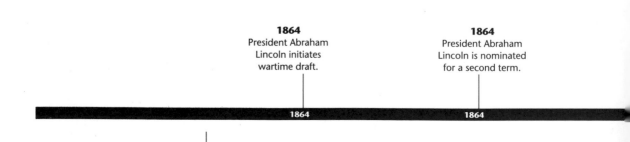

1864
President Abraham
Lincoln initiates
wartime draft.

1864

1864
President Abraham
Lincoln is nominated
for a second term.

1864

6/23/1864 Confederate forces led by Jubal Early begin a campaign in the Shenandoah Valley.

7/11/1864 Confederate troops commanded by Jubal Early reach outskirts of Washington, D.C., before being forced to return to the Shenandoah Valley.

7/17/1864 General **John Bell Hood** takes command of the Confederate Army of Tennessee.

7/30/1864 Union general **Ambrose Burnside** makes a disastrous attack in the Battle of the Crater.

8/5/1864 Admiral **David G. Farragut** leads the Union Navy to a major victory in the Battle of Mobile Bay, which closes off one of the Confederacy's last remaining ports.

8/29/1864 The Democratic Party nominates General **George B. McClellan** as its candidate for president of the United States and pushes a campaign promising an end to the war.

9/1/1864 General **William T. Sherman** captures Atlanta, Georgia, after a long campaign.

9/4/1864 General **William T. Sherman** orders all civilians to leave Atlanta, Georgia, as a way to hurt Southern morale.

9/19–22/1864 Union troops led by **Philip H. Sheridan** defeat Jubal Early's Confederate army in the Shenandoah Valley.

10/1/1864 **Rose O'Neal Greenhow** drowns in the Atlantic Ocean while trying to smuggle gold into the Confederacy in the hoops of her dress.

10/6/1864 **Philip H. Sheridan**'s Union troops begin a campaign of destruction in the Shenandoah Valley in

1864
A cyclone destroys most of Calcutta, India.

1864
"In God We Trust" first appears on U.S. coins.

1864

1864

order to wipe out Confederate sympathizers and sources of supplies.

10/19/1864 **Philip H. Sheridan**'s army drives Jubal Early's Confederate force out of the Shenandoah Valley.

10/31/1864 Nevada is admitted into the Union as the thirty-sixth state.

11/8/1864 **Abraham Lincoln** is reelected to the presidency of the United States by a comfortable margin.

11/15/1864 General **William T. Sherman** begins his famous March to the Sea, in which his Union army destroys a large area of Georgia on its way to the port city of Savannah.

12/16/1864 Union forces under the command of General **George Henry Thomas** crush **John Bell Hood**'s Army of Tennessee at the Battle of Nashville.

12/21/1864 **William T. Sherman**'s Union army completes its March to the Sea by taking control of Savannah, Georgia.

1/31/1865 The U.S. Congress submits the Thirteenth Amendment, which abolishes slavery, to the individual states for passage.

2/17/1865 General **William T. Sherman**'s army occupies the South Carolina capital of Columbia.

2/18/1865 Union forces seize control of Charleston, South Carolina.

2/22/1865 Confederate president **Jefferson Davis** returns command of the Army of Tennessee to General **Joseph E. Johnston** in a desperate attempt to stop **William T. Sherman**'s advance into North Carolina.

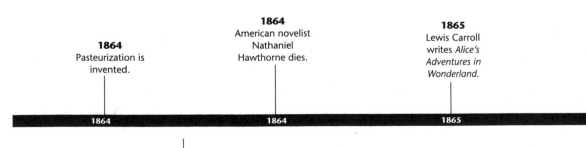

1864
Pasteurization is invented.

1864
American novelist Nathaniel Hawthorne dies.

1865
Lewis Carroll writes *Alice's Adventures in Wonderland.*

1864   1864   1865

2/27/1865 **Martin Delany** is commissioned as a major in the Union army, becoming the first black soldier to hold a field command in U.S. military history.

3/2/1865 Remaining Confederate troops in Shenandoah Valley go down to defeat at the hands of **Philip H. Sheridan.**

3/4/1865 President **Abraham Lincoln** is inaugurated for a second term of office.

3/13/1865 The Confederate Congress authorizes the use of slaves as Confederate combat soldiers.

4/1–2/1865 **Ulysses S. Grant**'s Army of the Potomac successfully breaks through Confederate defenses at Petersburg, forcing **Robert E. Lee**'s Army of Northern Virginia to evacuate the city and give up its defense of Richmond, Virginia.

4/3/1865 Union troops take control of Richmond, Virginia, and prepare for a visit from President **Abraham Lincoln** a day later.

4/9/1865 Trapped by pursuing Federal troops, General **Robert E. Lee** surrenders to General **Ulysses S. Grant** at Appomattox in Virginia.

4/14/1865 President **Abraham Lincoln** is shot by **John Wilkes Booth** while attending a play at Ford's Theatre in Washington, D.C.

4/15/1865 Vice president **Andrew Johnson** becomes president after **Abraham Lincoln** dies.

4/18/1865 Confederate General **Joseph E. Johnston** surrenders his Army of Tennessee to **William T. Sherman** near Raleigh, North Carolina.

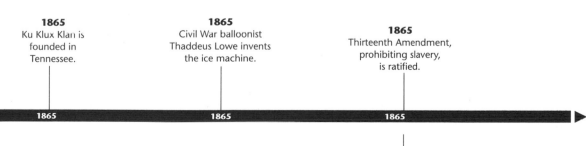

1865
Ku Klux Klan is founded in Tennessee.

1865
Civil War balloonist Thaddeus Lowe invents the ice machine.

1865
Thirteenth Amendment, prohibiting slavery, is ratified.

1865　　　　　　　　1865　　　　　　　　1865

4/26/1865 **John Wilkes Booth** is killed by Federal soldiers in a barn near Bowling Green, Virginia.

5/10/1865 Confederate president **Jefferson Davis** is taken prisoner by Federal troops at Irwinsville, Georgia.

5/26/1865 The very last Confederate troops put down their weapons, as a rebel army west of the Mississippi River led by Kirby Smith surrenders to Union officials.

6/6/1865 William Quantrill dies in federal prison.

11/10/1865 **Henry Wirz** becomes the only Confederate official to be executed for war crimes committed during the Civil War.

1866 **Ambrose Burnside** is elected governor of Rhode Island.

1866 **David R. Farragut** becomes the first admiral in U.S. naval history.

1866 The Republican Congress passes a Civil Rights Act over President **Andrew Johnson**'s veto. The Act gives citizenship and other rights to black people.

1866 Race riots between blacks and whites erupt during the summer in Memphis, Tennessee, and New Orleans, Louisiana.

1866 Tennessee is readmitted into the Union by Congress.

1866 George M. Maddox of Quantrill's Raiders is acquitted of murder charges from massacre at Lawrence, Kansas.

1867 Congress passes the Military Reconstruction Act over President **Andrew Johnson**'s veto.

1866
The first U.S. oil pipeline
is completed.

1866
Alfred Nobel
invents dynamite.

1866

1866

American Civil War: Biographies

1867   The Ku Klux Klan adopts a formal constitution and selects former Confederate general **Nathan Bedford Forrest** as its first leader.

1867   Former Confederate president **Jefferson Davis** is released from a Virginia jail after two years of imprisonment.

1867   Former slave and Union war hero **Robert Smalls** is elected to the South Carolina state legislature.

1868   Political disagreements between Congress and President **Andrew Johnson** become so great that the president is impeached. He avoids being removed from office by one vote in his Senate impeachment trial.

1868   Congress passes the Fifteenth Amendment, which extends voting rights to blacks, and sends the bill along to individual states for ratification.

1868   Alabama, Arkansas, Florida, Louisiana, North Carolina, and South Carolina are readmitted into the Union by Congress.

1868   Republican **Ulysses S. Grant** is elected the eighteenth president of the United States.

1868   Georgia expels black representatives, saying they are not eligible to hold political office. U.S. Congress responds by refusing to recognize Georgia representatives.

1868   Federal government sends troops back into Georgia to reestablish military law.

1870   The Fifteenth Amendment, guaranteeing voting rights for blacks, is ratified by the states and becomes law.

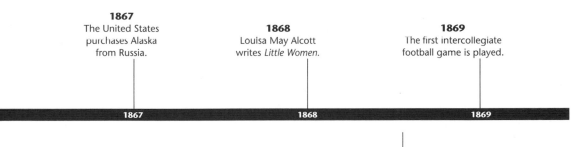

1867
The United States purchases Alaska from Russia.

1868
Louisa May Alcott writes *Little Women*.

1869
The first intercollegiate football game is played.

1867   1868   1869

1870 Congress passes the Enforcement Act of 1870 in an effort to protect the voting rights of all citizens—especially blacks—in the South.

1870 Georgia, Mississippi, Virginia, and Texas are readmitted into the Union by Congress.

1870 The Fifteenth Amendment guaranteeing voting rights for blacks is ratified by the states and becomes law.

1871 Congress passes the Ku Klux Klan Act, which outlaws conspiracies, use of disguises, and other practices of the white supremacist group.

1872 **Ulysses S. Grant** is reelected president of the United States.

1874 **Robert Smalls** is elected to the U.S. Congress.

1875 Congress passes a Civil Rights Act barring discrimination in hotels, theaters, railroads, and other public places.

1876 Republican Rutherford B. Hayes and Democrat Samuel J. Tilden run a very close race for the presidency of the United States. Tilden wins the popular vote, but neither candidate receives enough electoral votes for election. The two political parties eventually agree to a compromise in which Hayes becomes president in exchange for a guarantee that he remove federal troops from South Carolina, Florida, and Louisiana.

1877 President Rutherford B. Hayes removes Federal troops from the South. This withdrawal increases the vulnerability of blacks to Southern racism and marks the end of the Reconstruction period in American history.

1881 **Clara Barton** founds the American Red Cross.

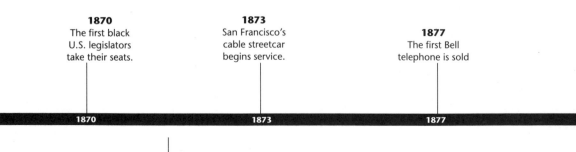

1870
The first black
U.S. legislators
take their seats.

1873
San Francisco's
cable streetcar
begins service.

1877
The first Bell
telephone is sold

1870   1873   1877

1891   **Ambrose Bierce** publishes *Tales of Soldiers and Civilians*, a collection of stories about the Civil War that includes his famous story "An Occurrence at Owl Creek Bridge."

1895   **Thomas Nast** completes his famous painting of **Robert E. Lee**'s surrender to **Ulysses S. Grant.**

1981   Southern writer **Mary Boykin Chesnut**'s diary of her Civil War experiences is published in its original form—over one hundred years after it was written—as *Mary Chesnut's Civil War* and wins the Pulitzer Prize.

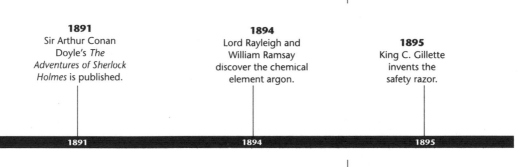

1891
Sir Arthur Conan Doyle's *The Adventures of Sherlock Holmes* is published.

1894
Lord Rayleigh and William Ramsay discover the chemical element argon.

1895
King C. Gillette invents the safety razor.

1891   1894   1895

A map of the United States east of the Mississippi River shows the key battles and events of the Civil War. *(Illustration by XNR Productions. Reproduced by permission of The Gale Group.)*

Robert E. Lee

Born January 19, 1807
Westmoreland County, Virginia
Died October 13, 1870
Lexington, Virginia

Confederate general
As commander of the Army of Northern Virginia,
became the Confederacy's most famous military
leader of the Civil War

General Robert E. Lee ranks as the most famous and beloved Confederate soldier to fight in the American Civil War. As commander of the Army of Northern Virginia, he masterminded many of the South's greatest military victories. Combining clever battlefield strategy with inspiring leadership, he nearly engineered an ultimate Confederate victory. As the conflict progressed, however, improved performance by the larger Union Army proved too much for Lee to overcome. Lee's decision to surrender in the spring of 1865 did not hurt his reputation among his fellow Southerners, though. In fact, the postwar South embraced Lee as its greatest symbol of nobility in defeat.

"With all my devotion to the Union and the feeling of loyalty and duty of an American citizen, I have not been able to make up my mind to raise my hand against my relatives, my children, my home."

Raised to believe in duty and honor

Robert Edward Lee was born in January 1807 to a wealthy Virginia family. His father, Harry Lee, was a Revolutionary War (1776–83) hero who had been one of George Washington's best friends. His mother, Anne Hill Carter Lee, also came from a wealthy and privileged background. Robert

Robert E. Lee. *(Courtesy of the Library of Congress.)*

251

E. Lee spent his first three years at Stratford Hall, a fine mansion along the banks of the Potomac River that had been home to the Lee family for several generations. In 1810, however, serious financial problems changed the family's living situation. Harry Lee lost the family fortune in a series of poor business decisions. The situation became so bad that he was thrown in debtor's prison (a special jail that held people who failed to pay off financial debts), and the Lee family was forced to leave Stratford.

They moved to a modest home in Alexandria, Virginia. Harry Lee did manage to secure his release from jail, but he did not provide much assistance to his family after his return. In May 1813, he abandoned them, sailing away to the Caribbean on a government-sponsored trip. He died five years later without ever returning to see his wife and children.

When Harry Lee set sail for the Caribbean, he left his wife to raise all five of their children alone. Anne Lee's family provided assistance, though. As her children grew up, Anne Lee did her best to teach them about concepts of duty and honor and sacrifice. Robert E. Lee took these lessons to heart. By young adulthood he was known as a person of deep religious faith and a strong sense of honor and integrity.

Begins life in military

In 1825, Lee managed to secure an appointment to the U.S. Military Academy at West Point, the finest officers' training school in the country. Determined to restore his family's reputation, the young cadet worked and studied very hard. He posted excellent grades and conducted himself so well that he did not receive a single demerit (a critical mark given to students who violate any of the school's many rules on conduct and appearance) in his four years of study at the academy.

In 1829, Lee graduated second in his class. After leaving West Point, he promptly joined the elite Army Corps of Engineers, which was responsible for forts, dams, and other major construction projects across America. Around this same time, his mother died, leaving him a small inheritance that included about ten slaves. In 1831, Lee married Mary Anna Randolph Custis (1806–1873), the great granddaughter of

Martha Washington (1732–1802), the wife of the first U.S. president, George Washington (1732–1799). They had seven children during the course of their long and happy marriage.

Lee's responsibilities with the Army Corps of Engineers took him all around the country during the 1830s and early 1840s. He worked on dams, levees (fortified shorelines designed to prevent rivers from overflowing their banks), forts, and other construction projects during this time, earning a promotion to the rank of captain.

In 1846, Lee's service in the Corps of Engineers was interrupted by the Mexican War (1846–48). This war was a fight between Mexico and the United States for ownership of huge sections of land in the West. Lee spent the next two years on the staff of U.S. general **Winfield Scott** (1786–1866; see entry). As the war progressed, Lee's understanding of military tactics and his bravery in combat impressed Scott so much that the general stated that "Robert E. Lee is the greatest soldier now living, and if he ever gets the opportunity, he will prove himself the great captain of history." The Mexican War ended in 1848, after the United States forced the Mexican government to give up its claims on California and other western lands in exchange for $15 million.

After returning from Mexico, Lee continued his work with the Army Corps of Engineers. In 1852, he accepted an offer to become superintendent at West Point. He guided the school for the next three years, but resigned in 1855 to accept a lieutenant colonel position in the Texas cavalry. In 1857, Lee took an extended leave of absence from the army in order to take care of legal and financial problems associated with the Arlington, Virginia, estate of his deceased father-in-law. He returned to active military service in October 1859 when abolitionist **John Brown** (1800–1859; see entry) tried to start a major slave uprising in Harpers Ferry, Virginia. Lee commanded the military detachment that captured Brown and ended his raid.

Joins the Confederacy

Lee and many other Americans viewed Brown's raid on Harpers Ferry as a sign that longstanding disagreements

The Origins of Arlington National Cemetery

In 1857, Robert E. Lee's wife, Mary Anna Randolph Custis Lee, learned that her father had died and left her his Virginia estate. This property, known as Arlington, included a fine mansion and beautiful grounds, but had fallen into a state of disrepair. Restoration of the estate became General Lee's responsibility, and he quickly took steps to improve the long-neglected land.

By 1861, Lee and his wife had made dramatic improvements in the Arlington estate. But two days after Lee resigned from the Federal Army in order to join the Confederate military, Union forces seized the property. Union officers promptly converted the mansion and surrounding grounds into a headquarters area for their army. The loss of Arlington, meanwhile, forced Lee's wife and other Custis family members to relocate to Richmond and other cities in Virginia. The Union Army officially confiscated (seized) the Arlington estate a short time later by taking advantage of a wartime law requiring property owners in occupied areas to pay taxes in person. Since General Lee could not pay his property taxes in person without being captured, the estate became the property of the federal government.

Arlington was first used as a cemetery for soldiers in 1864, when the Union Army set aside two hundred acres for burial of federal troops. By the end of the war the hills of the estate were dotted with graves marking the final resting place of thousands of Union soldiers. In 1882, Robert E. Lee's son George Washington Custis Lee sued the government for return of the land that had belonged to his ancestors. The government responded by offer-

within the United States over the issue of slavery might never be settled peacefully. These fears came true in the spring of 1861, when the nation's Northern and Southern regions went to war over the issue.

Many Northerners had become convinced that slavery was wrong. They wanted the Federal government to take steps to outlaw slavery or at least keep it from spreading beyond the Southern states where it was already allowed. But the Southern economy had become very dependent on slavery over the years, and white Southerners worried that their way of life would collapse if slavery was abolished (eliminated). They argued that each state should decide for itself whether to allow the practice. By 1861, Southern dissatisfac-

The Custis-Lee Mansion at Arlington National Cemetery. *(Courtesy of the Library of Congress.)*

ing him $150,000 to purchase the property. Lee accepted the offer, and the property subsequently became Arlington National Cemetery.

Today, Arlington National Cemetery is the most famous cemetery in the United States. More than 175,000 American soldiers, including troops from every major war in which the United States has fought, are buried within its borders. Arlington is also the site of the Tomb of the Unknown Soldier, which honors American servicemen who died in World War I (1914–18), World War II (1939–45), the Korean War (1950–53), and the Vietnam War (1955–75). Many famous Americans who devoted their lives to public service are buried at Arlington as well, including President John F. Kennedy (1917–1963) and his brother Robert Kennedy (1925–1968).

tion with the North had become so great that several states decided to secede from (leave) the Union and form a new country that allowed slavery, called the Confederate States of America. The Northern states, however, were unwilling to see the United States split in two. They vowed to force the South back into the Union.

When the Civil War began in early 1861, Lee agonized over what he should do. He felt deep loyalty both to his country and to his native state of Virginia, which had voted to secede. Finally, though, he made up his mind. Turning down an offer to command all Union forces, he submitted his resignation from the U.S. Army in order to join the Confederate military. "With all my devotion to the Union and the feel-

Lee Predicts a Long War

When the Civil War began, many people in both the North and the South expressed great confidence that their side would achieve total victory within a matter of months. General Robert E. Lee, though, believed that neither side really appreciated the courage and determination of their opponent. In the following letter written by Lee on May 5, 1861, he expresses deep concerns about the toll that the war might take on the two sides:

> [Politicians who predict an easy victory] do not know what they say. If it comes to a conflict of arms, the war will last at least four years. Northern politicians do not appreciate the determination and pluck [bravery] of the South, and Southern politicians do not appreciate the numbers, resources, and patient perseverance of the North. Both sides forget that we are all Americans. I foresee that the country will have to pass through a terrible ordeal, a necessary expiation (atonement or apology) . . . for our national sins.

As events turned out, Lee's prediction of a long and bloody conflict proved accurate. The Civil War lasted almost exactly four years and cost the lives of hundreds of thousands of young men.

ing of loyalty and duty of an American citizen, I have not been able to make up my mind to raise my hand against my relatives, my children, my home," he explained. "I have therefore resigned my commission in the army and, save in defense of my home state, with the sincere hope that my poor services may never be needed, I hope I may never be called upon to draw my sword."

Assumes command of Army of Northern Virginia

On April 23, 1861, Lee formally took command of all armed forces in Virginia. He spent most of his time, however, serving as a military advisor to Confederate president **Jefferson Davis** (1808–1889). He did not receive an important leadership position in the field until June 1862, when General **Joseph Johnston** (1807–1891; see entry) was wounded at the Battle of Seven Pines. President Davis then told Lee to take command of Johnston's army, which Lee renamed the Army of Northern Virginia.

Once Lee took the field, he quickly reversed the Confederacy's fortunes in Virginia, which had become the most fiercely contested region of the entire war. By the early summer of 1862, Union forces had advanced deep into the state, drawing to within a few miles of the Confederate capital of Richmond. But Lee halted the Northern offensive in a series of bloody clashes with the Yankee (Union) invaders. These clashes—known as the Seven Days' Battles—forced Union general **George B. McClellan** (1826–1885; see entry) to end his campaign against Richmond.

Lee followed up this success with a decisive triumph at the Second Battle of Bull Run (also known as the Second Battle of Manassas) in late August 1862. This victory over Union forces led by General John Pope (1822–1892) convinced Lee to attempt an invasion of the North. The Confederate general believed that a successful campaign into Union territory might convince Northerners to end their efforts to break the Confederacy. Lee's invasion ended on September 17, however, when Union forces fought his Army of Northern Virginia to a stalemate in the bloody Battle of Antietam in Maryland.

Lee dominates in the East

Lee's Army of Northern Virginia suffered enormous casualties in the Battle of Antietam. As a result, the Confederate commander decided to return to Virginia and rebuild his army over the winter. Eager to smash Lee's weary troops, Northern forces under the command of **Ambrose Burnside** (1824–1881; see entry) followed Lee to Fredericksburg, Virginia. When Burnside's Army of the Potomac attacked Lee's army on December 13, 1862, however, the offensive was smashed to pieces by Lee's well-prepared defenses. The rebel (Confederate) victory at Fredericksburg forced Burnside to abandon his offensive and cemented Lee's reputation as a brilliant and daring military strategist.

Lee's greatest triumph

In the spring of 1863, the Union Army mounted yet another offensive against Lee's Army of Northern Virginia. Northern military and political leaders knew that if they could crush Lee's army, Richmond and other important Southern cities would be vulnerable to Union attack, and the war could be brought to a close. With this in mind, Union general Joseph Hooker (1814–1879) led the Army of the Potomac into Virginia once again.

Armed with a huge force of approximately 130,000 troops, Hooker planned to use flank attacks and superior numbers to crush Lee's 60,000–man army, which remained entrenched in Fredericksburg. By late April, Hooker's army had taken up strong positions around Fredericksburg and the near-

by town of Chancellorsville. The Union Army appeared poised to strike. Lee, though, came up with a masterful strategy of countermoves that thoroughly puzzled Hooker. Relying on strong defensive positions, clever troop movements, and deadly attacks against Hooker's exposed flanks, Lee battered the Union force for three solid days. On May 6, the Army of the Potomac finally gave up and retreated to the North.

Lee's victory at Chancellorsville was his greatest triumph yet. "Unquestionably, this latest addition to the lengthening roster [list] of Confederate victories was a great one," wrote Shelby Foote in *The Civil War: Fredericksburg to Meridian*. "Indeed, considering the odds that had been faced and overcome, it was perhaps in terms of glory the greatest of them all; *Chancellorsville* would be stitched with pride across the crowded banners of the Army of Northern Virginia."

Gettysburg

Encouraged by his victory at Chancellorsville, Lee launched a second invasion of the North in June 1863. He knew that if Northern communities started to worry about their own safety, they would put tremendous pressure on Northern political leaders to negotiate a peace agreement with the Confederacy, even if it meant giving the Southern states their independence.

Lee's Army of Northern Virginia advanced into Pennsylvania, where they were met by the Union's Army of the Potomac and its new commander, General **George Meade** (1815–1872; see entry). On July 1, the two armies clashed outside of a little town called Gettysburg. The battle contin-

Union general Joseph Hooker. *(Reproduced by permission of the National Portrait Gallery.)*

ued for three days. Again and again, rebel troops crashed against Meade's defenses in hopes of smashing through and seizing victory. But the Army of the Potomac fought bravely, refusing to cave in to the rebel attacks.

The battle finally ended on July 3, when Lee ordered a disastrous charge at the heart of the Union defenses. This attack—known as "Pickett's Charge" after one of the Confederate officers who led the offensive—ended in complete failure for the South. Union weaponry easily shattered the advance. Shocked by this disastrous turn of events, Lee gathered his battered army together and retreated back to Virginia.

Lee faces a new enemy

In the days following the Battle of Gettysburg, Lee expressed great sadness and disgust with his performance in Pennsylvania. "It was all my fault," he told his troops. Lee even offered his resignation to President Davis, saying "no blame can be attached to the army for its failure to accomplish what was projected by me. I am alone to blame." Lee also pointed out that illness had begun to affect his ability to command (many historians believe that Lee began to suffer from heart disease around this time). Davis refused to accept the resignation, though, because Lee remained his finest general.

Lee worked hard to strengthen his Army of Northern Virginia throughout the winter of 1863–64. He wanted his army to be ready for the upcoming spring, when Northern armies would resume their efforts to restore the Union. When the spring of 1864 arrived, however, Lee found himself pitted against a tough new opponent in Union general **Ulysses S. Grant** (1822–1885; see entry).

Over the previous two years, Lee had defeated many different Union commanders, from George McClellan to Joseph Hooker. U.S. president **Abraham Lincoln** (1809–1865; see entry) had begun to believe he would never be able to find a general who could neutralize Lee's Army of Northern Virginia. In March 1864, however, Lincoln placed General Ulysses S. Grant in charge of Union forces.

Grant had been the Union's most successful general in the war's western theater (the region of the country between the Mississippi River and the Appalachian Mountains). When he arrived in the East in 1864, he took control of the Army of the Potomac and marched into Virginia in search of Lee. Grant hoped to use his superior force to smash the Army of Northern Virginia once and for all.

Lee and Grant clashed throughout the early summer of 1864. Fighting in engagements that ranged from bloody battles to small but deadly skirmishes, the two armies marched across the Virginia countryside in a desperate battle for survival. Lee avoided all of Grant's attempts to trap the Confederate Army and crush it. But Grant continued his steady pursuit of Lee's tired army. By mid-June, Lee's army had been forced to retreat to defensive positions around Petersburg, a city on the outskirts of Richmond.

In June 1864, Grant began a siege (a military effort to prevent food and other supplies from being delivered to a city or other location) of Petersburg. The siege did not starve Lee and his army into submission, but it prevented the Army of Northern Virginia from participating in the war. Lee and his men could only stand by helplessly as other Union armies marched across the South in triumph. "It must have been tragic for Lee to find himself ultimately bottled up at Petersburg because he loved the open fight and the war of maneuver," wrote Brian Pohanka in *Civil War Journal*. "With his army pinned down and besieged, he realized the end was in sight."

In April 1865, the Confederate defenses at Petersburg and Richmond finally began to crumble. Lee organized a desperate evacuation of his battered army. Grant quickly gave chase, however, and within a week he had surrounded Lee and his men. Lee surrendered his army on April 9. After signing the terms of surrender at the home of Wilmer McLean in Appomattox County, Virginia, Lee returned to his camp and told his loyal soldiers that "I have done the best I could for you. Go home now, and if you make as good citizens as you have soldiers, you will do well, and I shall always be proud of you."

College president and legend

After the war, Lee became president of Washington College (now Washington and Lee University) in Lexington, Vir-

ginia. He spent five years at the school, where he helped introduce the country's first educational departments of journalism and commerce. He also reshaped the school's curriculum to provide more training in subjects like science and engineering.

Lee also emerged as the war's most beloved and respected figure in the South. His fabulous military record and his lifelong emphasis on personal honor and dignity made

The Appomattox County home of Wilmer McLean, site of Robert E. Lee's Confederate surrender to Union general Ulysses S. Grant. *(Photography by Timothy O'Sullivan. Courtesy of the Library of Congress.)*

him very attractive to Southerners, who remained angry and upset over their defeat. "Southerners needed Lee to prove that good people can and do lose and to demonstrate that success in battle or elsewhere does not necessarily denote superiority," wrote historian Emory M. Thomas.

Lee died in October 1870, after suffering a stroke. News of Lee's death triggered a tremendous outpouring of grief all across the South. Ordinary citizens and thousands of devoted soldiers who had served under him offered testimonials (public statements declaring a person's merit) about his leadership and courage. Lee's funeral service in Lexington was attended by thousands of mourners, many of whom traveled for hundreds of miles to pay their respects. Today, more than a century after his death, Lee's status as a legend of the American South remains unchanged.

Where to Learn More

Archer, Jules. *A House Divided: The Lives of Ulysses S. Grant and Robert E. Lee.* New York: Scholastic, 1995.

Cannon, Marian G. *Robert E. Lee.* New York: Franklin Watts, 1993.

Connelly, Thomas Lawrence. *The Marble Man: Robert E. Lee and His Image in American Society.* New York: Knopf, 1977.

Davis, Burke. *Gray Fox: Robert E. Lee and the Civil War.* New York: Rinehart, 1956. Reprint, Short Hills, NJ: Burford Books, 1998.

Foote, Shelby, *The Civil War: A Narrative.* 3 vols. New York: Random House, 1958–74. Reprint, Alexandria, VA: Time-Life Books, 1999.

Freeman, Douglas Southall. *R. E. Lee: A Biography.* 4 vols. New York: Scribner's, 1934–35.

Harsh, Joseph L. *Confederate Tide Rising: Robert E. Lee and the Making of Southern Strategy, 1861–1862.* Kent, OH: Kent State University Press, 1998.

Kavanaugh, Jack, and Eugene C. Murdoch. *Robert E. Lee.* New York: Chelsea House, 1994.

Kerby, Mona. *Robert E. Lee: Southern Hero of the Civil War.* Springfield, NJ: Enslow, 1997.

Lee, Fitzhugh. *General Lee: A Biography of Robert E. Lee.* New York: Da Capo Press, 1994.

Marrin, Albert. *Virginia's General: Robert E. Lee and the Civil War.* New York: Atheneum, 1994.

National Park Service. *Arlington House: The Robert E. Lee Memorial.*[Online] http://www.nps.gov/arho/ (accessed on October 15, 1999).

Nolan, Alan T. *Lee Considered: General Robert E. Lee and Civil War History.* Chapel Hill: University of North Carolina Press, 1991.

Robert E. Lee Memorial Association. *Stratford Hall Plantation: The Birthplace of Robert E. Lee.* [Online] http://www.stratfordhall.org (accessed on October 15, 1999).

Snow, William P. *Lee and His Generals.* New York: Richardson & Co., 1867. Reprint, New York: Fairfax Press, 1982.

Taylor, Walter H. *General Lee, His Campaigns in Virginia, 1861–1865: With Personal Reminiscences.* Lincoln: University of Nebraska Press, 1994.

Thomas, Emory Morton. *Robert E. Lee: A Biography.* New York: W. W. Norton, 1995.

Wilkins, J. Steven. *Call of Duty: The Sterling Nobility of Robert E. Lee.* Nashville, TN: Cumberland House, 1997.

Woodworth, Steven E. *Davis and Lee at War.* Lawrence: University Press of Kansas, 1995.

Abraham Lincoln

Born February 12, 1809
Hodgenville, Kentucky
Died April 15, 1865
Washington, D.C.

Sixteenth president of the United States

A braham Lincoln is widely viewed as the greatest president in American history. He presided over the nation during one of its most difficult trials—the Civil War. Lincoln rose from humble beginnings in Kentucky to become a successful lawyer and state legislator in Illinois. In 1858, his growing concern over the expansion of slavery convinced him to join the antislavery Republican political party and oppose Democrat Stephen A. Douglas (1813–1861) for the U.S. Senate. Lincoln lost the election, but the spirited debates between the two candidates propelled him to national attention. In 1860, he became the sixteenth president of the United States.

But Lincoln's election convinced the slaveholding states of the Southern United States to secede (withdraw) from the Union and form a new country that allowed slavery, called the Confederate States of America. Lincoln considered this act an illegal rebellion against the national government, and the two sides soon went to war. During the war years, Lincoln struggled with incompetent generals and faced criticism over his policies. Yet his guidance and determination helped bring victory to the Union and freedom to millions of black Americans.

"I have no other [ambition] so great as that of being truly esteemed of my fellow men, by rendering myself worthy of their esteem."

Abraham Lincoln. *(Courtesy of the Brady National Photographic Art Gallery, Library of Congress.)*

Born poor in Kentucky

Abraham Lincoln was born in a log cabin in the slave state of Kentucky on February 12, 1809. He was the second child born to Thomas Lincoln, a hard-working carpenter and farmer, and his wife Nancy Hanks Lincoln. Although his parents' families had owned slaves in the past, the Lincolns came to oppose slavery. In fact, the Lincoln family joined an antislavery branch of the Baptist Church when Abraham was a boy.

Slavery had been practiced in North America since the 1600s, when black people were first taken from Africa and brought to the continent to serve as white people's slaves. The basic belief behind slavery was that black people were inferior to whites. Under slavery, white slaveholders treated black people as property, forced them to perform hard labor, and controlled every aspect of their lives. States in the Northern half of the United States began outlawing slavery in the late 1700s. But slavery continued to exist in the Southern half of the country because it played an important role in the South's economy and culture.

Lincoln mostly educated himself. His parents could not read or write, and they needed him and his older sister Sarah to help with the farm chores every day. As a result, it was rare when the children had time to attend school. Lincoln only went to school for a total of one year throughout his entire childhood. But he still managed to learn to read. He especially enjoyed reading poetry, because he liked the skillful ways poets put words together. He also became fascinated with a popular book called *Life of George Washington* by Mason Locke. This may have been the earliest indication of his future interest in politics.

In 1816, the Lincolns moved to the neighboring free state of Indiana. Sadly, Nancy Lincoln died in an epidemic two years later. In 1819, Thomas Lincoln married Sarah ("Sally") Bush Johnston, a widow with three young children. Young Abraham became very attached to his new stepmother. The Lincolns struggled financially during this time, so as a teenager Abraham worked at a series of odd jobs to help out. At nineteen, Lincoln took a flatboat loaded with produce down the Ohio and Mississippi Rivers to New Orleans along with another young man. During his time in the Deep South, he saw slaves in chains being sold at auction. The scene haunted him for many years and helped convince him that slavery was wrong. "The Negroes were strung together precisely like so many fish upon a trotline [a strong fishing line]," he recalled. "In this condition they were being separated forever from the scenes of their childhood, their friends, their fathers and mothers, and brothers and sisters, and many of them, from their wives and children, and going into perpetual [permanent] slavery."

Becomes a successful lawyer and politician

By the time Lincoln reached his twenties, he had become interested in the law. He started watching trials at the local courthouse, studying law books, and reading the Constitution and Declaration of Independence in order to understand the American justice system. When he was twenty-two, Lincoln left home and moved to New Salem, Illinois. As a clerk at the general store there, he met educated men who encouraged his interest in the law and politics. He practiced writing and public speaking, and joined a debating society. Within a year, he decided to run for the state legislature. "Every man is said to have his peculiar ambition," he said of his decision. "Whether it be true or not, I can say for one that I have no other so great as that of being truly esteemed [regarded] of my fellow men, by rendering [making] myself worthy of their esteem."

Upon losing his first election, Lincoln volunteered to serve in the Illinois militia during the Black Hawk War (1832). This conflict came about when white settlers attempted to force the Sauk and Fox Indians to move out of Illinois. Led by Chief Black Hawk (1767–1838), the Indians refused to leave their ancestral territory. Lincoln led a small militia unit through woods and swamps for several weeks, but they did not see any action before the Indians surrendered. After his term of military service ended, Lincoln became postmaster of New Salem and also worked as a surveyor (one who measures land to determine property or boundries, or to make maps).

In 1834, Lincoln ran for the state legislature again and won. He ended up serving four terms in office. He sponsored bills to improve the state's schools and also protested against measures designed to silence abolitionists (people who worked to end slavery). Lincoln also continued studying during this time and got a license to practice law in 1836. He showed great skill as an attorney. He was honest, funny, and sensitive in dealing with people. He also had a quick mind that allowed him to find weaknesses in his opponents' arguments and persuade juries to take his side. He moved to the new state capital of Springfield, Illinois, in 1837. Whenever the legislature was not in session, he traveled around the state as an attorney. He won most of his 250 cases before the State Supreme Court over the next several years.

In 1839, the successful young attorney and politician met Mary Todd, the daughter of a wealthy Kentucky family. After a rocky, on-again off-again courtship, they were married three years later. They eventually had four sons together, although only one of them survived to adulthood: Robert Todd (1843–1926), Edward Baker (1846–1850), William "Willie" Wallace (1850–1862), and Thomas "Tad" (1853–1871).

Bursts onto the national scene

In 1846, running as a member of the Whig political party, Lincoln was elected to represent Illinois in the U.S. House of Representatives. He soon emerged as an opponent of the Mexican War (1846–48). This was a conflict between the United States and Mexico for possession of lands in the West. Lincoln felt that the United States was illegally grabbing territory that belonged to its weaker neighbor. He also worried that westward expansion would complicate the already heated debate between North and South over slavery. Both sides would want to extend their political ideas and way of life to the new territories. Despite Lincoln's arguments, the U.S. government sent troops into the West and forced Mexico to give up huge areas of land in exchange for $15 million.

After Lincoln's term ended in 1849, he returned to his law practice in Springfield. But he continued to keep a close eye on politics and especially the ongoing debate over slavery. For almost thirty years, a federal law known as the Missouri Compromise of 1820 had prevented the spread of slavery to the Northern half of the country. This law basically established a line across the midsection of American territory above which slavery would not be permitted. By 1850, however, the addition of vast new lands in the West meant that neither side was happy with this arrangement any longer. People living in California, New Mexico, and other western territories wanted to be admitted into the Union as states. But both North and South wanted to influence whether or not slavery would be allowed in the new states. Finally, federal lawmakers came up with the Compromise of 1850. This law called for California to be admitted into the Union as a free state and authorized an end to slave trading in Washington, D.C. But it also provided Southern slaveholders with sweeping new powers to capture runaway slaves in the North.

The fragile peace achieved through this compromise was shattered a few years later. The two western territories of Kansas and Nebraska were next in line for statehood. In 1854, Illinois senator Stephen A. Douglas introduced the Kansas-Nebraska Act. It was based on the concept of "popular sovereignty," which held that the citizens of each new state should be able to decide for themselves whether to allow slavery. It explicitly abolished [eliminated] the Missouri Compromise of 1820 and gave the South a golden opportunity to expand the practice of slavery into new territories.

Most people accepted that Nebraska would enter the Union as a free state. But the status of Kansas was much less certain. Both abolitionists and proslavery forces rushed into Kansas in hopes of affecting the decision. Violence erupted throughout the region. But the impact of the Kansas-Nebraska Act also was felt far beyond the borders of Kansas. The entire nation was wracked with political change and uncertainty following its passage. The law triggered the disintegration of the national Whig political party, which divided into Northern and Southern factions over the slavery issue. The Southern Whigs joined the proslavery Democratic Party, while the Northern Whigs joined the antislavery Republican Party.

The Lincoln-Douglas debates

Lincoln joined the Republican Party and spoke out against the Kansas-Nebraska Act in letters and speeches. His strong opposition to the act convinced him to challenge the Democrat Douglas for his Senate seat in 1858. "I clearly see, as I think, a powerful plot to make slavery universal and perpetual in this nation. The effort to carry that plot through will be persistent and long continued," he said. "I enter upon the contest to contribute my humble and temporary mite [bit] in opposition to that effort."

Upon receiving the Republican Party's official nomination for the Senate, Lincoln gave a controversial speech that made headlines across the country. Some people, especially in the South, felt that he was calling for a war over slavery. "A house divided against itself cannot stand," he stated. "I believe this government cannot endure, permanently, half slave and half free. I do not expect the Union to be dissolved—I do not expect the house to fall—but I do expect it will cease to be divided. It will become all one thing, or all the other."

Lincoln ended up meeting Douglas in a series of debates. The two men were both excellent speakers, and their appearances attracted large crowds and a great deal of media attention. The debates reflected the growing division between the Republican and Democratic parties over slavery. Lincoln strongly opposed slavery because he believed it was morally wrong. He also thought that it contradicted the main principles upon which the country was founded. He felt that people of all races deserved an equal opportunity for "life, liberty, and the pursuit of happiness." But he did not necessarily believe that black people were equal to white people. Like most white people of his time, he held some racist views toward black people. He questioned whether black people and white people could live peacefully and equally together in American society. In fact, for many years he favored the idea of colonization, which involved sending the black residents of the United States to all-black countries in Africa and the Caribbean.

Lincoln recognized that it would be virtually impossible to outlaw slavery in the United States. That would require an amendment to the U.S. Constitution, and the Southern states would never support such a measure. So he and most other Republicans instead focused on preventing the spread of slavery outside of areas where it was already allowed. As the debates went on, Lincoln proved to be a strong force against slavery. "I have always thought that all men should be free; but if any should be slaves it should be first those who desire it for themselves, and secondly, those who desire it for others," he noted. "Whenever I hear anyone arguing for slavery, I feel a strong impulse to see it tried on him personally." Although Lincoln ended up losing the election, his views made him one of the most prominent members of the national Republican Party. Some people began mentioning him as a potential candidate for president in 1860.

President of the United States

As the presidential election neared, the issue of slavery continued to divide the country. When Lincoln won the Republican nomination, the Southern states threatened to secede (withdraw) from the United States if he were elected president. Lincoln tried to reassure the South that he did not intend to interfere with slavery where it already existed. But most Southerners still felt that a Republican president could not possibly represent their interests. In the meantime, the Democrats had trouble agreeing on a single candidate or platform. They ended up splitting their party into two factions, the Northern Democrats and the Southern Democrats, and running two separate candidates for president, Stephen Douglas and current vice president John C. Breckinridge (1821–1875). As a result, Lincoln was able to secure enough votes to be elected the sixteenth president of the United States.

Lincoln immediately began working to maintain peaceful relations with the South. In his first inaugural address, he argued against secession and let the South know that he would not make the first move toward war. He closed with a moving plea to his fellow countrymen: "We are not enemies but friends. We must not be enemies. Though passion may have strained, it must not break our bonds of affection. The mystic chords of memory, stretching from every last battlefield and patriot grave to every living heart and hearth-

Republican presidential nominee Abraham Lincoln. *(A drawing from a photograph by Mathew Brady. From* Harper's Weekly, *May 26, 1860.)*

stone, all over this broad land, will yet swell the chorus of the Union, when again touched, as surely they will be, by the better angels of our nature."

But Lincoln's words seemed to have little effect on the tense situation between North and South. Eleven Southern states had already announced their intention to secede from the Union and form a new country that allowed slavery, called the Confederate States of America, by the time Lincoln was inaugurated (sworn in). A few weeks later, the new Confederate government demanded that he remove the Federal troops stationed at Fort Sumter, located in the harbor at Charleston, South Carolina. Confederate president **Jefferson Davis** (1808–1889; see entry) viewed these troops as a symbol of Northern authority and wanted them to leave. But Lincoln refused to acknowledge the Confederacy as a legitimate country and claimed that the Southern states were engaged in an illegal rebellion against the U.S. government. When negotiations failed, Confederate forces opened fire on the fort on April 12, 1861. This event marked the beginning of the Civil War.

Wartime commander in chief

Lincoln faced an extremely difficult job as president during the war years. He had limited military experience, yet he was immediately expected to organize an army and devise a winning military strategy. He knew that every one of his actions could send thousands of young men to their deaths. As a result, conducting the war was difficult on him both emotionally and physically. But Lincoln possessed many traits that made him a great commander in chief. For example, he was able to analyze situations quickly and make good decisions. He was also good at dealing with difficult people. "His political experience had taught him how to win a political fight without making personal enemies out of the men he defeated, and he had as well the ability to use the talents of self-assured men who considered themselves his betters," Bruce Catton explained in *The Civil War*. Still, Lincoln did experience problems with incompetent and insubordinate (disobedient) generals in the early years of the war. He also faced constant criticism from opponents who disagreed with his policies. He even struggled to maintain order within his own cabinet (a group of advisors who head various government departments). But he overcame these difficulties with tact, diplomacy, and an unbending dedication to doing whatever was necessary to secure victory.

As soon as the war began, Lincoln called for seventy-five thousand volunteers to come to Washington, D.C., and defend the nation's capital against a possible Confederate attack. He also did everything in his power to keep the "border" states—which allowed slavery but remained loyal to the Union—from joining the Confederacy. For example, he suspended the legal provision known as habeas corpus in Maryland, a border state adjacent to Washington. Habeas corpus prevented government officials from imprisoning people without charging them with a crime. Lincoln knew that some people in the border states did not support the war effort, and he wanted the power to put these people in prison to stop them from helping the South. On several other occasions, he invoked the broad war powers granted to the president in the U.S. Constitution in order to keep control of the government and wage the war effectively. As a result, his political opponents called him a dictator and a tyrant.

The war forced Lincoln to remain flexible and periodically rethink his positions on various issues. For example, in the early part of the war he argued that his main purpose in fighting was to save the Union, not to end slavery. He said this in part because he wanted to avoid losing the loyalty of the border states. But black leaders and abolitionists in the North criticized him for moving too slowly toward emancipation (granting freedom to the slaves). In mid-1862, Lincoln decided that he could not forge (form) a lasting peace without putting an end to slavery. He also wanted to increase support for the war in the North and make it easier to recruit new soldiers. He began drafting his Emancipation Proclamation at this time. This war measure would declare all the slaves in the secessionist states to be free and allow black men to serve as soldiers in the Union Army. It would not affect the status of slaves in the border states or in areas of the South that were already under the control of Union troops. Lincoln issued a preliminary proclamation on September 22, 1862, following a narrow Union victory in the Battle of Antietam in Maryland. It warned the South that the final proclamation would take effect on January 1, 1863, unless they voluntarily rejoined the Union before that time. Of course, Lincoln could not force people in Confederate states to free their slaves. In fact, he had no power to enforce the proclamation until Union troops captured enemy territory. But the revolutionary document transformed the purpose of the war and ensured that there would be no further compromises on slavery.

In 1863, Union forces won a series of major battles, including a bloody one at Gettysburg, Pennsylvania. That November, Lincoln visited Gettysburg to dedicate a new military cemetery. There, he gave a brief speech that became one of the most famous addresses in the English language. Lincoln's Gettysburg Address laid out the principles of democracy for which the North was willing to fight. It introduced the idea of nationalism (a sense of loyalty and devotion to the country as a whole) into Northern debate about the Civil War. Instead of fighting to preserve the Union of fairly independent states with different interests and motivations, he explained, the North was fighting for the higher purpose of preserving the United States as a democratic nation. Lincoln believed deeply in democracy, which he described as "government of the people, by the people, for the people." He felt that if the South won the war and permanently separated from the United States, democracy would have failed.

As the war dragged on into 1864, many people in the North grew weary of fighting. Lincoln faced reelection that year and legitimately worried that he might lose to Democratic candidate **George B. McClellan** (1826–1885; see entry). To some Americans it seemed strange to proceed with a presidential election during the middle of a war. In fact, such an event had never occurred before in any other country. But Lincoln knew that holding the election was vital to continuing democracy in the United States. "We cannot have free government without elections," he stated, "and if the rebellion could force us to forego or postpone a national election, it might fairly claim to have already conquered and ruined us." Lincoln ran on a platform that backed his war measures and called for a constitutional amendment banning slavery. Shortly before the election took place, the Union Army claimed a string of stirring victories that changed public opinion toward the war and the president. Lincoln ended up winning reelection by a comfortable margin.

Death sends the North into mourning

By the beginning of 1865, it became clear that the Union was about to win the Civil War. Lincoln turned his attention to the task of putting the country back together as quickly and painlessly as possible. In his second inaugural address in March 1865, he seemed willing to forgive the Southern states for their rebellion. "Fondly do we hope—fervently [with intense feeling] do we pray—that this mighty scourge of war may speedily pass away," he stated. "With malice [ill will] toward none, with charity for all, with firmness in the right, as God gives us to see the right, let us strive on to finish the work we are in; to bind up the nation's wounds, to care for him who shall have borne the battle, and for his widow, and his orphan; to do all which may achieve a just and lasting peace, among ourselves and with all nations." Sadly, Lincoln would not live long enough to put his postwar plans into action.

On April 9, Confederate general **Robert E. Lee** (1807–1870; see entry) surrendered to Union general **Ulysses S. Grant** (1822–1885; see entry) at Appomattox, Virginia, to end the Civil War. People throughout the North poured into the streets in wild celebration. The end of the war gladdened Lincoln's heart, too. At times it had seemed to him that the war might never end, or that it would end in failure for the Union after years of heartache and pain. But Lee's surrender was a sure sign that Lincoln's heroic efforts to restore the Union had succeeded. When thousands of people gathered outside the White House to sing "The Star-Spangled Banner" and other patriotic songs, the president led them in loud cheers for General Grant and his soldiers.

President Abraham Lincoln's assassin, John Wilkes Booth. *(Reproduced by permission of AP/Wide World Photos, Inc.)*

The funeral train of President Abraham Lincoln.
(Reproduced with permission of UPI/Corbis-Bettmann.)

But the celebrations came to an abrupt end a few days later. On April 14, 1865, Lincoln and his wife attended a play at Ford's Theatre in Washington called *Our American Cousin.* They were seated in a fine balcony overlooking the stage. Midway through the performance, a fanatical supporter of the Confederacy named **John Wilkes Booth** (1838–1865; see entry) slipped into the rear of the balcony and shot Lincoln in the back of the head. Booth then leaped out of the balcony and landed on the stage below. He broke his leg in the fall, but still managed to limp off the stage and escape on horseback before anyone could capture him.

Physicians in the audience rushed to Lincoln's side, but they could do nothing for him. Concerned that the president would not survive any attempt to carry him to the White House, which was more than six blocks away, the doctors decided to take him to a boarding house across the street from the theater. Lincoln died there early the next morning.

News of Lincoln's death had an incredibly shattering impact on communities all across the North. After all, the Union's victory in the Civil War had made the president extremely popular. Northern communities realized that during the previous four years, Lincoln had managed to keep the dream of a restored Union alive despite many periods of doubt and discouragement. They also knew that victory would not have been possible without his guidance and determination. His assassination plummeted them into a mood of deep grief and rage. "While the nation is rejoicing . . . it is suddenly plunged into the deepest sorrow by the most brutal murder of its loved chief," wrote one Union veteran.

The nation remained in mourning in the weeks following Lincoln's death. Thousands of citizens paid their respects to their fallen president when the White House held a service in his honor. On April 20, Lincoln's body was placed on a train so that he could be buried in his hometown of Springfield, Illinois. As Lincoln's funeral car passed through the American countryside during the next few days, millions of farmers and townspeople gathered along the train's route to pay their respects.

Where to Learn More

Abraham Lincoln's Assassination. [Online] http://members.aol.com/RVS-Norton/Lincoln.html (accessed on October 8, 1999).

Abraham Lincoln Research Site. [Online] http://members.aol.com/RVSNorton/Lincoln2.html (accessed on October 8, 1999).

Assassination of President Lincoln and the Trial of the Assassins. [Online] http://www.tiac.net/users/ime/famtree/burnett/lincoln.htm (accessed on October 8, 1999).

Bishop, Jim. *The Day Lincoln Was Shot.* New York: Harper, 1955. Reprint, New York: Greenwich House, 1984.

Bruns, Roger. *Abraham Lincoln.* New York: Chelsea House, 1986.

Donald, David Herbert. *Lincoln.* New York: Simon & Schuster, 1995.

Dr. Samuel A. Mudd Society, Inc. *Dr. Samuel A. Mudd House Museum Home Page.* [Online] http://www.somd.lib.md.us/MUSEUMS/Mudd.htm (accessed on October 8, 1999).

Handlin, Oscar. *Abraham Lincoln and the Union.* Boston: Little, Brown, 1980.

Stern, Philip Van Doren. *The Life and Writings of Abraham Lincoln.* New York: Random House, 1940. Reprint, New York: Modern Library, 1999.

McPherson, James M. *Abraham Lincoln and the Second American Revolution*. New York: Oxford University Press, 1990.

Meltzer, Milton, ed. *Lincoln in His Own Words*. New York: Harcourt Brace, 1993.

National Park Service. *Ford's Theatre National Historic Site*. [Online] http://www.nps.gov/foth/index2.htm (accessed on October 8, 1999).

Oates, Stephen B. *With Malice Toward None: A Life of Abraham Lincoln*. New York: Harper and Row, 1977. Reprint, New York: HarperPerennial, 1994.

Surratt Society. *Surratt House Museum*. [Online] http://www.surratt.org/ (accessed on October 8, 1999).

Mary Todd Lincoln

Born December 13, 1818
Lexington, Kentucky
Died July 16, 1882
Chicago, Illinois

Wife of President Abraham Lincoln

Faced criticism and endured tragedy as first lady of the Union during the Civil War

Mary Todd Lincoln struggled with fears and depression that only grew worse with the untimely death of her husband in 1865.

Mary Todd Lincoln.
(Reproduced by permission of the National Portrait Gallery.)

Mary Todd Lincoln had a difficult job as first lady during the Civil War. She had to support her husband through stressful times and defend him against his opponents. She also faced a great deal of criticism herself for her expensive tastes and quick temper. Outwardly, she was well-equipped to deal with the job of first lady. After all, she came from a prominent family and had been a popular hostess in Lincoln's home state of Illinois. Inwardly, however, she struggled with fears and depression that only grew worse with the untimely death of her husband in 1865. Her battle with mental illness after the war made her a tragic figure.

Born into a wealthy Kentucky family

Mary Ann Todd Lincoln was born into a prominent family in Lexington, Kentucky, on December 13, 1818. She was the fourth of seven children born to Robert Smith Todd, a powerful banker, and his first wife. The Todds owned three slaves who acted as servants in their home and helped care for their children. Despite this fact, however, Robert Todd was not a strong supporter of slavery. When Mary was six years old, her mother died. Her father married Betsey Humphries the following year, and they eventually added eight more children to the family.

Mary was an intelligent, strong-willed, and highly emotional child. She often came into conflict with her stepmother and threw temper tantrums when she did not get her way. She struggled to get attention in such a large family, and later remembered her childhood as unhappy and lonely. As a young woman, Mary went away to school at the Shelby Female Academy. She received an excellent education at a time when few women had that opportunity.

In 1839, Mary moved to Springfield, which had recently become the capital of Illinois. She lived with one of her sisters, Elizabeth Edwards, who had married the son of the former governor of Illinois. Their home became the center of all the important social gatherings in Springfield. Mary proved to be a popular hostess and attracted a great deal of attention from the young men of the town. She was short and plump with an attractive face, and could make interesting and witty conversation on a wide range of subjects. But she remained insecure and sensitive to criticism, and she tended to hold a grudge against anyone who displeased her.

Marries the future president

Sometime shortly after her arrival in Springfield, Mary Todd met **Abraham Lincoln** (1809–1865; see entry), an attorney and member of the state legislature. He was ten years older than her, tall and thin, and quiet and awkward around women. But she saw the intensity and ambition behind his shyness. For his part, Lincoln was attracted to her intelligence and charm. They entered into a rocky, on-again off-again courtship, despite a lack of support from her family. They finally got married on November 4, 1842. They eventually had four sons together, although only one of them survived to adulthood: Robert Todd (1843–1926), Edward Baker (1846–1850), William "Willie" Wallace (1850–1862), and Thomas "Tad" (1853–1871).

Mary Lincoln had a difficult time during the early years of their marriage. Her husband was still working to establish himself as a lawyer and politician. Money was tight, and they initially rented a room in a hotel. It was a tremendous change for her, having grown up in luxury with servants to take care of her needs. She suddenly had to learn to cook, clean, wash, and care for her husband and young children. The Lincolns eventually moved into a nice house in Springfield and hired someone to help Mary with the chores. But these lean early years left her with a deep fear of poverty and a great love of expensive things.

Faces criticism and tragedy as first lady

By the late 1850s, the debate over slavery had created a huge rift between the Northern and Southern sections of the United States. Growing numbers of Northerners believed that slavery was wrong. Some people wanted to outlaw it, while others wanted to prevent it from spreading beyond the Southern states where it was already allowed. But many Southerners felt threatened by Northern efforts to contain slavery. They believed that each state should decide for itself whether to allow the practice. They did not want the national government to pass laws that would interfere with their traditional way of life. America's westward expansion only increased the tension between the North and South. Both sides wanted to spread their political views and way of life into the new states and territories.

Abraham Lincoln joined the antislavery Republican political party and ran for the U.S. Senate in 1858. He emerged as an outspoken opponent of slavery during a series of debates with Democrat Stephen Douglas (1813–1861). Although Lincoln lost the election, he gained a national reputation. In 1860, he was elected president of the United States. At this point, several Southern states decided that the U.S. govern-

Mary Todd Lincoln's husband, Abraham, and son, Thomas (Tad). *(Photograph by Anthony Berger. Courtesy of the Library of Congress.)*

ment and its antislavery president could no longer represent their interests. They announced their intention to secede (withdraw) from the United States and form a new country that allowed slavery, called the Confederate States of America. But Lincoln and other Northern politicians were determined to keep the Southern states in the Union. The Civil War began in April 1861, just a few weeks after Lincoln took office.

Once the Lincolns moved to the White House in Washington, D.C., Mary Lincoln decided to redecorate their new home. She felt that the president's house should reflect his important position. She purchased new china, furniture, carpets, and artwork for the White House. Although the items she chose reflected her good taste, they were also very expensive. In fact, she ended up exceeding the $20,000 budget for redecoration—which was supposed to cover the entire four-year term of her husband's presidency—within the first year. She also bought a striking new wardrobe for herself. People in the North criticized the first lady's spending habits. They thought it was inappropriate for her to live so extravagantly when thousands of young men were suffering and dying in the war.

Some people even questioned Mary Lincoln's loyalty to the Union. After all, she had been born in Kentucky, and her family had owned slaves. Four of her brothers and three of her half-brothers served in the Confederate Army during the Civil War. But in reality, Mary Lincoln felt a deep commitment to the Union cause and strongly endorsed her husband's policies. The stress of the war created some strain in their marriage, but she stood by the president and defended him against his critics. She also supported him by visiting sick and wounded soldiers in hospitals, and by helping to entertain important military and political leaders in the White House.

Mary Lincoln also faced a great deal of personal tragedy during the war years. The Lincolns' beloved son Willie died of typhoid fever in 1862. She struggled to deal with his death and remained secluded in her room for several months. Afterward, she refused to enter the room where Willie had died. She also held a mystical meeting called a séance to try to contact his spirit. Then in 1865, just as the Union celebrated victory in the Civil War, Abraham Lincoln was shot in the head, as he and the first lady attended a play at Ford's Theatre in Washington. He died the next day, April 15, 1865. The shock and grief over her husband's violent death left Mary Lincoln deeply depressed and virtually unable to function.

Struggles with mental illness

As she began to recover, Mary Lincoln went to Chicago to be with one of her sisters. While there, she learned that Abraham Lincoln's former law partner, William Herndon (1818–1891), was spreading ugly lies about her late husband and their marriage. Herndon claimed that Lincoln had never loved his wife, and had spent his whole life thinking about a childhood sweetheart named Ann Rutledge. The humiliation Mary Lincoln felt as a result of Herndon's statements caused her to suffer an emotional breakdown. She never fully recovered and struggled with mental illness for the rest of her life.

Mary Lincoln became obsessed with the idea that she was broke, but still could not stop herself from spending money extravagantly. During the late 1860s, she tried to sell some of her expensive clothing, jewelry, and furniture under an assumed name. This led to another embarrassing scandal, and she moved to Europe in order to avoid public criticism. She eventually returned to Chicago, and she received an annual pension (payment) from the U.S. Congress in 1870.

In 1875, however, Mary Lincoln became involved in another traumatic and highly publicized episode. The Lincolns' oldest son, Robert, went to court to have his mother declared insane. He was worried that she would spend all her money and become a financial burden to him, so he decided to commit her to a mental institution. Robert Lincoln won the first court battle. Mary Lincoln spent four months in an asylum in Batavia, Illinois, before being released to the custody of her sister. But she appealed the decision with the help of Myra Bradwell (1831–1894)—the first woman to practice law in the United States—and was found sane.

Again hoping to avoid public attention, Mary Lincoln moved to Europe for a few years. Upon her return to the United States, she became ill and was crippled by a back injury. She died on July 16, 1882. She was buried beside her husband in Springfield, Illinois.

Where to Learn More

Baker, Jean H. *Mary Todd Lincoln: A Biography.* New York: Norton, 1987.

Collins, David. *Shattered Dreams: The Story of Mary Todd Lincoln.* Greensboro, NC: Morgan Reynolds, 1994.

Neely, Mark E., Jr., and R. Gerald McMurtry. *The Insanity File: The Case of Mary Todd Lincoln.* Carbondale: Southern Illinois University Press, 1993.

Oates, Stephen B. *With Malice Toward None: A Life of Abraham Lincoln.* New York: Harper and Row, 1977. Reprint, New York: HarperPerennial, 1994.

Mary Todd Lincoln Research Site. [Online] http://members.aol.com/RVS-Norton/Lincoln15.html (accessed on October 8, 1999).

Sandburg, Carl. *Mary Lincoln: Wife and Widow.* New York: Harcourt, Brace and Co., 1932. Reprint, Bedford, MA: Applewood Books, 1995.

Santow, Dan. *Mary Todd Lincoln.* New York: Children's Press, 1999.

James Longstreet

Born January 8, 1821
Edgefield District, South Carolina
Died January 2, 1904
Gainesville, Georgia

Confederate general

**Controversial military leader whose reputation as
General Robert E. Lee's "old war horse" was
shaken at Gettysburg**

James Longstreet is perhaps the most controversial of the generals who served the Confederacy during the American Civil War. Longstreet's supporters point out that he fought courageously at many of the war's biggest battles, and that General **Robert E. Lee** (1807–1870; see entry) had such high regard for Longstreet that he affectionately referred to him as the Confederacy's "Old War Horse." But Longstreet's critics argue that he devoted too much time and energy to trivial political quarrels, and that he did not always do a good job of supporting Lee. Much of this still-lively debate about Longstreet centers on the Battle of Gettysburg, during which he and Lee had a famous dispute over military strategy.

A Georgia childhood

Longstreet was born on January 8, 1821, in Edgefield District, South Carolina, to James and Mary Ann Dent Longstreet. Within weeks of his birth, however, he was taken to his parents' cotton plantation outside of Gainesville, Georgia. "My earliest recollections were of the Georgia side of the

"James Longstreet made three mistakes that have denied him his deserved place in Southern posterity: He argued with Lee at Gettysburg, he was right, and he became a Republican."

Writer Stewart Sifakis

James Longstreet. *(Courtesy of the Brady National Photographic Art Gallery, Library of Congress.)*

285

Savannah River, and my school days were passed there," Longstreet recalled.

As Longstreet grew older, he developed a keen interest in fishing, hunting, and other outdoor activities. Encouraged by his father, he also dreamed of someday building a career for himself in the military. "From my early boyhood [my father] conceived that he would send me to West Point [Military Academy] for army service," Longstreet remembered. "But in my twelfth year he passed away [from cholera]." Longstreet's mother then moved her family to northern Alabama. A few years later, one of Longstreet's relatives helped him gain admittance to West Point.

West Point and Mexico

Longstreet entered West Point in 1838. He struggled in some of his classes, but his athletic abilities and his outgoing personality helped him to get by. Longstreet's many friends from this period of his life included **Ulysses S. Grant** 1822–1885; see entry), a boy from Ohio who would later take command of the Union Army during the Civil War.

After graduating from the academy in 1842, Longstreet entered the U.S. Army. He was first stationed to a military outpost in St. Louis, Missouri. During Longstreet's stay in St. Louis he met Louise Garland, the daughter of his regimental commander. The two became close, and in March 1848 Longstreet and Garland married. They eventually had ten children, but only five of them survived to adulthood.

Longstreet's first battlefield experiences came during the Mexican War, a conflict between Mexico and the United States that lasted from 1846 to 1848. This war came about when the United States became interested in acquiring significant sections of Mexican territory in order to expand its own land holdings. In 1845, America annexed (added) Texas to the Union and tried to negotiate the purchase of California and New Mexico from Mexico. But Mexico regarded Texas as one of its own provinces, and it refused to give up California and New Mexico. America's determination to take possession of these lands did not diminish, however, and the two countries ended up going to war over the territories.

Longstreet first served in the Mexican War under General Zachary Taylor (1784–1850) as part of the U.S. Eighth Infantry. His steady performance during the first year of the conflict brought him considerable attention, and he began to rise through the ranks. In early 1847, the Eighth Infantry joined an offensive led by General **Winfield Scott** (1786–1866; see entry) into the heart of Mexico. Scott's campaign included a successful assault on the Mexican fortress of Chapultepec. During this attack, Longstreet carried the flag of the Eighth Infantry over the fortress walls, only to be shot in the leg. He quickly turned and handed the flag to a fellow soldier named George Pickett (1825–1875), who waved the flag in triumph as he charged into the fort. Longstreet's bravery during the storming of Chapultepec further added to his growing reputation.

As Scott's campaign unfolded, American forces captured most of Mexico's major cities, including the capital of Mexico City. The offensive broke Mexico's ability to resist the American push to expand its territory. When a treaty ending the war was signed in early 1848, Mexico ceded (gave up) two-fifths of its territory to the United States in exchange for $15 million.

Joins the Confederate Army

Longstreet continued to serve in the U.S. Army in the 1850s. But his years of military service under the American flag came to an end on June 1, 1861, when he joined the newly formed army of the Confederate States of America. The Confederate States of America was composed of eleven Southern states which seceded from (left) the United States in late 1860 and early 1861. The root causes of this wave of secession were bitter disagreements between the nation's Southern and Northern regions over the issues of slavery, states' rights, and Federal authority.

Many Northerners believed that slavery was wrong and wanted to abolish (eliminate) it. In addition, they argued that the Federal government had the authority to pass laws that applied to all citizens of the United States. But much of the South's economy and culture had been built on the slave system, and Southerners resented Northern efforts

Naming Civil War Battles

Many famous Civil War battles are actually known by two different names, because the North and the South used different ways to name the engagements. The Union Army, for example, usually named battles for nearby creeks or rivers, while the Confederate forces often named battles for nearby towns. As a result, some battles came to be known by two different names:

Union Name for Battle	Confederate Name for Battle
Stones River	Murfreesboro
Antietam	Sharpsburg
Bull Run	Manassas
Fair Oaks	Seven Pines

This system was also used by the two sides to name their armies. For example, the Union used river names like the Potomac and the James as names for their forces. The Confederacy, meanwhile, named armies based on the geographic region in which they operated (Army of Northern Virginia, Army of Tennessee, Army of Mississippi, etc.)

to halt or contain the practice. In addition, they argued that the Federal government did not have the constitutional power to institute national laws on slavery or other issues. White Southerners argued that each state should decide for itself whether to allow slavery. In early 1861, these differences broke out into open war, as the South declared its independence, and the North vowed to use force to keep the country together.

Lee's "old war horse"

After joining the Confederate Army, Longstreet quickly established himself as an able officer and a tough fighter. Assigned to the South's Army of Northern Virginia, he was immediately promoted to brigadier general because of his West Point background and service in the Mexican War. In January 1862, however, Longstreet's concentration on military duties was shattered when three of his children died from scarlet fever. According to some historians, Longstreet never fully recovered from this loss.

Despite his personal problems, Longstreet distinguished himself during the first two years of the war. Emerging as one of General Robert E. Lee's most trusted officers, Longstreet helped secure Confederate triumphs in several major battles, including the First Battle of Bull Run (July 1861), the Seven Days' Campaign (June 1862), the Second Battle of Bull Run (August 1862), and the Battle of Fredericksburg (December 1862). Of course, not every battle went in favor of the South. But even in engagements like the bloody Battle of Antietam (September 1862), in which the North clawed out a narrow victory in western Maryland, Longstreet's troops displayed great spirit.

Longstreet's divisions filled vital roles in many of these clashes. In some battles, they led offensive charges that sparked rebel (Confederate) victory. In others, Longstreet used his knowledge of military tactics (movement of troops and ships) and strategy to erect strong defensive positions that were difficult for Union forces to penetrate. But whatever the assignment, Longstreet's troops seemed to do a good job of it. As Longstreet's reputation for steady battlefield performance increased, Lee began referring to him admiringly as "my old war horse."

The Battle of Gettysburg

During the summer of 1863, Lee decided to follow up a smashing May victory at Chancellorsville, Virginia, with an invasion of the North. The Confederate general hoped that by bringing the war into the Northern states, he could capture badly needed provisions (food and supplies) and create a surge of antiwar sentiment in the North. Lee knew that President **Abraham Lincoln** (1809–1865; see entry) would not be able to continue the war against the South if he did not have the support of the Northern people.

Lee moved his Army of Northern Virginia into Pennsylvania. His army of seventy-five thousand troops was a dangerous one. But the extended absence of Lee's cavalry on a raid made it hard for him to obtain accurate information about enemy troop movements. As a result, the Confederate force nearly walked right into the Union's Army of the Potomac, a ninety thousand–man force led by General **George Meade** (1815–1872; see entry).

On July 1, the two armies finally came together in the vicinity of a village called Gettysburg. Neither side gained a big advantage during the afternoon. Instead, leaders of both armies maneuvered for the best possible strategic position. When the day's fighting was over, Lee gathered Longstreet and his other officers together to discuss their next move. Longstreet believed that the Union Army had managed to secure superior positions. Concerned that the rebels would be unable to push the Yankees (Northerners) from those positions, he urged Lee to leave the area and establish a strong defensive position elsewhere. "[Longstreet] reasoned that because a Confederate army was in Union territory, Meade . . . would be forced by political pressures to take the offensive to drive the enemy out of Pennsylvania," stated historian James M. McPherson in *Civil War Journal*. "So he recommended to Lee that they find a strong position, wait for the inevitable [unavoidable] Union attack, and then break it to pieces."

But Lee was confident that his army could win, and he disregarded Longstreet's advice. When it became clear that Lee intended to order a large-scale offensive on the Union defensive positions, Longstreet sulked and muttered his doubts about the plan to other officers.

On the following day, Lee ordered his troops forward in a large-scale assault on the Yankee enemy. Longstreet's performance during this attack has been a source of bitter debate ever since. Some historians contend that Longstreet was so mad at Lee that he deliberately did a poor job of leading his troops. But other historians believe that while Longstreet strongly disagreed with Lee's strategy, he did his best to fulfill his commander's wishes.

In any event, Lee's frontal assault of July 2 failed. But after retreating for the evening, Lee decided to attempt another offensive against the Union defenses the following day. Targeting a center of Union defenses called Cemetery Ridge, he told Longstreet to prepare his troops to lead the assault the next morning.

On the morning of July 3, Longstreet once again expressed deep reservations about Lee's plan. Noting that the open terrain in front of Cemetery Ridge offered no protection for his soldiers, he flatly predicted catastrophe. But when Lee refused to change his mind, Longstreet prepared his men for the assault. "Never was I so depressed as upon that day," he later wrote. "I thought that my men were to be sacrificed and that I should have to order them to make a hopeless charge."

As Longstreet had predicted, the attack on Cemetery Ridge ended in disaster for the Confederates. Led by a division of soldiers under the command of George Pickett—Longstreet's old comrade from the Mexican War—Longstreet's corps (a military division) made a heroic but doomed effort to break through the Union defenses. The Union cannons and rifles lined up along Cemetery Ridge cut

A military bridge near Knoxville, Tennessee. James Longstreet's attempt to overtake Union-occupied Knoxville failed. *(Photograph by George N. Barnard. Courtesy of the Library of Congress.)*

the advancing rebel force to pieces and brought Lee's dreams of Northern invasion to an end. "That day at Gettysburg was one of the saddest of my life," Longstreet later said.

Longstreet moves West

The failure of "Pickett's Charge," as the July 3 attack came to be known, forced Lee to retreat back to Virginia with the battered remains of his army. Two months later Longstreet was transferred out of the Army of Northern Virginia at his own request. He joined the Army of Tennessee, commanded by General **Braxton Bragg** (1817–1876; see entry).

At first, the switch to the war's western theater (the region of the South between the Mississippi River and the Appalachian Mountains) seemed to rekindle Longstreet's spirits. For example, in September 1863, he helped Bragg gain a decisive victory over Union troops in northern Georgia at the Battle of Chickamauga. But Longstreet became infuriated when Bragg fumbled away a chance to crush the remainder of the enemy army. After that, Longstreet engaged in bitter quarrels with several subordinate (lower ranked) officers and launched a siege of Union-occupied Knoxville, Tennessee, that ended in complete failure.

Rejoining General Lee

After the failed siege of Knoxville, Longstreet became so depressed that he asked to be relieved of command. The Confederate Army refused to accept his resignation, but it did send Longstreet and his troops back to Virginia, where they were reunited with Lee.

In May 1864, Lee's Army of Northern Virginia faced Ulysses S. Grant's Army of the Potomac in the bloody Wilderness campaign. During the course of this violent struggle, Longstreet was accidently shot in the throat by his own troops. He eventually recovered from the wound, but by the time he returned to active service, the Civil War was in its final stages. He helped defend Petersburg and Richmond from the advancing Union armies during the spring of 1865, but the Confederate resistance became hopeless. In April 1865, he accompanied Lee when he surrendered at Appomattox, Virginia.

Loved and hated in the South

After the war, Longstreet became a successful New Orleans insurance and cotton broker. But while some Southerners continued to honor him for his wartime efforts, his popularity in the region dropped dramatically when he allied himself with the Republican political party, which had led the fights to end slavery and preserve the Union. Ignoring his critics, Longstreet served in a variety of federal Republican administrations until his death in 1904.

Longstreet also became very unpopular in some quarters because of his postwar criticism of Lee. General Lee was beloved all across the South, and no one liked to hear him criticized. When Longstreet dared to complain about

Lee's decisions at Gettysburg, Southerners instead blamed him for the loss.

Debates about Longstreet's performance at Gettysburg continue today. Some historians are among his strongest critics. For example, Steven E. Woodworth wrote in *Jefferson Davis and His Generals* that "At Gettysburg . . . Longstreet demonstrated that he could be anything but reliable and more than a little childish when the plan chosen by his commander did not meet with his approval." Other historians, however, believe that Longstreet was one of the South's strongest corps commanders, and that he has been treated unfairly. "Corps commander James Longstreet made three mistakes that have denied him his deserved place in Southern posterity," commented Stewart Sifakis in *Who Was Who in Civil War History*. "He argued with Lee at Gettysburg, he was right, and he became a Republican."

Where to Learn More

DiNardo, R. L., and Albert A. Nofi, eds. *James Longstreet: The Man, the Soldier, the Controversy.* Conshohocken, PA: Combined Pub., 1998.

Eckenrode, H. J., and Bryan Conrad. *James Longstreet: Lee's War Horse.* Chapel Hill: University of North Carolina, 1936. Reprint, 1986.

Hallock, Judith Lee. *General James Longstreet in the West: A Monumental Failure.* Fort Worth, TX: Ryan Place, 1995.

The Longstreet Chronicles. [Online] http://www.chickasaw.com/~rainbow/ (accessed on October 15, 1999).

Longstreet, James. *From Manassas to Appomattox: Memoirs of the Civil War in America.* Philadelphia: Lippincott, 1896. Reprint, New York: Da Capo Press, 1992.

Piston, William Garrett. *Lee's Tarnished Lieutenant: James Longstreet and His Place in Southern History.* Athens: University of Georgia Press, 1987.

Wert, Jeffry D. *General James Longstreet: The Confederacy's Most Controversial Soldier—A Biography.* New York: Simon & Schuster, 1993.

Thaddeus Lowe

Born August 20, 1832
Jefferson Mills, New Hampshire
Died January 16, 1913
Pasadena, California

Balloonist for Union Army
Conducted military reconnaissance for
Union forces during Civil War

Thaddeus Lowe developed and supervised a fleet of manned balloons that provided valuable information to Union forces on enemy troop positions and movements. Lowe's balloons thus became the first aviation aircraft used in American military history. The U.S. government never really appreciated the value of Lowe's Balloon Corps, however. By mid-1863, administrative errors and general lack of support brought Lowe's balloon operations to an end.

Difficult childhood fosters independent spirit

Thaddeus Soieski Constantine Lowe was born in Coos County, New Hampshire, on August 20, 1832, to a family whose ancestors had fought in the Revolutionary War (1776–83). His parents, Clovis and Alpha Lowe, had four other children in addition to Thaddeus. By the time he was ten years old they decided that they could no longer provide for all of them. They arranged to hire Thaddeus out to a neighboring farmer who agreed to provide him with food, shelter, and adult guidance in exchange for work. Saddened

"[I] would lie in a field or sit astride a picket fence, gazing for hours at the great white clouds hanging like banners or floating slowly across the skies."

Thaddeus Lowe in one of his balloons. *(Courtesy of the Library of Congress.)*

at the idea of separation from his parents and siblings, Lowe reluctantly went off to live with his new guardians.

Lowe was treated poorly by the farmer and his wife. They were harsh disciplinarians who behaved as if he were their personal servant. They refused his requests for books to read and made little effort to provide for his education. Lowe, though, was very curious about the world around him. He borrowed books whenever he was able, and spent long hours exploring the neighboring countryside. Years later, Lowe recalled that he loved to look up into the sky during these excursions. "[I] would lie in a field or sit astride a picket fence, gazing for hours at the great white clouds hanging like banners or floating slowly across the skies," he said. Lowe's early interest in the sky and its mysterious properties eventually grew into a deep fascination with ballooning and aerial navigation.

By the time that Lowe was eleven years old, he had become so unhappy on the farm that he decided to run away. He chose the Fourth of July as his day of departure because of its status as a symbol of independence. He set out alone into the world with a small bag of belongings and eleven cents. He spent the next several years in small farming communities and Portland, Maine, before moving to Boston, Massachusetts.

Lowe spent his teenage years working at a variety of odd jobs in order to feed and clothe himself. But even though he had to devote a great deal of his time and energy to these jobs, he worked hard to increase his knowledge of chemistry and other subjects. His interest in the skies also remained strong, and he began using kites and balloons to conduct various experiments in aeronautics (the study of aircraft navigation).

Passion for flying

By the mid-1850s, Lowe had gained enough education in chemistry and other fields of science to support himself as a lecturer on these subjects. He spent nearly all of his free time, however, trying to develop a reliable balloon that would allow him to explore the skies that had fascinated him for so long.

People had been traveling through the air by balloon since 1783, when a Frenchman named Jean François de Rozier flew over Paris. (De Rozier died a few months later during an attempted flight over a European waterway known as the English Channel.) By the 1850s, American John Wise and other balloonists—sometimes called aeronauts—had made repeated ascents up into the skies in manned balloons. But ballooning remained an expensive and dangerous occupation that few people dared to attempt.

In February 1855, Lowe married Leontine Gachon, a Frenchwoman who encouraged his study of aeronautics. They settled in New England, where Lowe earned enough money to buy a balloon. In 1856, Lowe ascended in his balloon for the first time. His first ride was a "captive" ascent—one in which the balloon rises but is connected to the ground by a system of ropes. Within a short period of time, however, Lowe was making "free" ascents. He could then roam wherever he wished because no ropes kept the vessel tethered to the ground. "More ascensions followed as Lowe perfected his ballooning techniques, and he learned to make free ballooning flights across country," wrote Eugene B. Block in *Above the Civil War.* "He loved the silence in the air, the apparent stillness while the balloon, borne by the wind, moved effortlessly far above the surface of the earth."

By 1858, Lowe was constructing his own balloons and making flights of ever greater distance. In 1859, he constructed a huge balloon called the *City of New York.* He dreamed of flying that balloon across the Atlantic Ocean to Europe. But two attempts to make this voyage ended in failure because his airship had problems retaining enough gas to stay inflated.

Lowe's most famous flight

In early 1861, Lowe abandoned his efforts to cross the Atlantic in favor of a flight across America's heartland. He and several other leading scientists believed that this flight would prove their theory that an eastward flowing air stream existed in the upper levels of the atmosphere, and that this air stream could someday be used to float across the ocean to Europe. Early in the morning of April 20, 1861, Lowe launched his bold experiment. Departing from Cincinnati, Ohio, he rose skyward until he was almost three miles above the earth. Just as he and his fellow scientists expected, he en-

Thaddeus Lowe sets up balloon gas generators near the U.S. Capitol in Washington, D.C.
(Reproduced by permission of Corbis.)

tered into a powerful air stream that carried him steadily eastward. His exhilarating voyage carried him over the Allegheny Mountains at altitudes that sometimes exceeded four and a half miles above the earth's surface. He finally landed outside Unionville, South Carolina, nine hours later, only to be taken into custody as a Union spy.

Lowe, as it turned out, had launched his flight in the opening days of the American Civil War. This conflict between the nation's Southern and Northern states began in April 1861. The two sides had become extremely angry with one another over the years, especially over the issue of slavery. Many Northerners believed that slavery was immoral. Some people wanted to outlaw it, while others wanted the Federal government to stop it from spreading beyond the Southern states where it was already allowed. But slavery played a big role in the Southern economy and culture, and white Southerners felt threatened by Northern efforts to contain slavery. They believed that each state should decide for itself whether to allow slavery. They did not want the national government to pass laws that would interfere with their traditional way of life. The two sides finally went to war in the spring of 1861 when the Southern states tried to secede from (leave) the United States and form a new country that allowed slavery, called the Confederate States of America.

When Lowe first landed in South Carolina, he worried that he might be thrown into prison or even executed. The local townspeople who watched him land had never seen anything like his balloon before, and they viewed its "Yankee" (Northerner) owner with suspicion and alarm. They grew even more doubtful of his truthfulness when he insisted that he had flown all the way from Cincinnati, more than nine hundred miles away. But Lowe finally convinced them of his honesty when he pulled out a Cincinnati newspaper that explained the details of his flight. The Southern authorities promptly released him and his balloon. But when he returned North, he made his way to Washington, D.C., to volunteer his balloon expertise to the Union cause.

Balloonist for the Union

Within a few weeks of his arrival in Washington, Lowe was granted an audience with President **Abraham Lincoln** (1809–1865; see entry). During his meeting with the president, Lowe explained his belief that balloons could be used by the Union Army as a valuable tool in tracking Confederate positions and troop movements. After all, they could rise to heights that would allow passengers to peer onto the other side of forests and hills and mountains, where Confederate camps and armies might be lurking. Lowe noted that this information would greatly help Union generals in devising their military strategies.

Lincoln was intrigued by Lowe's presentation. A few days later, Lowe further demonstrated the value of his balloons by sending a telegraphic message to the ground from a height of five hundred feet. This demonstration impressed Lincoln so much that he assigned the civilian (non-military) balloonist to the Army of the Potomac and named him chief of army aeronautics. Lowe remained a civilian, but he received an army salary that was equivalent to that earned by a colonel.

Over the next two years, Lowe provided valuable assistance to Union forces. He developed a fleet of seven balloons, each of which was capable of taking army officers thousands of feet above the ground. From these high vantage points, Union observers were able to develop accurate maps, determine effective transportation routes, and scout possible campsites. Best of all, Lowe's small but effective Balloon Corps enabled Union officers to observe Confederate activities. Union artillery officers, for example, sometimes used the balloons to help them determine where to aim their cannons in the middle of battles. The balloons also allowed the Union to track enemy movements and see where rebel (Confederate) armies were camped. In fact, it was not unusual for observers in Lowe's balloons to detect smoke from enemy camps at distances of twenty-five miles or more.

Not surprisingly, Lowe's balloons became a prime target for Confederate gunfire and artillery shells. The rebels knew that the balloons were used by the Union to gather military information. With the balloons in use, the Confederates had a difficult time launching surprise attacks and keeping the size of their armies secret. Confederate forces subsequently fired on Lowe and other members of his Balloon Corps whenever they could in hopes of bringing one of the airships down. This desire to shoot Lowe down led one historian to call the balloonist "the most shot-at man in the war."

Lack of support causes frustration

As the war progressed, Lowe and his fleet of balloons gained many admirers in the Union Army. Army of the Potomac commander **George B. McClellan** (1826–1885; see entry) and his cavalry commander George Stoneman (1822–1894) became particularly vocal supporters of Lowe. They praised the usefulness of the balloons in their reports and urged the Federal government to increase its financial support for Lowe's corps.

Despite these expressions of support, though, Lowe experienced great frustration during his service to the Army of the Potomac. His Balloon Corps received little financial or

Longstreet's View of Lowe's Balloon Corps

Many Confederate soldiers and officers admitted that they were very relieved when Lowe's Balloon Corps disbanded in 1863. Years after the Civil War concluded, the famous Confederate general **James Longstreet** (1821–1904; see entry) wrote Thaddeus Lowe a letter in which he expressed admiration for Lowe's ballooning exploits. He also talked about the South's failed effort to launch a balloon of its own:

> I was . . . in the woods May 2, 1862, when I saw your balloon about to rise. Then commenced [began] a heavy cannonading from the Confederate works [artillery]. Shots went over our heads, tearing six branches from the trees.
>
> The balloon rose, and the firing was soon directed at this air target, shot after shot, shells exploding way up, and occasionally the sharp crack of a rifle would be heard when our sharpshooters took a chance shot—and it kept up for half a day. No damage was done, except slaughter of five old trees and great holes in the ground where the solid shot struck.
>
> At all times we were fully aware that you Federals [Union forces] were

using balloons to examine our positions and we watched with envious eyes their beautiful observations as they floated high in the air, well out of range of our guns. While we were longing for balloons that poverty denied us, a genius arose and suggested that we send out and get every silk dress in the Confederacy and make a balloon.

> It was done and soon we had a great patchwork ship of many and various hues [colors] which was ready for use in the Seven Days' campaign [a battle in Virginia that lasted from June 25 to July 1, 1862].
>
> We had no gas [for the balloon] except in Richmond and it was the custom to inflate the balloon there, tie it securely to an engine, and run it down the York River Railroad to any point at which we desired to send it up. One day it was on a steamer down the James River when the tide went out and left the vessel and the balloon high and dry on a bar [sandbar]. The Federals gathered it in, and with it the last silk dress in the Confederacy. This capture was the meanest trick of the war and one I have never yet forgiven.

administrative support from the U.S. War Department. In addition, many Union officers stubbornly refused to consider using the balloons, even though their effectiveness had been proven. Instead, they relied on cavalry and other traditional scouting methods with which they were familiar. Finally, Lowe's repeated requests to be given a military commission (an officer ranking in the army) were ignored.

The army's refusal to grant Lowe a military commission infuriated him. After all, he and his fellow balloonists had braved enemy cannonfire and stormy weather for almost two years in order to provide the Union Army with valuable reconnaissance information. This disappointment, along with continued bureaucratic interference, finally convinced Lowe to resign his position in May 1863. Lowe's Balloon Corps remained in operation a few months longer, but it quickly fell apart without its leader. The Corps formally disbanded (broke up) on August 1, 1863, marking an end to aerial scouting activity in the war.

Lowe's resignation did not attract that much attention in the North. But several officers and scientists who had witnessed his exploits (bold deeds) sent him letters expressing their appreciation for his efforts on behalf of the Union. Major General George Stoneman, for example, offered heartfelt words of thanks to the balloonist for his service: "I beg to testify to you in writing, as I often have in words, my appreciation of the valuable services you have rendered the government during your connection with the Army of the Potomac. . . . I have been up in [your balloons] often and never made an ascent without coming down much better informed in regard to everything in my vicinity than I could possibly have been by other means. Valuable as your balloons have been, I feel satisfied that you would have made them still more so had you been encouraged by having more facilities [resources] extended to you."

Inventor and businessman

After the war, Lowe became a noted inventor and entrepreneur. He devised a new process for manufacturing artificial ice in 1866, and in 1873 he developed a manufacturing process that greatly improved the use of gaslight illumination. He also introduced new processes in the steelmaking industry and financed the construction of an observatory and an electric railway in California. In the late 1890s, however, Lowe experienced financial difficulties that dogged him for the rest of his life. He died in California in 1913.

Where to Learn More

Block, Eugene B. *Above the Civil War: The Story of Thaddeus Lowe, Balloonist, Inventor, Railroad Builder.* Berkeley, CA: Howell-North Books, 1966.

Hoehling, Mary. *Thaddeus Lowe: America's One-Man Air Corps.* New York: Messner, 1958.

Karr, Kathleen. *Spy in the Sky.* New York: Hyperion Books for Children, 1997.

Sims, Lydel. *Thaddeus Lowe: Uncle Sam's First Airman.* New York: Putnam, 1964.

George B. McClellan

Born December 3, 1826
Philadelphia, Pennsylvania
Died October 29, 1885
Orange, New Jersey

Union general known as "the young Napoleon"
Commander of the Army of the Potomac in 1861–62
Democratic nominee for the presidency in 1864

George B. McClellan was one of the top Union military leaders during the early years of the Civil War. He took command of the Army of the Potomac in July 1861—following the Union's humiliating defeat at the First Battle of Bull Run—and soon proved to be a great organizer and motivator of troops. When it came time to lead his forces into battle, however, McClellan became slow and indecisive. His shortcomings as a battlefield leader may have prevented the Union from capturing the Confederate capital of Richmond, Virginia, during the Peninsula Campaign of spring 1862. In September of that year, his extreme caution allowed Confederate forces under **Robert E. Lee** (1807–1870; see entry) to escape after the Battle of Antietam in Maryland. McClellan was very popular with his troops, but his failures and his arrogance strained his relationship with Union political leaders. President **Abraham Lincoln** (1809–1865; see entry) finally removed him from command in November 1862.

"McClellan was capable and skilled in creating an army, but he had too much of a mother's instinct in him, too much of the protective instinct."

From Civil War Journal: The Leaders

George B. McClellan
(Courtesy of the Library of Congress.)

A high-achieving young man

George Brinton McClellan was born in Philadelphia, Pennsylvania, on December 3, 1826. He was the third of five children born to George McClellan, a doctor and founder of a medical school, and his wife, Elizabeth Brinton McClellan. Both of his parents belonged to old and distinguished Philadelphia families. As a result, McClellan had many advantages growing up. He attended a top preparatory school as a boy, then enrolled in the University of Pennsylvania at the age of thirteen. In 1842, he received an appointment to attend the prestigious U.S. Military Academy at West Point in New York. At fifteen, McClellan was actually too young to become a cadet at West Point, but the school made an exception to its age rule for him. He had a brilliant career as a cadet (military student) and graduated second in his class in 1846.

After leaving West Point, McClellan joined the U.S. Army as an engineering officer. He served in the Mexican War (1846–48; a dispute between the United States and Mexico over large sections of territory in the West) and won two awards for distinguished service. After the United States forced Mexico to give up its claims on California and other areas in 1848, McClellan remained in the military and built forts, harbors, and railroads. He also became an instructor at West Point for three years. In the mid-1850s, McClellan traveled to Europe to study the latest military advancements. This was an important assignment for the young officer. Upon his return, he designed a new saddle for military use and introduced the pup tent to American forces. In 1857, McClellan resigned from the army to become an engineer in the rapidly growing railroad industry. By 1860, he had become president of the Ohio and Mississippi Railroad. He also married Ellen Marcy that year. They eventually had a son and a daughter together.

Rejoins the military at the start of the Civil War

McClellan's work in the railroad industry made him a wealthy man. But he remained interested in military matters, especially as ongoing disputes between the Northern and Southern sections of the country threatened to erupt into war. The main issue dividing the two regions was slavery. Growing numbers of Northerners believed that slavery was wrong. Some people wanted to outlaw it, while others wanted to prevent it from spreading beyond the Southern states where it was already allowed. But slavery played an important role in the South's economy and culture. As a result, many Southerners felt threatened by Northern efforts to contain slavery. They believed that each state should decide for itself whether to allow the practice. They did not want the national government to pass laws that would interfere with their traditional way of life.

America's westward expansion further increased the tension between the North and South. Both sides wanted to spread their political views and way of life into the new states and territories. By 1861, the situation convinced a group of Southern states to secede (withdraw) from the United States and form a new country that allowed slavery, called the Confederate States of America. But Northern political leaders would not let the Southern states leave the Union without a fight. The Civil War began a short time later.

George McClellan and his wife, Ellen. *(Courtesy of the Library of Congress.)*

McClellan lived in Cincinnati, Ohio, when the war started. As the Northern states began to raise armies for the conflict, the governor of Ohio asked McClellan to take command of that state's volunteer forces. Even though his main army service had been as an engineer, McClellan eagerly accepted the rank of major general in the Ohio Volunteers. His forces fought in some of the earliest clashes of the Civil War. They entered western Virginia—a region that remained sympathetic to the Union despite Virginia's decision to secede—in July 1861. Their successful offensive (attack) chased most Confederate troops out of the area and cleared the way for Union supporters to separate from Virginia and establish their own state, known as West Virginia. McClellan took a great deal of credit for this early Northern success. He soon came to national attention as the Union's first war hero.

Commands the Union's Army of the Potomac

While McClellan was running Confederate forces out of western Virginia, the main Union Army was suffering an embarrassing defeat in July 1861 at the First Battle of Bull Run (also known as the First Battle of Manassas) in the eastern part of the state. Poorly prepared and terribly disorganized, the Army of the Potomac ended up making a panicked retreat back to Washington, D.C. President Abraham Lincoln reacted to the defeat by naming McClellan commander of the Army of the Potomac. At the age of thirty-four, McClellan took control of the North's largest army. He became the second-highest ranking officer in the American military. The only soldier who outranked him was General **Winfield Scott** (1786–1866; see entry), the commander of all U.S. armed forces.

Within a short time, McClellan proved himself to be a great organizer and trainer of troops. He used tough training schedules and strict discipline to improve the army's preparation and confidence. He made sure his men had the best arms and equipment, were well fed, and got paid on time. He also mingled with the troops and showed that he cared about them, which helped raise their morale. Over time, McClellan turned the inexperienced and demoralized Army of the Potomac into a strong fighting force. Thanks to the general's personal style of leadership, the soldiers in the ranks almost worshiped him. In fact, he was more popular among his men than any other Civil War general.

Unfortunately, McClellan was not as popular among Northern political leaders. He tended to be arrogant and boastful, and he resented having civilian (non-military) officials tell him what to do. As a result, he clashed with President Lincoln, Secretary of War Edwin Stanton (1814–1869), and General Scott on many occasions. In fact, he actively worked against Scott and ended up forcing the elderly general to retire in November 1861. McClellan then took his place as general-in-chief of all the Union armies. By this time, Northern newspapers were calling McClellan the "Young Napoleon," after the famous French military leader and emperor Napoléon Bonaparte (1769–1821).

Once McClellan had trained and supplied his troops, Northern political leaders expected him to launch an offensive strike against the Confederates in Virginia. But McClellan continually found excuses to delay the attack. "So soon as I feel that my army is well organized and well disciplined and strong enough, I will advance and force the Rebels [Confederates] to a battle on a field of my own selection," he stated. "A long time must elapse before I can do that."

Part of the problem was that McClellan consistently overestimated the size and strength of the opposing forces. He became convinced that the Confederate Army waiting for him in Virginia consisted of 250,000 men, when in fact it was more like sixty thousand. By November 1861, he decided that he should wait for the end of winter before moving against the enemy. In December, he became ill with typhoid fever, which led to another delay of several weeks. But the main reason behind McClellan's extreme caution and indecision was that he was unwilling to commit troops to battle unless he was guaranteed of success. "McClellan was capable and skilled in creating an army, but he had too much of a mother's instinct in him, too much of the protective instinct," according to William C. Davis, Brian C. Pohanka, and Don Troiani in *Civil War Journal: The Leaders*. "He was creating an army, and he wanted that army to be as good as any that had ever taken a battlefield, but at the same time he wanted no harm to come to it."

The Peninsula Campaign

Lincoln finally forced McClellan into action. In January 1862, the president released General War Order No. 1, which called for a Union offensive into Virginia to begin by February 22. When the Army of the Potomac remained in Washington past that date, Lincoln punished McClellan for his inaction by stripping him of his title as general-in-chief over all Union forces. McClellan, who remained in charge of the Army of the Potomac, finally began his ambitious Peninsula Campaign in mid-March. Rather than marching through northern Virginia, he transported about one hundred thousand troops by boat to the Virginia coast. His army then marched inland up the peninsula toward the Confederate capital of Richmond.

At first, it appeared that McClellan's plan would be successful. The Union forces met with little resistance and

Allan Pinkerton—
The Detective Who Convinced McClellan He Was Outnumbered

One of the main reasons Union general George B. McClellan was so reluctant to move against the Confederate Army was that he always believed he was outnumbered. For example, McClellan delayed the start of his Peninsula Campaign for six months because he thought there were 250,000 Confederate troops waiting for him in Virginia. But the real number of enemy forces was more like sixty thousand. The man who provided McClellan with these inflated estimates of Confederate troop strength was Allen Pinkerton, one of the best-known detectives of his day.

Pinkerton was born in 1819 in Glasgow, Scotland. He grew up in the city's slums and eventually became involved in protests against conditions there. After a clash with police in 1841, Pinkerton smuggled himself aboard a boat heading across the Atlantic Ocean to Nova Scotia, Canada. He eventually moved to the United States and settled in Chicago, Illinois.

During his early years in Chicago, Pinkerton worked as a barrel maker. One time, his work led him directly to a band of counterfeiters (people who illegally produce and use fake money). He gave the police information about the band that led to their arrest. Soon afterward, Chicago merchants began hiring Pinkerton to help them track down other criminals.

In 1850, Pinkerton founded the Pinkerton National Detective Agency. It eventually became the nation's largest private investigation firm. During the early years, his agency specialized in providing security for the rapidly growing railroad industry. In the late 1850s, he worked closely with McClellan, who was the vice president of an Illinois railroad company at that time.

In November 1860, Abraham Lincoln was elected as the new president of the United States. He was scheduled to travel from Illinois to Washington, D.C., to be inaugurated (sworn in) in early 1861. Pinkerton's detectives learned of a plan to assassinate Lincoln as he made his way to Washington. Pinkerton spoiled the plan by changing the president's transportation plans at the last minute.

When the Civil War began a short time later, McClellan took command of volunteer forces in western Virginia. He asked Pinkerton to join his staff and provide military intelligence (information about the enemy) to assist in his war efforts. Before long, some of Pinkerton's best detectives were moving behind Confederate lines in the South and collecting secrets to help the

Allan Pinkerton. *(Reproduced by permission of Archive Photos, Inc.)*

Union. Pinkerton also spent a great deal of time interviewing prisoners, refugees, and fugitive slaves who crossed into Union territory to find out what they knew about the enemy. He regularly produced long, detailed reports about conditions in the Confederate Army.

Pinkerton remained with McClellan as the young officer took command of the Army of the Potomac and then of all the Union forces. By this time, the famous detective's most important job involved estimating the number of Confederate troops McClellan could expect to encounter in any given area. Pinkerton came up with a formula to help him determine enemy troop strength. Unfortunately, his assumptions were so far off that his estimates consistently turned out to be wrong. In fact, Pinkerton provided wildly inflated numbers that were often double or triple the actual figures. "Each step in Pinkerton's collection of this military intelligence was marked by error, adding up finally to colossal [gigantic] error," Stephen W. Sears explained in *George B. McClellan: The Young Napoleon.*

Nevertheless, McClellan believed Pinkerton's estimates without question. "McClellan accepted these reports with no more critical analysis than went into their making," Sears noted. "They were, after all, exactly what he expected: confirmation of his own conclusions." Due in part to Pinkerton, McClellan was extremely hesitant to move his army against the Confederates. His slowness prevented the Union from claiming major victories on two occasions, and forced Lincoln to remove McClellan from command in November 1862. Pinkerton quit working for the military at this time as well. He continued his detective agency after the war and died in 1884.

In early fall of 1862, President Abraham Lincoln visited George McClellan and his troops at Antietam. Here, Lincoln speaks with McClellan's intelligence expert, Allan Pinkerton (left) and Major General John A. McClernand. *(Courtesy of the Library of Congress.)*

claimed victory in several minor battles as they moved toward Richmond. But then McClellan was tricked into thinking that the Confederates had established a major defensive position in Yorktown. He spent a month setting up a siege (a blockade intended to prevent delivery of food and supplies) of the town, only to have the small enemy force leave before he attacked. The delay enabled Confederate general **Joseph E. Johnston** (1807–1891; see entry) to prepare his troops for the defense of Richmond.

McClellan pushed past Yorktown in early May, but his army continued to move slowly. The long-awaited clash between McClellan's and Johnston's armies finally took place on May 31 at Fair Oaks, only six miles from Richmond. Although the fighting ended in a virtual draw, it resulted in a change in Confederate leadership. Johnston suffered a serious wound in the battle, and Robert E. Lee took his place. Lee soon proved that he was more cunning and aggressive than Johnston. On June 25, he led a force of seventy thousand Confederate troops against McClellan. The two sides engaged in a series of fierce battles across the Virginia peninsula over the next week. These clashes, which came to be known as the Seven Days' Battles, convinced McClellan to abandon his offensive. Some historians claim that McClellan could have captured Richmond and ended the Civil War three years earlier if he had acted more quickly and decisively.

For his part, McClellan blamed Lincoln and the war department for his defeat. He claimed that they did not provide him with the reinforcements and supplies that he needed to win. "The president is an idiot!" he declared. "I only wish to save my country and find the incapables around me will not permit it." By August 1862, Lincoln decided that he had endured enough of McClellan's indecision and disrespect. He placed the Army of the Potomac under the command of Major General John Pope (1822–1892), who had already commanded the Federal Army of Virginia, and ordered them to return to Washington. But before McClellan's troops could get back from the Virginia peninsula, Confederate forces attacked Pope's army in northern Virginia. This contest, known as the Second Battle of Bull Run, resulted in another costly defeat for the Union.

Replaced as commander following the Battle of Antietam

As the losses continued to mount for the Union Army, many Northerners became concerned that the Confederates might win the war. President Lincoln knew that the lack of success in battle had left Union soldiers feeling fearful and discouraged. Recognizing the intense loyalty the troops felt toward McClellan, Lincoln made the difficult decision to return him to command of the Army of the Potomac. Once again, the young general turned the army around, improving the men's discipline and morale.

In the meantime, Confederate general Robert E. Lee decided to take advantage of his recent victories to invade the North. He believed that if the Confederate Army proved that it was capable of seizing control of Northern territory, Lincoln might be forced to negotiate an end to the war. Lee led fifty-two thousand troops across the Potomac River into Maryland in early September. A few days later, McClellan left Washington with seventy-five thousand troops from the Army of the Potomac. On September 13, McClellan received an incredible stroke of good luck. One of his men found a copy of Lee's orders to his army. The papers had been dropped by a careless Confederate officer.

McClellan's discovery of Lee's orders spurred him to close on the Confederate Army more quickly. But many historians claim that he was still too slow to act. Although his army reached Antietam Creek in western Maryland on September 16, McClellan decided to wait until the following day to launch an attack. The delay allowed Confederate troops under General **Thomas "Stonewall" Jackson** (1824–1863; see entry) to arrive and reinforce Lee's position. On September 17, the two armies finally met in a vicious day-long battle that killed or wounded more than twenty-three thousand Union and Confederate soldiers. This one-day casualty total marked the single bloodiest day in Civil War history.

By September 19, Lee decided to retreat back to Virginia. But it took his men some time to cross the swollen Potomac River. Some historians claim that if McClellan had launched another attack, he could have destroyed the Southern army. But the Union general was shaken by the high casualties his troops had suffered. "This Army is not now in condition to undertake another campaign nor to bring on another battle," he stated. "I am tired of the sickening sight of the battlefield with its mangled corpses and poor, suffering wounded. Victory has no charms for me when purchased at such a cost." As a result, McClellan did not pursue Lee's army when it retreated. He thus gave up another opportunity to bring an earlier end to the war.

In November 1862, Lincoln relieved McClellan of his command for good. The young general had demonstrated great skills as an organizer and motivator. But when it came to leading troops into battle, he was a failure. "The tragedy of McClellan," Davis, Pohanka, and Troiani wrote, "is that he failed to utilize his greatest strengths. His army would have done anything for him. . . . Yet he did not grant them that opportunity because it would mean that his beloved army would suffer."

Runs for president in 1864

After being stripped of his command, McClellan returned home to Trenton, New Jersey, and waited for new orders. But no orders ever came. He continued to watch the war closely, however, and before long he decided that he might be able to affect the outcome through politics. In 1864, McClellan challenged Lincoln as the Democratic political party's candidate for president. At first it appeared that he might be successful. But the Union Army claimed several important victories before the election that increased Northern support for Lincoln and the war effort. As a result, Lincoln returned to office by a comfortable margin. "For my country's sake I deplore [regret] the result—but the people have decided with their eyes wide open and I feel that a great weight is removed from my mind," McClellan said afterward.

Following his failed presidential bid, McClellan took his family to Europe for several years. Upon returning to the United States, he went back to work in engineering. In 1878, he was elected governor of New Jersey. During his three-year term in office, he improved the state's schools and built up a state militia. By the 1880s, McClellan finally decided that he was ready to face his Civil War record. He began speaking to veterans' groups and visiting battlefields during this time. He also wrote a memoir of his days with the Army of the Potomac called *McClellan's Own Story*. He defended his actions in the book, but also admitted that he lacked the killer instinct required of great battlefield generals. McClellan died suddenly of heart failure in Orange, New Jersey, on October 29, 1885. Many of the soldiers who had fought under him attended his funeral.

Where to Learn More

Davis, William C., Brian C. Pohanka, and Don Troiani. *Civil War Journal: The Leaders*. Nashville, TN: Rutledge Hill Press, 1997.

Green, Carl R., and William R. Sanford. *Union Generals of the Civil War*. Springfield, NJ: Enslow, 1998.

McClellan, George B. *McClellan's Own Story*. New York: C. L. Webster, 1887. Reprint, Scituate, MA: Digital Scanning, 1999.

McClellan Society. *MG George B. McClellan Pages*. [Online] http://www.civilwarreader.com/mcclellan/ (accessed on October 15, 1999).

Rowland, Thomas J. *George B. McClellan and Civil War History: In the Shadow of Grant and Sherman*. Kent, OH: Kent State University Press, 1998.

Sears, Stephen W. *George B. McClellan: The Young Napoleon*. New York: Ticknor and Fields, 1988. Reprint, New York: Da Capo Press, 1999.

Waugh, John C. *The Class of 1846: From West Point to Appomattox: Stonewall Jackson, George McClellan, and Their Brothers*. New York: Warner Books, 1994.

George G. Meade

Born December 31, 1815
Cádiz, Spain
Died November 6, 1872
Philadelphia, Pennsylvania

Union general
Led Northern forces to victory
at the Battle of Gettysburg

General George G. Meade will always be best remembered for his involvement in the famous Battle of Gettysburg. During this mid-1863 battle in the Pennsylvania countryside, Meade guided the Union's Army of the Potomac to a smashing victory over the South's Army of Northern Virginia, commanded by General **Robert E. Lee** (1807–1870; see entry). This Union victory is often cited as a major reason why the North eventually was able to win the war.

But despite his role in this important Northern triumph, Meade has received less praise for his performance than a number of other Civil War generals. His cautious pursuit of Lee's battered army after Gettysburg has been criticized by many historians. In addition, the decision of General **Ulysses S. Grant** (1822–1885; see entry) to take personal command of the Army of the Potomac in 1864 put Meade in Grant's shadow for the remainder of the war. Nonetheless, Meade's triumph at Gettysburg has assured him a prominent place in Civil War history.

"The results of [Meade's] victory [were] priceless. . . . The charm of Robert Lee's invincibility [was] broken.

Writer George Templeton Strong

George G. Meade.

Early career in engineering

George Gordon Meade was born in Spain on New Year's Eve, 1815. His father, Richard Worsam Meade, was stationed in Spain as a naval agent for the United States government. The Meade family lived comfortably during young George's first years, but mounting debts gradually began to threaten their economic well-being. Richard Meade brought his family back to the United States in an effort to regain his financial footing. He died a short time later, however, leaving his family deeply in debt. The family's strained financial circumstances forced young George to withdraw from a public school in Philadelphia that he had been attending.

In 1831, Meade managed to gain admission into the U.S. Military Academy at West Point in New York. He did not have a driving desire to build a career for himself in the army. He studied hard, though, because he knew that a good performance at the academy would aid him in whatever career he decided to pursue. Meade graduated from the academy in 1835. One year later he resigned from the army and took a series of jobs in the area of civil engineering (design and construction of bridges, canals, forts, and other public works).

Meade's civil engineering career took him all around the country in the late 1830s and early 1840s. He performed engineering work for Southern railroad lines and assisted in surveying (determining the boundaries of) the Mississippi and Texas border. As time passed, however, he realized that much of the engineering work taking place across the nation was being handled by the U.S. Army. He decided to return to active military duty, and on May 19, 1842, he was appointed a second lieutenant in the army's Corps of Topographical Engineers.

Meade spent most of the next two decades working on various engineering projects along the eastern seaboard and the Great Lakes coastlines. These projects ranged from conducting surveys of the Great Lakes boundaries to design work on coastal lighthouses. His only break from engineering work during this time came during the late 1840s, when he fought in the Mexican War (1846–48).

Tough Civil War soldier

Meade's career as an army engineer came to an end in April 1861, when hostilities between America's Northern and

Southern states erupted into war. These two regions had long been angry with one another over the issue of slavery. The Northern states thought slavery was wrong and wanted to abolish it. But the agriculture-based Southern economy had grown dependent on slavery, and white Southerners worried that their way of life would collapse if slavery was abolished (eliminated). As Northern calls to end slavery persisted, Southerners became increasingly resentful and defensive. The two sides finally went to war when the Southern states tried to secede from (leave) the Union and form a new country that allowed slavery, called the Confederate States of America.

When the Civil War began, Meade was promoted to brigadier general in the Union reserve army. Commanding a brigade of Pennsylvania soldiers, he helped build defenses around Washington, D.C. In June 1862, he was assigned to the Union's Army of the Potomac, commanded by Union general **George B. McClellan** (1826–1885; see entry). The Army of the Potomac was the Union's largest army in the war's eastern theater (the region of the country east of the Appalachian Mountains), so Meade knew that his new assignment meant that he would likely see a great deal of combat.

Meade's instincts were right. Over the course of the following year, he repeatedly found himself pitted against Confederate forces on battlefields throughout Virginia and southern Maryland. Leading commands in both minor skirmishes and major battles (Seven Days' Campaign [June 1862], Second Bull Run [August 1862], Antietam [September 1862], Fredericksburg [December 1862], and Chancellorsville [May 1863]), Meade acquired a reputation as a tough and steady officer. By mid-1863, his battlefield courage and aggressive style had captured the attention of President **Abraham Lincoln** (1809–1865; see entry) and his advisors.

Takes command of Army of the Potomac

Ever since the Civil War started back in 1861, Lincoln had been dissatisfied with the performance of the generals leading the Army of the Potomac. The president felt that the army's first commander, General George B. McClellan had been too cautious in confronting the Confederate enemy. Lincoln thus fired McClellan, only to watch in dismay as his successors—**Ambrose Burnside** (1824–1881; see entry) and

Joseph Hooker (1814–1879)—suffered costly defeats at the hands of General Robert E. Lee and his rebel (Confederate) Army of Northern Virginia.

When Lee launched a daring invasion of Northern territory in June 1863, Lincoln decided to replace Hooker with Meade. The president knew that if Lee's invasion was successful, pressure to negotiate an end to the war would increase throughout the North. If these calls became loud enough, he would have no choice but to negotiate a peace agreement with the South that would grant the secessionist states their independence.

When Meade took command of the Army of the Potomac on June 28, he knew that the entire course of the war might rest on his ability to beat back Lee's advance. He concentrated his army of ninety thousand troops together in the vicinity of a small Pennsylvania town called Gettysburg to prepare for the arrival of the Confederate Army.

Battle of Gettysburg

The two armies met outside of Gettysburg on July 1, 1863. During the battle's first day, Lee's seventy-five thousand–troop force pushed hard against Meade's defensive lines. But Meade had selected his position well, and Lee's forces were unable to dislodge the Federal Army. The following day, Lee launched a second major assault on the Army of the Potomac in hopes of breaking Meade's army and moving deeper into Union territory. Once again, however, the Army of the Potomac held its ground, delivering punishing blows of its own on the rebel army.

On July 3, the fighting resumed. As the battle wore on, it became clear to Lee that he would not be able to defeat Meade using ordinary measures. He gambled that a full frontal assault on the center of the Union's defenses might cripple the Northern army. He ordered fifteen thousand troops under the command of James J. Pettigrew (1828–1863) and George E. Pickett (1825–1875) to rush Cemetery Ridge, the heart of the Northern defenses. Some of Lee's officers urged him to abandon the plan, but the Confederate general refused to change his strategy.

This assault on Cemetery Ridge—commonly known as "Pickett's Charge"—ended in disaster for Lee's army. As Pettigrew and Pickett urged their troops on across the open ground that separated the two armies, Union artillery destroyed the advance with deadly cannon fire. Stunned by this disastrous turn of events, Lee gathered his battered army together and retreated back to Virginia.

The Battle of Gettysburg took a terrible toll on both armies. Meade's Army of the Potomac sustained more than twenty-three thousand casualties in the three days of fighting, while the Confederates lost approximately twenty-eight thousand troops. But while both sides suffered enormous losses in the clash, it was clear that the Union had won a major victory. Meade's triumph ended Lee's dreams of forcing a peace treaty and showed the North that the Confederate general could be defeated. As Northern writer George Templeton Strong exclaimed, "The results of this victory are priceless. . . . The charm of Robert Lee's invincibility is broken. The Army of the Potomac has at last found a general that can handle it, and has stood nobly up to its terrible work in spite of its long disheartening list of hard-fought failures. . . . Government is strengthened four-fold at home and abroad."

Everyone in the North reacted with excitement to news of Meade's great victory. But his cautious pursuit of Lee's bloodied army disappointed some observers, including Lincoln. These critics felt that if Meade had acted aggressively, he might have been able to destroy the Army of Northern Virginia completely and bring the war to an end. Today, some historians continue to criticize Meade for letting Lee get away. But others point out that a continuation of the fighting might not have ended in a Union victory, for Lee still had thousands of veteran troops at his disposal. "A heavy load of responsibility weighed on Meade's shoulders [at Gettysburg]," explained James M. McPherson in *Battle Cry of Freedom*. "He had been in command only six days. For three of them his army had been fighting for the nation's life, as he saw the matter, and had narrowly saved it. Meade could not yet know how badly the enemy was hurt, or that their artillery was low on ammunition."

Major General George G. Meade stands in front of his tent in June 1864.

(Reproduced by permission of the National Portrait Gallery.)

Grant takes over

On July 3, 1863, Meade was promoted to brigadier general in the regular Union Army. He continued to lead the Army of the Potomac throughout the fall and winter of that year. In the spring of 1864, however, Lieutenant General Ulysses S. Grant decided to accompany the Army of the Potomac. As the chief of all Union forces, Grant assumed leadership of the army. His arrival dropped Meade to second in command. But the hero of Gettysburg handled the new arrangement with dignity. He carried out Grant's orders with efficiency, and in August 1864, Grant arranged Meade's promotion to the rank of major general.

During the final months of the war, Meade assisted Grant as he slowly squeezed the life out of the disintegrating Confederate armies. He fought with distinction in several battles. In addition, he helped Grant develop the siege of Petersburg, Virginia, a maneuver that trapped Lee's army in the city for months. By the spring of 1865, it was clear that the Confederacy was on the verge of collapse. In April 1865, General Lee finally surrendered the battered remains of his army to Grant, bringing the war to a close.

After the war, Meade spent two years as commander of the Military Division of the Atlantic and the Department of the East in Philadelphia. In January 1868, he was reassigned to Atlanta, Georgia, where he enforced federal Reconstruction policies in a fair and reasonable manner (Reconstruction was the period in American history immediately following the Civil War when the nation struggled to resolve its differences and readmit the Southern states into the Union). He died in Philadelphia on November 6, 1872, as a result of pneumonia and the lingering effects of old war wounds.

Where to Learn More

Cleaves, Freeman. *Meade of Gettysburg.* Norman: University of Oklahoma Press, 1960.

Lyman, Theodore. *With Grant and Meade from the Wilderness to Appomattox.* Lincoln: University of Nebraska Press, 1994.

The Meade Archive. [Online] http://adams.patriot.net/~jcampi/welcome. htm (accessed on October 15, 1999).

John Singleton Mosby

Born December 6, 1833
Powhatan County, Virginia
Died May 30, 1916
Washington, D.C.

Confederate guerrilla leader
Tormented Union forces in northern Virginia from 1863 to 1865 as commander of "Mosby's Rangers"

During the course of the Civil War, groups of armed raiders known as "guerrillas" or "rangers" sprouted up all across the Confederacy to fight against invading Union armies. A number of these groups amounted to little more than semiorganized bands of outlaws who became best known for episodes of drunkenness and mindless violence. But other Southern guerrilla units operated with great effectiveness against important Union patrols and supply lines. The best of these guerrilla companies was commanded by John Singleton Mosby, a native Virginian whose bravery and dedication made him one of the most feared and respected of Confederate military leaders.

Born and raised in Virginia

John Singleton Mosby was born in Virginia in 1833 to Alfred and Virginia Mosby. Both sides of Mosby's family had lived in Virginia for generations. As he grew up, his relatives instilled in him a great love for his home state. Mosby entered the University of Virginia at the age of nineteen, but his

"Mosby has annoyed me considerably."

Union general William T. Sherman

John Singleton Mosby.
Reproduced by permission of the National Portrait Gallery.)

studies were abruptly cut short when he killed a man in an angry dispute.

When Mosby was brought to trial, the court decided that he did not deserve to receive a long prison term. Nonetheless, he was expelled from the university and imprisoned for nine months on a charge of unlawful shooting. Mosby spent much of his time in jail reading law books. When he was released, he became a legal assistant in the office of the local prosecutor who had convicted him.

Mosby worked and studied hard during this time. Within a year or so of his release from prison, he launched a successful career for himself as an attorney. In 1857, Mosby married Pauline Clark, the daughter of a Kentucky politician, and the couple soon started a family. Mosby's peaceful life was shattered, though, when the American Civil War broke out in April 1861.

Mosby sides with Virginia

The Civil War came about because of long-standing differences between the Northern United States and the Southern United States over a variety of issues, especially slavery and the concept of states' rights. Many Northerners believed that slavery was wrong and wanted to abolish (eliminate) it. They also contended that the Federal government had the authority to pass laws that applied to all citizens of the United States. But a large part of the South's economy and culture had been built on slavery, and Southerners resented Northern efforts to halt or contain the practice. In addition, they argued that the Federal government did not have the constitutional power to institute national laws on slavery or other issues. Instead, white Southerners argued that each state should decide for itself whether to allow slavery. Finally, America's westward expansion worsened these disputes, since both sides wanted to spread their way of life—and their political ideas—into the new territories and states.

By the spring of 1861, these bitter differences had caused a dramatic split in the country. At that time, a number of Southern states seceded from (left) the United States to form a new country that allowed slavery, called the Confederate States of America. The U.S. government, however, declared that those states had no right to secede and that it was willing to use force to make them return to the Union. In April 1861, the two sides finally went to war over their differences.

When the war began, Mosby promptly joined Virginia's Confederate army as a private. During the first six months of his service, however, Mosby did not make much of an impression on his superiors. Bored with routine military duties, he showed little initiative or interest in advancing to a higher rank. "We all thought he was rather an indifferent soldier," admitted one Confederate officer who knew Private Mosby.

Mosby becomes a ranger

By the spring of 1862, Mosby was spending most of his time helping Confederate colonel William E. Jones with paperwork and other administrative affairs. Desperate to escape these routine duties, he occasionally managed to grab an assignment to go scout enemy positions.

Within a few months, the detail and accuracy of Mosby's scouting reports caught the attention of General **Jeb Stuart** (1833–1864; see entry), a dashing cavalry officer in the Confederate Army of Northern Virginia. Impressed by Mosby's scouting abilities, Stuart used the young Virginian whenever he could. In fact, Mosby's scouting reports proved vital in helping Stuart execute a famous reconnaissance (exploration and spying) mission around Union troops in the summer of 1862. After the mission was completed, Mosby could barely contain his enthusiasm. "My dearest Pauline," he wrote to his wife. "I returned yesterday with General Stuart from the grandest scout of the war. I not only helped to execute it, but was the first one who conceived and demonstrated that it was practicable. Everybody says it was the greatest feat of the war. I never enjoyed myself so much in my life."

Mosby's experiences on the reconnaissance mission convinced him that he could better serve the Confederacy as the leader of one of the guerrilla units that were popping up across the South. These guerrilla or ranger companies used violent raids and sabotage (destruction or vandalism of property) to strike against Union outposts and supply lines. Loosely connected with the Confederate Army, they were supposed to operate under the direction of the South's regular military commanders. In many cases, though, these guerrilla companies functioned with little supervision from the army.

At first, Stuart resisted Mosby's requests for permission to start a new guerrilla group that would operate behind enemy lines in northern Virginia. But in December 1862, Stuart finally approved the request. On January 1, 1863, Mosby officially became the captain of a nine-man guerrilla group that eventually became the most effective ranger company in the entire South.

"Mosby's Confederacy"

Mosby spent the first two months of 1863 adding new recruits to his band. Then, as springtime arrived in northern Virginia, Mosby launched a series of raids that rocked Union forces throughout the region. Sometimes they ambushed (lied in wait to attack) Union patrols or captured Union horses and other supplies. At other times they destroyed Union railroads or cut telegraph lines. On a number of occasions, he and his men even struck on the outskirts of the Federal capital of Washington.

Mosby's most daring escapade of 1863 came in March, when he traveled into Northern territory and captured a Union general, thirty-two other Federal soldiers, and fifty Union horses. According to Mosby, the Union general was sound asleep in his bedroom when he walked in. Mosby promptly drew the covers back, pulled up the general's nightshirt (a long shirt worn in bed), and swatted him on the rear with the blunt side of his sword blade. As the general bolted upright in bed, Mosby said, "Do you know Mosby?" The still-sleepy Union commander responded, "Yes, have you captured him?" Smiling, Mosby answered, "No, but he has captured you."

Mosby's raids angered Union commanders in the region, but they seemed helpless to stop his band. The Union's inability to catch "Mosby's Rangers," as they came to be called, was due in no small part to pro-Confederate feelings in northern Virginia, which Mosby's guerrillas continued to use as a base of operations. In fact, most people who lived in that area were so sympathetic to Mosby and his fellow guerrillas that a few counties came to be known as "Mosby's Confederacy." "The people of Mosby's Confederacy were overwhelmingly pro-Virginia, pro-Confederacy, and therefore pro-Mosby," wrote William C. Davis in *Civil War Journal: The Leaders*. "They opened their homes, silos, barns, hayricks, and cellars to Mosby's men, and they fed and hid them. Without this informal civilian volunteer infrastructure, Mosby could not have operated."

In June 1863, Mosby formally organized his rangers into the Forty-third Battalion of Virginia Cavalry. By this time, many men were asking to join Mosby's company. They were drawn by his spectacular successes and the idea of serving the Confederacy without putting up with lots of military rules and regulations. But even as the size of his band grew—an estimated one thousand guerrillas rode with Mosby at one time or another during the war—the Virginian never gave up control. In fact, he was known as a tough disciplinarian who commanded complete respect, even though he was one of the smallest men in the entire company.

Triumphs and setbacks

From mid-1863 through early 1865, Mosby's Rangers continued to steal Union supplies, destroy Union communication lines, and ambush Union patrols with great effectiveness. Mosby recognized that he was a hunted man, and he barely escaped death in a couple of battles with Union pursuers. But he never gave any thought to quitting his guerrilla activities. "The true secret was that it was a fascinating life, and its attractions far more than counterbalanced its hardships and dangers," he later admitted.

Mosby's leadership enabled his band of guerrillas to avoid disaster on numerous occasions. But in early 1864, his fortunes took a turn for the worse. On January 10, eight of Mosby's Rangers—including his two best lieutenants—were killed by Union cavalry forces outside of Harpers Ferry, Virginia. Then, in May 1864, Mosby learned that his close friend

Jeb Stuart had been killed in battle outside of the Confederate capital of Richmond.

In August 1864, Mosby faced his greatest challenge yet when Union cavalry under the command of General **Philip Sheridan** (1831–1888; see entry) entered northern Virginia. Sheridan's mission had two primary elements. First, he had been ordered to destroy fields and farms in the area so that they could not be used by Confederates. Second, he had been instructed to clear northern Virginia's Shenandoah Valley of the troublesome Confederate cavalry and guerrilla units that had used it as their home for the previous few years.

Battling Sheridan

Over the next few months, Mosby's Rangers and regular Confederate cavalry under the command of Lieutenant General Jubal Early (1816–1894) repeatedly struck against Sheridan's invading army. Mosby's raids on the Union Army's supply lines were so effective that Sheridan admitted that "Mosby has annoyed me considerably." But Sheridan diverted large numbers of troops to protect his supply lines. He then continued with his brutally effective demolition of the Shenandoah Valley.

In September, Mosby suffered a gunshot wound that forced him to the sidelines for a few weeks. During his absence, Sheridan's cavalry captured seven of Mosby's men and executed them. They killed their captives because they believed that a Union cavalryman had earlier been murdered while trying to surrender. Before leaving, the Union troops pinned a note on one of the bodies that indicated that death would "be the fate of all Mosby's guerrillas caught hereafter."

Mosby decided that he had to take firm action to put a halt to such executions. In October, Mosby's Rangers derailed a train outside Harpers Ferry and stole more than $170,000. Union cavalry under the command of Major General George A. Custer (1839–1876) gave chase, but over the next two weeks Mosby captured thirty of his pursuers. On November 6, the guerrilla leader ordered all of the prisoners to pull a piece of paper out of a hat. The seven men who selected papers with marks on them were to be killed in revenge for the executions of his men a few weeks before. When Mosby saw that one of the unlucky drawers was a teenage drummer boy, he spared his life. But he forced the other prisoners to draw again to see who would take his place. Of the seven condemned Union prisoners, four actually lived (two survived their gunshot wounds, and two escaped). But Mosby felt that he had made his point. If any more of his rangers were executed, he would execute the same number of Union prisoners.

By late October 1864, Sheridan had swept Jubal Early's cavalry out of the Shenandoah Valley and burned many of the farms and crops in northern Virginia. He never fully crushed Mosby and his raiders, but ultimately the guerrillas could do little to stop Sheridan, as he pushed his way through the region. In December 1864, Mosby was wounded once again. Rumors of his impending death swirled around the Confederacy until February 1865, when he made an appearance in Richmond.

Mosby joins the Republican Party

By the spring of 1865, the Confederacy was tottering on the brink of defeat. On April 9, the largest of the remaining rebel armies surrendered, and the other Confederate forces quickly followed suit. Instead of formally surrendering, however, Mosby disbanded his company of rangers on April 21.

After the war, Mosby returned to his law practice. The size of his family continued to grow (he and his wife eventually had eight children), and he became increasingly involved

Dressed in his military uniform, John Singleton Mosby poses in front of a painted landscape.
(Reproduced by permission of Corbis.)

in politics. During the presidency of **Ulysses S. Grant** (1822–1885; see entry), Mosby decided to join the Republican political party. This decision shocked and angered many of Mosby's Southern friends, since the party was viewed as an organization of Northerners and abolitionists. But Mosby refused to budge from his decision. Over the next several years he served in Republican administrations in a variety of positions, including assistant attorney in the Department of Justice. He died in 1916 at the age of eighty-two.

Where to Learn More

Carter, Samuel. *The Last Cavaliers: Confederate and Union Cavalry in the Civil War.* New York: St. Martin's Press, 1980.

Col. John Mosby and the Southern Code of Honor. [Online] http://xroads. virginia.edu/~class/am483_97/Projects/anderson/intro.html (accessed on October 15, 1999).

Jones, Virgil Carrington. *Ranger Mosby.* Chapel Hill: University of North Carolina Press, 1944. Reprint, McLean, VA: EPM Publications, 1987.

Longacre, Edward C. *Mounted Raids of the Civil War.* South Brunswick, NJ: A. S. Barnes, 1975. Reprint, Lincoln: University of Nebraska Press, 1994.

Ramage, James A. *Gray Ghost: The Life of Colonel John Singleton Mosby.* Lexington: University of Kentucky Press, 1999.

Siepel, Kevin H. *Rebel: The Life and Times of John Singleton Mosby.* New York: St. Martin's Press, 1983. Reprint, New York: Da Capo Press, 1997.

Wert, Jeffry D. *Mosby's Rangers.* New York: Simon & Schuster, 1990.

Thomas Nast

Born September 27, 1840
Landau, Germany
Died December 7, 1902
Guayaquil, Ecuador

Northern newspaper artist
Drew sentimental pictures and harsh editorial cartoons that increased public support for the Union cause during the Civil War

In the days before photography enjoyed wide use, American newspapers hired artists to draw pictures to accompany news stories. Thomas Nast was one of the best-known and most influential newspaper artists of this period. He produced over three thousand pictures during his career, ranging from sentimental paintings to harsh editorial cartoons. His work inspired public support for the Union cause during the Civil War, and helped end government corruption in New York City in the years afterward. "For nearly a quarter of a century, through the pages of *Harper's Weekly,* Nast gave his strength to the American people," Albert Bigelow Paine wrote in *Thomas Nast: His Period and His Pictures.* "He was profoundly moved by every public question, and his emotions found expression in his pictures. Such a man can but awaken a powerful response."

"Thomas Nast has been our best recruiting sergeant. His emblematic cartoons have never failed to arouse enthusiasm and patriotism. . . .

Abraham Lincoln

Thomas Nast. *(Reproduced by permission of Archive Photos, Inc.)*

Shows artistic talent from an early age

Thomas Nast was born in Landau, Germany, on September 27, 1840. When he was six years old, his family moved to the United States and settled among other German immigrants in New York City. Nast showed an interest in art from an early age. Since he could not speak English when he first came to America, he communicated with his friends and classmates by drawing pictures. During Nast's early school years, his teachers praised his drawing ability. But they also noticed that he did not perform so well in other subjects. As a result, Nast ended his regular schooling as a teenager and began taking art classes at New York's Academy of Design.

When he was fifteen, Nast took some of his drawings to the offices of *Frank Leslie's Illustrated Newspaper.* Leslie recognized that Nast had talent, but doubted whether someone so young would be responsible enough to hold a job as a newspaper artist (in those days, photography was a new and complicated process, so newspapers used artists to provide illustrations for news stories). Leslie decided to test the young man with a difficult assignment—he told Nast to go to the ferry dock and bring back a picture of a crowd boarding a boat. When Nast returned the next day with a first-rate picture, Leslie gave him a job.

For the next few years, Nast traveled to various news events around New York City and drew pictures of the people and places involved. In 1857, he began expanding his role at the newspaper to include drawing cartoons that expressed his opinion about certain issues. One of his first cartoons was a satire (a work that uses sarcasm or wit to comment on social problems and other issues) about an ongoing police scandal in New York. In 1860, Nast traveled to Europe, where he covered political events in England and Italy and visited the town where he was born in Germany. He returned the following year and married Sarah Edwards, the daughter of a theater family for whom he had designed sets. They eventually had four children and bought a house in Morristown, New Jersey.

Pictures inspire support for the Union during the Civil War

By the time Nast returned to the United States in 1861, long-standing disagreements between the Northern and Southern sections of the country had erupted into war. The two sides had been arguing over several issues—including slavery and the power of the national government to regulate it—for many years. Growing numbers of Northerners, like Nast, believed that slavery was wrong. Some people wanted to outlaw it, while others wanted to prevent it from spreading beyond the Southern states where it was already allowed. But slavery played a big role in the Southern economy and culture. As a result, many Southerners felt threatened by Northern efforts to contain slavery. They believed that each state should decide for itself whether to allow slavery. They did not want the national government to pass laws that would interfere with their traditional way of life.

This ongoing dispute came to a crisis point when **Abraham Lincoln** (1809–1865; see entry) was elected president of the United States. Lincoln was a Northerner who opposed slavery, although he wanted to eliminate it gradually rather than outlaw it immediately. Following Lincoln's election, many people in the South felt that the national government could no longer represent their interests. Several Southern states decided to secede (withdraw) from the United States and form a new country that allowed slavery, called the Confederate States of America. But it soon became clear that Northern leaders were willing to fight to keep the Southern states in the Union. The Civil War began a short time later.

Upon his return, Nast briefly covered the war for *New York Illustrated News* and for *Frank Leslie's Illustrated Newspaper.* In 1862, he accepted a position as an artist at *Harper's Weekly*—the best paper of its time—which he would hold for the next twenty-five years. Nast felt intense loyalty toward the Union and expressed his feelings through his skillful drawings and witty cartoons. Both his scenes of battle and his cartoon commentaries on political issues inspired Northern support for the war effort. In fact, President Abraham Lincoln once declared that "Thomas Nast has been our best recruiting sergeant. His emblematic [symbolic] cartoons have never failed to arouse enthusiasm and patriotism, and have always seemed to come just when these articles were getting scarce."

One of Nast's most famous works from the war years was "Christmas Eve," published in the winter of 1862–63. The two-paneled picture showed a woman at home praying for the safe return of her husband, and a soldier sitting by a campfire looking longingly at a picture of his family. This picture inspired hundreds of Northerners to write letters of thanks to the paper, and even encouraged some young men to volunteer to join the Union Army.

But not all of Nast's wartime pictures were sentimental. He also produced many satiric cartoons that showed exactly what he thought about Southerners, as well as certain generals and politicians. "They were not works of art—Nast did not so consider them," Paine said of the cartoons. "War is not a time of culture and discrimination, but of blows, and those dealt by Thomas Nast were swift and savage and aimed to kill." In fact, some of his cartoons were so harsh that he received death threats from offended Southerners.

Becomes a social reformer and statesman

The Civil War ended in a Union victory in 1865. Nast became a vocal critic of President **Andrew Johnson** (1808–1875; see entry) during Reconstruction (1865–77)—the period in American history immediately following the Civil War, when the country struggled to settle its differences and bring the Southern states back into the Union. Nast believed that Johnson's lenient (easy) policies toward the South would allow Confederate leaders to return to power and prevent former slaves from gaining equal rights. He drew caricatures (portraits in which the subject's features are exaggerated or distorted) of Johnson in order to call attention to these concerns.

In 1869, Nast turned his attention to New York City politics. A powerful man named William Marcy "Boss" Tweed (1823–1878) led a ring of officials that controlled all business dealings in the city. Tweed's government was corrupt and used trickery and deception to steal millions of dollars. After investigating the situation, Nast produced numerous cartoons criticizing the Tweed ring. For example, one cartoon showed Tweed wearing a king's robes and sitting on a throne. For a while, Nast was one of the only people who dared to say anything bad about the powerful political leader. But as he increased public awareness of the situation, more and more citizens of New York became outraged. His work helped cause Tweed's fall from power in 1872.

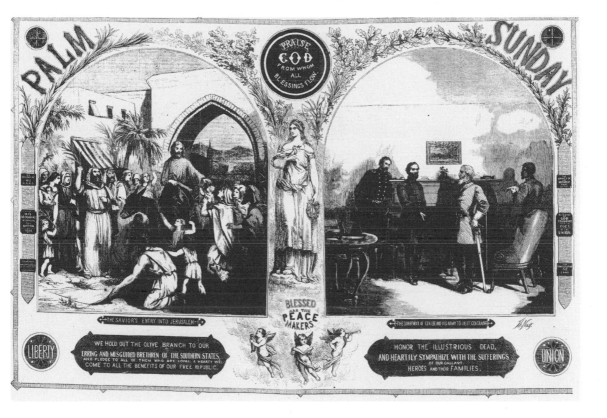

PALM

SUNDAY

PRAISE
GOD
FROM WHOM
ALL
BLESSINGS FLOW.

BLESSED
THE
PEACE
MAKERS

-THE SAVIOR'S ENTRY INTO JERUSALEM-

-THE SURRENDER OF GEN. LEE AND HIS ARMY TO LIEUT. GEN. GRANT-

LIBERTY

UNION

WE HOLD OUT THE OLIVE BRANCH TO OUR
ERRING AND MISGUIDED BRETHREN OF THE SOUTHERN STATES,
AND PLEDGE TO ALL OF THEM WHO ARE LOYAL, A HEARTY WEL-
COME TO ALL THE BENEFITS OF OUR FREE REPUBLIC.

HONOR THE ILLUSTRIOUS DEAD,
AND HEARTILY SYMPATHIZE WITH THE SUFFERINGS
OF OUR GALLANT
HEROES AND THEIR FAMILIES.

In 1874, Nast used an elephant as a symbol of the Republican political party in one of his cartoons. The idea caught on, and the party still uses an elephant as its symbol today. In the late 1870s, Nast's contributions to newspapers lessened as he spent more time painting and illustrating books. In 1886, he broke off his long relationship with *Harper's Weekly*. A few years later, he tried unsuccessfully to start his own paper. In 1895, Nast completed one of his best-known paintings. It showed Confederate general **Robert E. Lee** (1807–1870; see entry) surrendering to Union general **Ulysses S. Grant** (1822–1885; see entry) at Appomattox, Virginia, to end the Civil War.

In 1902, some of Nast's old friends in the U.S. government offered him a position as consul (an official government representative) to the South American nation of Ecuador. Nast did not feel qualified for the job, but he wanted to serve his country and also needed the money. Unfortu-

One of George Nast's most well-known paintings shows the surrender of Confederate general Robert E. Lee to Union general Ulysses S. Grant. *(From Harper's Weekly.)*

nately, he became ill shortly after his arrival in Ecuador and died there on December 7, 1902.

Where to Learn More

Hoff, Syd. *Boss Tweed and the Man Who Drew Him.* New York: Coward, McCann, and Geoghegan, 1978.

Keller, Morton. *The Art and Politics of Thomas Nast.* New York: Oxford University Press, 1968.

Paine, Albert Bigelow. *Thomas Nast: His Period and His Pictures.* New York: Chelsea House, 1980.

Shirley, David. *Thomas Nast: Cartoonist and Illustrator.* New York: Franklin Watts, 1998.

Thomas Nast Homepage. [Online] http://www.buffnet.net/~starmist/nast/main.htm (accessed on October 15, 1999).

Edward A. Pollard

Born February 27, 1831
Albemarle County, Virginia
Died December 12, 1872
Lynchburg, Virginia

Editor of the *Richmond Examiner*
Early historian of the Confederacy

Edward A. Pollard emerged as one of the South's best known commentators on Confederate leadership and military strategy during the Civil War. As the editorial page editor of the *Richmond Examiner,* Pollard's harsh criticism of Confederate president **Jefferson Davis** (1808–1889; see entry) and other political leaders turned him into one of the South's most controversial writers. In addition, he published an annual series of books during the Civil War in which he provided his own interpretations of the war's progress. These volumes, which also attracted a lot of attention, made Pollard one of the first historians of the Confederacy.

Born into Virginia aristocracy

Edward Alfred Pollard was born in February 1831 in Albemarle County, Virginia. His parents were members of the state's planter (plantation owner) aristocracy (a privileged and influential class of people with distinguished ancestors). Unlike most other members of that group, however, Pollard's parents were not wealthy. The farmland that they owned was

"Morning broke on a scene never to be forgotten. . . . The smoke and glare of fire mingled with the golden beams of the rising sun. . . ."

not very fertile, and Pollard's father, Richard Pollard, had lost a lot of money in bad business deals. As a result, young Edward and his eight brothers and sisters knew that they would have to find careers for themselves.

Fortunately for Edward, the generosity of several relatives enabled him to gain admittance into the region's finest schools, including the University of Virginia and the College of William and Mary. By the time Pollard left William and Mary in 1850, he had excellent writing skills and a growing knowledge of the law. But he never earned a degree, in part because he spent a lot of his time gambling and engaging in other distracting activities.

Pollard spent much of the 1850s wandering around the globe. He spent the first part of the decade in Europe, where he supported himself as a writer for newspapers and magazines. He then moved on to California and Mexico before landing in the Central American country of Nicaragua. Once he arrived in Nicaragua, he allied himself with slave-owners who were trying to expand slavery into the region. "The path of our destiny on this continent lies in . . . tropical America [where] we may see an empire as powerful and gorgeous as ever was pictured in our dreams of history," Pollard wrote in 1859. "An empire . . . representing the noble peculiarities of Southern civilization. . . . The destiny of Southern civilization is to be consummated [completed] in a glory brighter even than that of old." In the end, however, these efforts to establish Southern-style slavery in Nicaragua failed.

Defender of slavery

During the late 1850s, Pollard watched the growing tensions between America's Northern and Southern regions with great interest. The main issue dividing the two regions was slavery. Growing numbers of Northerners believed that slavery was wrong. Some people wanted to outlaw it, while others wanted to prevent it from spreading beyond the Southern states where it was already allowed. But slavery played an important role in the South's economy and culture. As a result, most white Southerners felt threatened by Northern efforts to contain slavery. They believed that each state should decide for itself whether to allow the practice. They did not want the national government to pass laws that would interfere with their traditional way of life.

Pollard strongly supported the South's point of view regarding slavery. He believed that blacks were terribly inferior to whites, and saw nothing wrong with keeping blacks enslaved. As a result, Northern claims that slavery was an immoral system angered and frustrated him. These feelings led Pollard to write and publish a book called *Black Diamonds Gathered in the Darkey Homes of the South* in 1859. Using his own childhood memories as the foundation for his book, Pollard portrayed slaves as being happy in their captivity and characterized all slaveowners as kind and gentle masters. "In these sketches," wrote historian Jon L. Wakelyn, "Pollard had created a fantasy world of old Virginia, a world he believed worth preserving."

Writing in Richmond

In early 1861, relations between the North and South became so bad that a group of Southern states decided to secede (withdraw) from the United States and form a new country that allowed slavery, called the Confederate States of America. But Northern political leaders would not let the Southern states leave the Union without a fight. By April it was clear that the differences between the two regions were going to be settled through warfare.

As the two sides prepared for war, Pollard established himself as one of the Confederacy's most vocal defenders. In addition to helping his brother Henry Rives Pollard edit a strongly pro-Southern newspaper in Baltimore, Maryland, he completed a book called *Letters of a Southern Spy*. This collection of essays, published in the spring of 1861, viciously attacked President **Abraham Lincoln** (1809–1865; see entry) and all Northerners as cowardly and dishonest people who wanted to stir up a race war in the South.

Letters of a Southern Spy angered many people who lived in and around Baltimore. After all, the city, which was located only thirty miles from the Federal capital of Washington, D.C., was home to many people who opposed slavery and remained loyal to the Union. As threats against Pollard poured in, he hurriedly left town and relocated to the Confederate capital of Richmond.

Once Pollard arrived in Richmond, he joined the staff of John M. Daniel's *Richmond Examiner* as the editor of its editorial page. During his first weeks in Richmond, Pollard wrote many editorials praising the Confederate people and their civilian leaders, such as President Jefferson Davis. He also expressed great confidence in the South's military leaders. As time passed, however, Pollard grew more critical of Davis and other civilian authorities. Statements of hopefulness about the Confederacy gradually gave way to nasty, gossipy attacks on Davis, Vice President **Alexander Stephens** (1812–1883; see entry), and many other rebel (Confederate) leaders. The only group of Confederate leaders toward which Pollard remained friendly was the military command. Eventually, however, even some military leaders felt the sting of Pollard's critical editorials. Today, many historians point to Pollard's harsh words as prime examples of the sort of attacks that Davis was forced to endure throughout the course of the war. These attacks, they agree, hindered Davis's ability to lead and unify the Confederacy.

Imprisonment

Pollard's criticism of Southern leaders finally became so strong that he lost the support of Daniel, the owner of the *Examiner.* As a result, Pollard resigned from the newspaper and boarded a ship for England, where he hoped to resume his writing career. The ship upon which he was traveling, however, was stopped by a Union ship that was part of a Northern blockade (a military operation designed to cut an enemy area off from outside supplies or communications) of the entire East Coast. When the Union sailors discovered Pollard's identity, they immediately arrested him as a spy.

Pollard was sent to prison in Boston, Massachusetts. His jailers let him go when they determined that he was not really a spy. But when he was released, he attempted to resume his anti-Northern writings in New York. His activities angered the Union authorities, who arrested him again and threw him in jail.

Pollard Describes the Fall of Richmond

In early April 1865, the Confederate defense of the capital city of Richmond finally crumbled. As General Robert E. Lee evacuated his army from the city, the atmosphere on Richmond's streets became scary and chaotic. Writing for the *Richmond Examiner,* Edward Pollard described the scene with a heavy heart:

As the day wore on, clatter and bustle in the streets denoted the progress of the evacuation and convinced those who had been incredulous [doubtful] of its reality. The disorder increased each hour. The streets were thronged [crowded] with fugitives making their way to the railroad depots [stations]; pale women and little shoeless children struggled in the crowd; oaths and blasphemous shouts [swearing] smote [struck] the air. . . .

When it was finally announced by the Army that . . . the evacuation of Richmond was a foregone [unavoidable] conclusion, it was proposed to maintain order in the city by two regiments of militia [army composed of citizens]; to destroy every drop of liquor in the warehouses and stores; and to establish a patrol through the night. But the militia ran through the fingers of their officers . . . and in a short while the whole city was plunged into mad confusion and indescribable horrors.

It was an extraordinary night; disorder, pillage [looting], shouts, mad revelry. . . . In the now dimly lighted city could be seen black masses of people crowded around some object of excitement . . . swaying to and fro in whatever momentary passion possessed them. The gutters ran with a liquor freshet [overflow], and the fumes filled the air. Some of the straggling soldiers . . . easily managed to get hold of quantities of the liquor. Confusion became worse confounded; the sidewalks were encumbered [littered] with broken glass; stores were entered at pleasure and stripped from top to bottom; yells of drunken men, shouts of roving pillagers [robbers], wild cries of distress filled the air and made night hideous.

But a new horror was to appear upon the scene and take possession of the community. To the rear-guard of the Confederate force . . . had been left the duty of blowing up the iron-clad vessels in the James [River] and destroying the bridges across the river. . . . The work of destruction might well have ended here. But the four principal tobacco warehouses of the city were fired; the flames seized on the neighboring buildings and soon involved a wide and widening area; the conflagration [fire] passed rapidly beyond control. And in this mad fire, this wild, unnecessary destruction of their property, the citizens of Richmond had a fitting souvenir of the imprudence [lacking in judgment] and recklessness of the departing Administration.

Morning broke on a scene never to be forgotten. . . . The smoke and glare of fire mingled with the golden beams of the rising sun. . . . The fire was reaching to whole blocks of buildings. . . . Its roar sounded in the ears; it leaped from street to street. Pillagers were busy at their vocation, and in the hot breath of the fire were figures as of demons contending [fighting] for prey.

Pollard finally won his release from jail in January 1865. He promptly returned to Richmond and returned to the staff of the *Examiner*. But by this time, Union armies were marching to victory throughout the South. As the war drew to a close, many of Pollard's editorials reflected shock and sadness at the Confederacy's collapse.

Historian of the Confederacy

Pollard's work as a wartime editor of the *Richmond Examiner* brought him considerable attention. In the years immediately after the war, however, he became best known as one of the first people to provide a historical account of the Confederacy's brief existence.

Pollard's work as a historian actually began during the war, when he published annual volumes devoted to summarizing the previous year's events. As with his editorials for the *Examiner,* these volumes praised the actions of General **Robert E. Lee** (1807–1870; see entry) and other rebel generals and attacked President Davis as incompetent and stubborn. According to historian Jon L. Wakelyn, these volumes "probably [did] more than any other of the early histories to fix the reputations of Confederate leaders for the future."

Pollard continued his work as a historian of the Confederacy during the postwar years. In 1866, he published *The Lost Cause,* a book that described the South's bid to leave the Union as a heroic effort that was undertaken to preserve Southern honor and virtue. In this and other works of the late 1860s he continued to criticize both the North and the Confederacy's civilian (nonmilitary) leaders, while simultaneously urging whites to maintain their superior social positions over blacks.

Pollard's writing output dwindled in the early 1870s, when his health began to decline. He died on December 12, 1872, in Lynchburg, Virginia, after a long illness.

Where to Learn More

Maddex, Jack P., Jr. *The Reconstruction of Edward A. Pollard: A Rebel's Conversion to Postbellum Unionism.* Chapel Hill, University of North Carolina Press, 1974.

Pollard, Edward A. *Letters of a Southern Spy.* E. W. Ayres, 1861.

Pollard, Edward A. *The Lost Cause.* New York: E. B. Treat, 1866. Reprint, New York: Gramercy Press, 1994.

Wakelyn, Jon L. "Edward Alfred Pollard" in *Leaders of the American Civil War.* Edited by Jon L. Wakelyn and Charles F. Ritter. Westport, CT: Greenwood Press, 1998.

Dred Scott

Born 1795?
Southampton County, Virginia
Died September 17, 1858
St. Louis, Missouri

Slave who sued unsuccessfully to obtain his freedom

The U.S. Supreme Court's controversial ruling in *Dred Scott v. Sandford* increased the hostility between North and South that led to the Civil War

red Scott was a slave who challenged the institution of slavery in court. He filed a lawsuit arguing that he should be free since his master had taken him to live in free territory for several years. The historic case, known as *Dred Scott v. Sandford*, made it all the way to the U.S. Supreme Court in 1857. At this time, the Northern and Southern halves of the country were involved in a fierce debate about slavery and the extent to which the government should be allowed to control it.

The Supreme Court ruled that black Americans did not have the rights of citizens, so Scott was not entitled to file his lawsuit. The sweeping ruling also said that the U.S. government could not limit the spread of slavery to new states and territories—or even prevent people from holding slaves in free states—because the Constitution does not allow the government to deprive citizens of their property. The court's decision upset many people in the North, but thrilled many people in the South. It also increased the hostile (unfriendly) feelings between the two sections of the country that led to the Civil War a few years later.

Dred Scott v. Sandford placed the entire institution of slavery on trial.

Dred Scott. *(Courtesy of the Library of Congress.)*

Born a slave

The man who became famous in court as Dred Scott was born in Virginia around 1795. He was originally called Sam, but he changed his name sometime before he filed his historic lawsuit. Scott never knew the exact date of his birth because he was born a slave.

Black people were taken from Africa and brought to North America to serve as slaves for white people beginning in the 1600s. The basic belief behind slavery was that black people were inferior to whites. Under slavery, white slaveholders treated black people as property, forced them to perform hard labor, and controlled every aspect of their lives. States in the Northern half of the United States began outlawing slavery in the late 1700s. But slavery continued to exist in the Southern half of the country because it played an important role in the South's economy and culture.

Most slave owners tried to prevent their slaves from learning much about themselves or the world around them. They believed that educated slaves would be more likely to become dissatisfied with their lives. For this reason, Scott received no information about his birth. He also never learned to read and write. Years later, he used a symbol to represent his name whenever he was required to sign legal documents.

As a young man, Scott belonged to Peter Blow, who owned a farm in Virginia. Blow eventually decided that the land was not fertile enough to farm successfully. In 1819, he moved west along with his family and their six slaves, including Scott. They settled in the busy frontier town of St. Louis, Missouri, where Blow opened a boarding house called the Jefferson Hotel. Since he did not need Scott's help in the boarding house, Blow hired his slave out as a deckhand on riverboats that went up and down the Mississippi River. Slave owners often rented their extra slaves to other people and received payment for the work they did.

Sold and taken to free territory

In 1832, Peter Blow became ill and was forced to give up his hotel business. He ended up selling his slaves in order to pay off his debts. He sold Scott to Dr. John Emerson for

$500. It is not clear how Scott felt about being sold. One story says that he was so upset that he ran away and hid in a swamp. But another story says that he asked to be sold because Blow had whipped him. Shortly after buying Scott, Emerson received a commission as a surgeon in the U.S. Army. He went to live at Fort Armstrong in Illinois in 1833 and took Scott with him. Illinois was a free state, meaning that it did not allow slavery. But at that time, the laws were unclear about what happened when a master brought a slave into free territory. Most people generally agreed that slaveowners could travel into free states with their slaves and remain there for short periods of time. If slaveowners wanted to settle in a free state permanently, however, they might have to free their slaves.

In 1836, Emerson was transferred to Fort Snelling. This fort was located on the Mississippi River, near what would later become St. Paul, Minnesota. At that time it was part of Wisconsin Territory, which did not allow slavery. Emerson took Scott with him to Fort Snelling. During this time, Emerson also arranged to purchase a female slave named Harriet Robinson. Scott and Robinson became romantically involved and considered themselves married, although slaves were not legally permitted to marry. They eventually had four children, although only their daughters Eliza and Lizzie survived to adulthood.

In 1837, Emerson moved back to St. Louis, but Dred and Harriet Scott remained behind. The doctor eventually got married and moved to Fort Jesup in Louisiana. He then sent for his servants. When the Scotts arrived in Louisiana, they again lived in a slave state. But later that year Emerson returned to Fort Snelling with his slaves. In 1840, they returned to St. Louis. Dr. Emerson died in December 1843. Some slaveowners put provisions in their wills that freed their slaves upon their death. Instead, Dr. Emerson's will said that ownership of Scott and his family would pass to his widow, Irene Emerson.

Sues to obtain freedom

Shortly after the death of his master, Scott tried to purchase freedom for himself and his wife. But Mrs. Emerson refused to set them free. On April 6, 1846, Scott took the un-

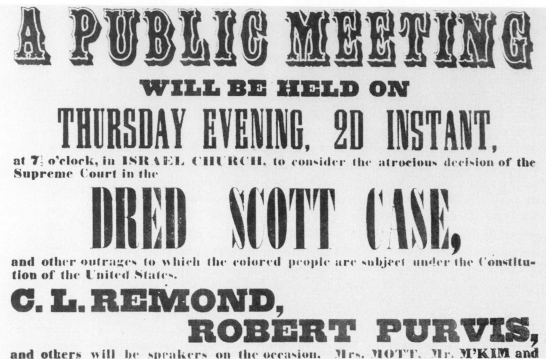

A PUBLIC MEETING

WILL BE HELD ON

THURSDAY EVENING, 2D INSTANT,

at 7½ o'clock, in ISRAEL CHURCH, to consider the atrocious decision of the Supreme Court in the

DRED SCOTT CASE,

and other outrages to which the colored people are subject under the Constitution of the United States.

C. L. REMOND,
ROBERT PURVIS,

and others will be speakers on the occasion. Mrs. MOTT, Mr. M'KIM and B. S. JONES of Ohio. have also accepted invitations to be present.
All persons are invited to attend. Admittance free.

A handbill announces a public meeting for individuals interested in discussing the Supreme Court's decision in the *Dred Scott* case in 1857.

usual step of filing a lawsuit against the widow. The suit claimed that he should be given his freedom because he had spent long periods of time with Dr. Emerson in areas of the country where slavery was banned. Scott knew that slaves had won their freedom in similar cases before. The courts had ruled that masters who took their slaves to live in free territory for a certain period of time must set them free. Scott just had to prove in court that he had lived in free territory and that the Emersons treated him as a slave.

After several delays, a Missouri circuit court judge ruled in Scott's favor on January 12, 1850. But the Emerson family appealed the ruling to the state supreme court. In 1852, that court reversed the earlier decision and found in favor of the Emersons. Shortly afterward, Mrs. Emerson sold Scott and his family to her brother, John F. A. Sanford. Sanford lived in New York but often traveled to St. Louis on business. Scott brought a new lawsuit against Sanford. Since the suit now involved people from two different states, Scott was entitled to take his case to the U.S. Supreme Court.

Appears before the Supreme Court

The case known as *Dred Scott v. Sandford* finally appeared before the Supreme Court in February 1856. (The trial name offically, though erroneously, spelled Sanford's name with two d's.) By this time, the entire nation had become involved in an intense debate over slavery. Growing numbers of Northerners believed that slavery was wrong. Some people wanted to outlaw it, while others just wanted to prevent it from spreading beyond the Southern states where it was already allowed. But slavery played a big role in the Southern economy and culture. As a result, many Southerners felt threatened by Northern efforts to contain slavery. They believed that each state should decide for itself whether to allow the practice. They did not want the national government to pass laws that would interfere with their traditional way of life. This dispute grew even more heated as the United States expanded westward. Both sides wanted to spread their political ideas into the new territories and states.

Scott's case concerned several issues that both abolitionists (people who wanted to end slavery) and slavery supporters considered important. For example, it would decide whether slaves who were brought to free states had a right to freedom. Since Scott brought the suit as a citizen of Missouri, it would also decide whether black Americans could be considered citizens. Finally, it would decide whether the federal government had the authority to limit the spread of slavery to new states. Basically, the impact of the case extended far beyond Dred Scott and his family. The entire institution of slavery was placed on trial.

Chief Justice Roger B. Taney (1777–1864) announced the court's decision on March 6, 1857. Led by five justices who were Southerners, a majority of the nine-person court ruled against Scott. According to the Supreme Court, no black man—whether he was free or a slave—could ever become a U.S. citizen. Since only citizens were allowed to sue in federal court, Taney explained that Scott had no legal right to file his lawsuit in the first place. This ruling alone would have shocked and angered abolitionists all across the North. But Taney also said that the federal government did not have the right to outlaw slavery in any U.S. territories. He claimed that laws banning slavery were unconstitutional (went against the principles outlined in the U.S. Constitution) because they deprived slaveholders of property. He also stated that slaveholders could legally transport their slaves anywhere in the country since slaves were considered property.

Ruling increases hostility between North and South

Antislavery organizations immediately spoke out against the verdict. They were upset that the Supreme Court had opened the door to slavery anywhere in the country. Some Northerners saw the court's decision as proof of a Southern conspiracy to spread the institution of slavery into free states as well as the disputed western territories. After all, the ruling theoretically made it possible for slaveholders to move permanently into a free state without ever releasing their slaves from captivity. Many people worried that the Northern states would be powerless to prevent slavery from being practiced within their borders.

On the other hand, many Southerners were thrilled with the Supreme Court's decision. Northerners had been trying to force them to make major changes to their economy and social system for years. But with the *Dred Scott* decision, the Supreme Court had supported the South's view of the slavery issue. It had firmly rejected the efforts of abolitionists and black Americans to limit the spread of slavery and gain equal rights for people of all colors. Over the next few years, Northern abolitionists used the *Dred Scott* decision as evidence that slavery and freedom could not exist together in the United States. Sure enough, the North and South went to war over the issue in 1861.

As reaction to the court's decision swept through the country, the slave Dred Scott—whose lawsuit had sparked the whole controversy—faded from view. In 1858, he and his wife were purchased by Taylor Blow, a member of the family that had owned Scott many years earlier. Blow granted Scott his freedom in May of that year. Sadly, Scott did not have much time to enjoy his hard-won freedom. He died on September 17, 1858, in St. Louis.

Where to Learn More

Fehrenbacher, Don E. *The Dred Scott Case: Its Significance in American Law and Politics*. New York: Oxford University Press, 1978.

Finkelman, Paul. *Dred Scott v. Sandford: A Brief History with Documents*. Boston: Bedford Books, 1997.

Fleischner, Jennifer. *The Dred Scott Case: Testing the Right to Live Free*. Brookfield, CT: Milbrook Press, 1997.

Herda, D. J. *The Dred Scott Case: Slavery and Citizenship*. Hillside, NJ: Enslow, 1994.

Lukes, Bonnie L. *The Dred Scott Decision*. San Diego: Lucent Books, 1997.

Winfield Scott

Born June 13, 1786
Petersburg, Virginia
Died May 27, 1866
West Point, New York

Union general in chief at the beginning of the Civil War

Developed the "Anaconda Plan," which eventually helped the Union win the war

A veteran of the War of 1812 (1812–15), the Seminole Wars (1835–42), and the Mexican War (1846–48), General Winfield Scott had achieved the position of commander over all Federal forces when the Civil War began in 1861. His advanced age and poor health made it impossible for him to lead troops into combat personally, and he was forced to resign his position a few months after the war started. Before resigning, though, he developed a war strategy for the Union that helped it gain victory in the conflict. Scott's strategy helped cement his reputation as one of America's most successful military figures of the nineteenth century.

A famous American soldier

Winfield Scott was born to William and Ann Mason Scott on June 13, 1786, on a large farm about fourteen miles from Petersburg, Virginia. Scott's father died when he was six years old, leaving his mother to raise him alone. He credited her and two teachers with his training in manners as well as his passion for books. His mother died when Scott was seventeen.

Winfield Scott was one of America's great military heroes of the nineteenth century.

Winfield Scott. *(Courtesy of the Library of Congress.)*

After a year of high school, Scott entered the College of William and Mary in Williamsburg, Virginia. But he stayed only one year, leaving to study law with a prominent attorney, David Robinson. Shortly thereafter, Scott began his own practice, travelling around the area to provide legal aid wherever it was needed.

In 1807, President Thomas Jefferson (1743–1826) announced the need for a militia (a group of citizens who volunteer to provide military services) to help the U.S. government keep British troops at bay during a foreign trade conflict. Hearing of the president's need, Scott rode twenty-five miles in one night to borrow a friend's old uniform and report for duty. Shortly thereafter, he was put in charge of a small group patrolling a section of coastline. A year later, Scott achieved the rank of captain of artillery. A few years later, he performed with great distinction in the War of 1812. This war, which lasted from 1812 to 1815, pitted the United States against Great Britain in a struggle for possession of lands in the North American West. Neither side was able to claim a clear victory in the struggle, and they finally agreed to a treaty that ended the war.

Scott built a very good reputation for himself during this conflict. Despite being wounded twice and captured once, he emerged as one of America's best officers. By the time the war ended, his exploits (brave deeds) fighting British troops along the Canadian border and elsewhere had made him one of the nation's best known soldiers.

Scott spent the next four decades serving his country in the military. During the 1830s and 1840s, he led American troops in important campaigns against several different Indian tribes, including Cherokee, Seminole, Winnebago, Sac (Sauk), and Fox groups. These clashes pushed the tribes onto reservations or forced them to relocate further West so that white settlers could move onto the land they had previously inhabited.

In 1841, Scott was appointed general in chief over all federal forces. A few years later, he and General Zachary Taylor (1784–1850) led American forces in the Mexican War. This war, which began in 1846, was a fight between Mexico and the United States for ownership of huge sections of land in the West. Mexico's leaders did not want to give up their claims on these lands, because they recognized that the territory was quite valuable. By 1848, though, Scott and Taylor guided American forces to a series of dramatic military victories in the heart of Mexico. These triumphs forced the Mexican government to give up its claims on California and other western lands in exchange for $15 million. The treaty that ended the war enlarged the territory held by the United States by nearly one quarter. It also reduced the size of Mexico's territory by almost one half.

Preparing for the Civil War

By the time the Mexican War ended, Scott was known across America as a fierce fighter and a bold military strategist. In 1852, the Whig political party nominated him for the presidency of the United States. They

Winfield Scott and future U.S. president Zachary Taylor (above) led American forces in the Mexican War. *(Courtesy of the Library of Congress.)*

hoped to take advantage of his fame and popularity. Divisions within the party over the issue of slavery hurt Scott's cause, though, and he was soundly defeated by Democratic Party candidate Franklin Pierce (1804–1869) in the general election.

Scott remained in charge of America's army through the remainder of the 1850s, acquiring the nickname of "Old Fuss and Feathers" because of his affection for military rules and conduct. His health and conditioning declined during this time, however, as advancing age and various physical ailments took their toll. By the end of the decade he was so overweight that he could not even mount a horse, and he sometimes fell asleep in the middle of important meetings. People began to wonder if perhaps he should be replaced.

Questions about Scott's ability to command the Federal military intensified in the spring of 1861, when the American Civil War began. This war came about because of longstanding differences between the nation's Northern and

**Winfield Scott returned
from the Mexican War a
military hero.** *(Courtesy of the
Library of Congress.)*

Southern regions over several major issues. The most important of these issues was slavery. Many Northerners believed
that slavery was wrong. They wanted the federal government
to take steps to outlaw slavery or at least keep it from spreading beyond the Southern states where it was already allowed.
But slavery played an important role in the Southern economy and culture. Many Southerners resented Northern attempts to contain slavery. They felt that each state should decide for itself whether to allow the practice. They did not
want the federal government to pass laws that would interfere with their traditional way of life. The two sides finally
went to war in 1861, after the Southern states tried to secede
from (leave) the Union and form a new country that allowed
slavery, called the Confederate States of America.

When it became clear that the Southern states were
going to attempt to form their own country, both North and
South scrambled to convince leading military officers to join

their side. Scott remained with the Federal army in the North, even though he had been born and raised in the secessionist state of Virginia. He decided that his greatest loyalty was to his country and the army to which he had devoted his life. But he recognized that his age (seventy-four) and poor health would make it impossible for him to lead armies into combat in the upcoming war. He asked an army officer and fellow Virginian named **Robert E. Lee** (1807–1870; see entry) if he would accept field command of the Union Army in the upcoming war. But Lee informed Scott that he had reluctantly decided to join the Confederate Army because he could not "raise my hand against my birthplace, my home, my children" of Virginia. When Scott heard this, he replied, "You have made the greatest mistake of your life, but I feared it would be so."

Scott's second choice as field commander of Union forces was Major General **George B. McClellan** (1826–1885; see entry). McClellan gladly accepted the offer, and in May 1861, he became the second-highest ranking general in the U.S. Army. During the summer of 1861, both men worked hard preparing defenses around the U.S. capital of Washington. They recognized that if the city's defenses were not strong, Confederate forces might try to capture it in hopes of ending the war with one big victory. But while the generals succeeded in establishing effective fortifications around Washington, their relationship became strained.

Scott's "Anaconda Plan"

As Scott, McClellan, President **Abraham Lincoln** (1809–1865; see entry), and other officials prepared the Union forces for the upcoming war, disagreements arose between them over the best strategy for obtaining victory. Many people in the North—from politicians and military officers to newspaper editors and ordinary citizens—believed that the Union Army would easily defeat the Confederate force. They called for a full-scale invasion of the South, arguing that the Union Army's advantages in manpower, weapons, supplies, and veteran officers would enable it to smash the Confederate rebellion within a matter of months.

Winfield Scott did not agree with this strategy, however. He believed that a big invasion of the South was a terrible idea for several reasons. For one thing, he thought that the South might be a far tougher opponent than most Northerners realized. He also did not have a lot of confidence in the inexperienced soldiers that the Union was training for the war. Scott worried that it would take months before these men developed into competent troops. Finally, he believed that a successful full-scale invasion might produce "devastated [slave states] not to be brought into harmony with their conquerors, but to be held for generations, by heavy garrisons [large numbers of troops]."

Instead of an invasion plan, Scott developed a strategy to "envelop the insurgent [secessionist] States and bring them to terms with less bloodshed than by any other plan," as he stated in a May 1861 letter to McClellan. Under Scott's proposed plan, the North would hold off on a major invasion and instead concentrate its efforts on blockading Southern ports and controlling the Mississippi River, which ran through the western section of the Confederacy.

The general believed that these waterways held the key to Union victory. Northern control of the seas would prevent the Confederacy from receiving weapons and other supplies from other nations. Northern control over the Mississippi River, meanwhile, would drive a wedge between Texas, Louisiana, and Arkansas and the rest of the Confederacy. Scott firmly believed that if the North could establish an effective blockade and divide the South by taking control of the Mississippi, the Confederacy would eventually collapse from supply shortages and economic weakness. The Union could then invade and smash the remains of the Confederate Army into pieces.

Scott believed that his plan would eventually work, and that it would cause less bloodshed than other strategies. But many Northerners did not like Scott's plan. Political leaders, newspaper writers, and ordinary farmers and townspeople all said that his plan was too cautious and that it would take too long to execute. They called Scott's strategy the Anaconda Plan, after the large snake that kills its victims by slowly squeezing them to death. Impatient and overconfident, these critics continued to call for a massive military invasion of the South. Public demand for a big offensive (attacking) campaign finally became so great that Lincoln agreed to an invasion plan.

McClellan pushes Scott into retirement

During the summer of 1861, the North mounted a major offensive into Virginia. The invasion ended in disaster, though, when Southern troops smashed the Union Army at Manassas Junction on July 21. Many Northerners called on Scott to retire when they learned the results of this battle, called the First Battle of Bull Run or the First Battle of Manassas. Since he was general in chief over all Union troops, they argued that he deserved some of the blame for the defeat, even though he had been at his offices in Washington, D.C., when the actual battle took place.

General McClellan maneuvered to push Scott into retirement as well. McClellan ignored the general, saying that "he understands nothing, appreciates nothing." Submitting his reports directly to Lincoln, he tried to convince Northern political leaders that Scott should resign. Lincoln tried to calm the bitter rivalry between the two generals, but his efforts failed. On November 1, Scott retired from active military service "for reasons of health." In reality, though, it was the actions of McClellan and his political allies that forced him to retire.

Scott spent the rest of the war watching from the sidelines. As the war progressed, he noted with great satisfaction that the Union used a great deal of his Anaconda Plan to defeat the Confederacy. The Union Navy established a blockade of Southern ports that eventually became extremely effective, and his proposal to seize control of the Mississippi Valley became a key part of Union strategy by 1862. In the spring of 1865, the Union finally won the war.

Scott lived to see the Union restored, although health problems plagued him throughout the Civil War years. He died in 1866 while staying at the U.S. Military Academy at West Point in New York.

Where to Learn More

Eisenhower, John S. D. *Agent of Destiny: Life and Times of General Winfield Scott.* New York: Free Press, 1997.

Johnson, Timothy D. *Winfield Scott: The Quest for Military Glory.* Lawrence: University Press of Kansas, 1998.

William Henry Seward

Born May 16, 1801
Florida, New York
Died October 10, 1872
Auburn, New York

Secretary of state in the
Lincoln and Johnson administrations

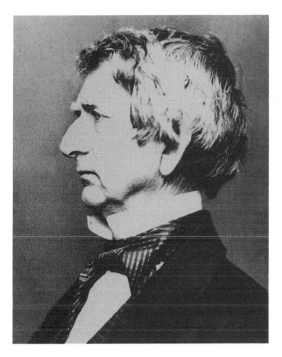

William Henry Seward was an important political figure throughout the Civil War era. In the 1840s and 1850s, he became known as one of America's leading advocates of abolitionism (the movement to end slavery). During the war, he joined the administration of President **Abraham Lincoln** (1809–1865; see entry) as secretary of state and became one of the president's most trusted advisors. Seward remained in his position as secretary of state through the first years of Reconstruction (the period from 1865 to 1877 during which the Southern states were rebuilt and rejoined the United States) as well. During this period, Seward supported President **Andrew Johnson** (1808–1875; see entry) and his generous policies toward the South and negotiated the purchase of Alaska from Russia.

Growing up in rural New York

William Henry Seward was born in 1801 in Florida, New York, a small village in the southern region of the state. His father was Samuel Seward, a wealthy landowner who was

"There is no law of this State which recognizes slavery, no statute which admits that one man can be the property of another, or that one man can be stolen from another."

William H. Seward. *(Courtesy of the National Archives and Records Administration.)*

363

very strict with young William and his five brothers and sisters. His mother was Mary Jennings, who treated her children with kindness and affection.

As a boy, Seward had his full share of chores around the family farm. Health problems bothered him throughout his childhood, though, leading his parents to wonder if he had the strength to succeed at farming or other strenuous pursuits. "My health caused me to be early set apart for a collegiate education, [which was regarded at the time] by every family . . . as a privilege so high and so costly that not more than one son could expect it," remembered Seward.

In 1816, Seward's father enrolled him in Union College, an all-male school in Schenectady, New York. Seward excelled in his studies, graduating four years later with top honors. In October 1822, he passed the state bar exam, which enabled him to practice law in New York. Soon after passing the exam, he accepted a position at a law firm in Auburn, New York, where he maintained a home for the rest of his life. In 1824, he married a local girl named Frances Miller, with whom he eventually had four children.

Law and politics

Seward's law practice became very successful during the 1820s. As the years passed, however, Seward never really warmed up to the idea of being an attorney. Instead, he became attracted to local and state politics. In 1830, he was elected to the state senate, where he quickly emerged as one of New York's brightest young legislators. He maintained his flourishing law practice during this time, but devoted most of his energy to his senatorial duties.

In the mid-1830s, Seward became a dedicated member of the Whigs, a new political party that believed in a strong national bank, high tariffs (taxes on imported goods), and social reforms designed to help poor people. In 1834, he ran for governor of New York as the Whig nominee, only to be decisively defeated. Four years later, however, he won the governor's office by a sizable margin.

Governor of New York

Seward served as governor of New York for two terms, from 1839 to 1843. During this time he became widely known for his efforts to improve education, increase economic development, expand state canal and railroad systems, and improve conditions in prisons. He worked hard to expand educational opportunities for immigrant children, for example, and tried to relieve the terrible conditions in the New York prison system.

Seward's opposition to slavery also became evident during this period. He endorsed bills that increased the civil rights of both free blacks and fugitive slaves, and changed laws to make it easier for black children to obtain an education. Seward's views on slavery became even better known, however, when he got in a bitter fight with Virginia slaveowners.

Seward's dispute with Virginia erupted in 1839, when three black sailors from New York state unsuccessfully attempted to smuggle (secretly carry) a Virginia slave aboard their ship. When Virginia's governor learned about the scheme, he demanded that the three sailors be turned over to Virginia officials for trial. Seward responded by launching an attack on the institution of slavery and ignoring Virginia's demands. "There is no law of this State which recognizes slavery, no statute which admits that one man can be the property of another, or that one man can be stolen from another," wrote Seward. "[The sailors' act] is not a felony [major crime] nor a crime within the meaning of the constitution." The New York governor's stand "placed Seward squarely in the antislavery camp at a time when the abolitionists were gaining prominence on the national political scene," wrote John M. Taylor in *William Henry Seward: Lincoln's Right Hand.*

Seward joins the U.S. Senate

Seward decided not to seek the governorship of New York in 1842. The political battles of the previous few years had exhausted him, and he decided that he needed to take a break. He returned to his law practice, where he made enough money to pay off several large debts that he had accumulated as governor.

By the mid-1840s, though, Seward's enthusiasm for politics had returned. In 1849, he was elected to the U.S. Senate, where his criticism of slavery intensified. Alarmed at Southern efforts to expand slavery into America's western territories, he warned of a future war between the slavery-dependent South and the Northern states, where slavery was increasingly viewed as immoral. In the mid-1850s, Seward left the Whig Party, which was falling apart because of disagreements over slavery. He joined a new antislavery party known as the Republicans.

Within a matter of months, Seward emerged as one of the leading antislavery voices of the new party. On October 25, 1858, for example, he delivered a famous speech in Rochester, New York, where he warned of an approaching "irrepressible conflict" between the South's slave-based economy and the North's free labor economy. "The United States must and will, sooner or later, become either entirely a slave-holding nation or entirely a free-labor nation," he stated. "I know, and you know, that a revolution has begun. . . . While the government of the United States, under the conduct of the Democratic party, has been all that time surrendering one plain and castle after another to slavery, the people of the United States have been no less steadily and perseveringly [persistently] gathering together the forces with which to recover back again all the fields and castles that have been lost."

By 1860, Seward was completing his second full term as senator (he was reelected in 1855) and thinking about running for president of the United States. After all, he was one of America's best known political leaders, and he knew he could count on support from many influential Republican Party leaders. As the time drew near for Republicans to select their candidate for president in the fall 1860 elections, Seward was sure that he would win the nomination.

As it turned out, however, Seward did not receive the party's nomination. Some delegates (representatives) opposed him because of his past policies as New York governor. Others voted against him because they knew that Seward's strong antislavery reputation would make him unpopular with Southern voters. These factors enabled a relatively unknown politician named Abraham Lincoln to capture the Republican nomination for the presidency. Lincoln's victory shocked Seward and his supporters, as well as the rest of the nation. But after spending a few weeks at his home in Auburn, Seward actively campaigned for Lincoln's election.

The American Civil War begins

In November 1860, widespread support from Northern voters enabled Lincoln to defeat Democratic candidates Stephen Douglas (1813–1861) and Vice President John C. Breckinridge (1821–1875) to become the sixteenth president of the United States. Lincoln's victory infuriated America's Southern states, though. Republicans had hoped that their decision to nominate Lincoln instead of a "radical abolitionist" like Seward would reassure white Southerners that the party wanted to settle North-South differences over slavery through negotiation and compromise. But most white Southerners believed that all Republicans were alike. They worried that Lincoln would take immediate steps to abolish (eliminate) slavery, which they viewed as the cornerstone of their economic and social lives.

As a result, a number of Southern states seceded from (left) the United States following Lincoln's election. With their enemies in control of the U.S. government, they felt that the only way they could protect their rights as independent states was to leave the Union. But it soon became clear that the North was willing to fight to keep the Southern states in the Union. Within a matter of months, the two sides were at war.

Lincoln's secretary of state

When Lincoln won the presidential election of 1860, he asked Seward to serve as his secretary of state. Seward accepted the position, which was the most important one in the entire cabinet (a group of advisors who guide various departments of government). Upon arriving in Washington, D.C., however, Seward acted as if he were the president. Skeptical about Lincoln's abilities to lead the country, he lectured the president about various policy issues and tried to dictate military strategy.

Lewis Paine, the man who stabbed William Seward the night of President Abraham Lincoln's assassination. *(Reproduced by permission of the National Portrait Gallery.)*

Seward's actions angered Lincoln. But the president knew that the New York native was a bright legislator and a talented statesman. As a result, he skillfully neutralized Seward's maneuvers until mid-1861, when the secretary of state realized that Lincoln knew what he was doing. From that point on, Seward accepted his role and became an important member of the Lincoln administration.

As the Civil War progressed, Seward proved his value to Lincoln in many ways. For example, Lincoln recognized that if Great Britain or France declared support for the Confederate government, the Union might have to let the Southern states go or risk a disastrous trade war with Europe. Seward used his diplomatic skills to convince Great Britain and France to withhold recognition of the Confederacy's claim of independence. He also intervened to prevent foreign nations from providing the South with ships, weapons, and other supplies.

By the time the war ended in the spring of 1865, Seward had become a close friend and trusted advisor to Lincoln. After all, they had spent the previous four years laboring together to restore the Union and defending each other from critics who did not like their wartime policies. On April 14, 1865, however, their friendship and alliance came to a tragic end. That evening, fanatical Southern sympathizers attacked both men in separate incidents. Seward was attacked in the bedroom of his Washington, D.C., home, where he was recovering from a carriage accident. He suffered several stab wounds at the hands of Lewis Paine, but survived the assault. Lincoln was murdered by John Wilkes Booth while attending a play at Washington's Ford Theatre.

"Seward's Folly"

Lincoln's death vaulted Vice President Andrew Johnson into the presidency on April 15, 1865. Seward continued to serve as secretary of state in the Johnson administration. He supported Johnson's Reconstruction policies, which were widely criticized for being too lenient on the South. Defending Johnson's approach to restoring the Southern states to the Union, Seward argued that "history shows that the more generous and magnanimous [forgiving] the conqueror to the conquered, the sooner victory has been followed by conciliation and a lasting peace."

In 1867, Seward made his most remarkable postwar contribution when he negotiated the purchase of Alaska from Russia for $7.2 million. Some people referred to the acquisition of Alaska as "Seward's Folly," because they could not believe that he had paid so much money for a distant land of ice and mountains. As time passed, however, Americans realized that Seward's purchase of the land was one of the great bargains of all time.

Seward left his government position in March 1869, when **Ulysses S. Grant** (1822–1885; see entry) became president of the United States. He returned to Auburn, but soon became restless in retirement. He subsequently went on a tour of the world with some family friends. Shortly after his return to Auburn, however, his health began to decline. He died on October 10, 1872.

Where to Learn More

Lothrop, Thonrton Kirkland. *William Henry Seward.* Boston: Houghton Mifflin, 1895. Reprint, 1972.

Taylor, John M. *William Henry Seward: Lincoln's Right Hand.* New York: HarperCollins, 1991.

Van Deusen, Glyndon G. *William Henry Seward.* New York: Oxford University Press, 1967.

Robert Gould Shaw

Born October 10, 1837
Boston, Massachusetts
Died July 18, 1863
Morris Island, South Carolina

Union colonel of the all-black Fifty-Fourth Massachusetts Regiment

Led the assault on Fort Wagner in South Carolina that proved the courage of black soldiers in combat

Robert Gould Shaw became a hero as commanding officer of the Fifty-Fourth Massachusetts Regiment—the first all-black regiment to be organized in the North. Black men were not allowed to join the Union Army in the early days of the Civil War. Even when the law was changed in mid-1862, many people still doubted whether black men could be good soldiers. Prominent black leaders and abolitionists (people who wanted to eliminate slavery) organized the Fifty-Fourth Massachusetts and selected Shaw as its leader in the hope of changing people's views. In July 1863, the regiment led an assault on Fort Wagner, a Confederate stronghold guarding the harbor in Charleston, South Carolina. The bravery of Shaw and the Fifty-Fourth Massachusetts during the assault convinced people across the North that black soldiers deserved to fight for the freedom of their race.

"Isn't it extraordinary that the Government won't make use of the instrument that would finish the war sooner than anything else—the slaves?"

Robert Gould Shaw. *(From Harper's Weekly, August 15, 1863.)*

Son of wealthy abolitionists

Robert Gould Shaw was born into a life of wealth and privilege on October 10, 1837, in Boston, Massachusetts. His parents, Francis George Shaw and Sarah Blake Sturgis Shaw, were both descended from early American colonists. They put their money and influence to work as social reformers. One of the issues that concerned them deeply was slavery.

Black people were taken from Africa and brought to North America to serve as slaves for white people beginning in the 1600s. The basic belief behind slavery was that black people were inferior to whites. Under slavery, white slaveholders treated black people as property, forced them to perform hard labor, and controlled every aspect of their lives. States in the Northern half of the United States began outlawing slavery in the late 1700s. But slavery continued to exist in the Southern half of the country because it played an important role in the South's economy and culture.

The Shaws believed that slavery was wrong and wanted to abolish (put an end to) it. They frequently spoke out on the subject and held meetings of fellow abolitionists at their home. As a result, Robert was exposed to the arguments against slavery from an early age.

Educated in Europe

When Robert was nine years old, his family moved to Staten Island, New York. At this time, Staten Island was a rural area populated by a few wealthy families who lived on large estates. Shaw loved being outdoors and exploring the fields and woods near his home. He attended a small private school there, and then went to boarding school for a short time. In 1848, Shaw went to Europe with his family. He lived there for most of the next eight years, studying in Switzerland and Germany.

In 1856, Shaw returned to the United States and enrolled at Harvard University. He found the schoolwork easy compared to his education in Europe, so he spent most of his two years there enjoying an active social life. He joined a boating club and played violin in string quartets. He also struggled with the question of what he wanted to do with his life. Hoping to do more traveling, he took a job in the New York City offices of an overseas trading company owned by his uncle in 1859. He did not like the work, however, and worried that he lacked the ability to move up into management.

Joins the Union Army

By 1860, the issue of slavery had caused a huge division between the Northern and Southern sections of the country. Thanks to the efforts of Shaw's parents and other abolitionists, growing numbers of Northerners believed that slavery was wrong. Some people wanted to outlaw it, while others wanted to prevent it from spreading beyond the Southern states where it was already allowed. But many Southerners felt threatened by Northern efforts to contain slavery. They believed that each state should decide for itself whether to allow slavery. They did not want the national government to pass laws that would interfere with their traditional way of life.

This situation exploded when **Abraham Lincoln** (1809–1865; see entry) was elected president of the United States. Since Lincoln was a Northerner who opposed slavery, the Southern states believed that the nation's government could no longer represent their interests. In early 1861, several Southern states seceded (withdrew) from the United States and formed a new country that allowed slavery, called the Confederate States of America. But Northern political leaders were determined to keep the Southern states in the Union. The two sides soon went to war.

Shaw was glad when the Civil War began because he was tired of seeing the North compromise with the South. "As for making concessions [compromises], it is only patching up the affair for a year or two, when it would break out worse than ever," he stated. He also felt that force was justified to settle the issue of slavery. When the Southern states began to secede, Lincoln called for volunteers to come defend the U.S. capital in Washington, D.C. Shaw immediately joined the Seventh New York National Guard as a private. This military unit was made up almost entirely of young men like Shaw, from wealthy New England families. Huge crowds of people lined the streets to see them off on their trip to Washington. They ended up being the first regiment to arrive in the capital. But Shaw's first experience of military life did not prove very exciting. He spent most of his time doing chores during his ninety-day term of service.

Becomes an officer in the Second Massachusetts

When his time with the Seventh New York ended, Shaw applied for a commission as an officer in the Second Massachusetts Regiment. Under the direction of Colonel George H. Gordon, Shaw learned military discipline and his self-confidence increased. He finally seemed to have found something meaningful to do with his life. Within a short time, the Second Massachusetts began to see action in the war. They were sent to the Shenandoah Valley in western Virginia, where they engaged in a number of skirmishes (brief fights) with Confederate forces under the command of **Thomas "Stonewall" Jackson** (1824–1863; see entry).

During breaks in the fighting, Shaw began thinking and talking with other officers about the wisdom of using black soldiers, and especially former slaves, in the Union Army. At this point, Federal law prohibited black men from joining the army. Many Northern whites wanted to keep it that way. Some whites claimed that the purpose of the Civil War was to restore the Union rather than to settle the issue of slavery. And since the war was not about slavery, they felt that there was no need to change the law so that black people could join the fight. Another reason that many Northern whites did not want black men to be allowed to join the army was deep-seated racial prejudice. Some whites believed that they were superior to blacks and did not want to fight alongside them. Finally, some Northerners worried that allowing blacks to become soldiers would convince the border states—four states that allowed slavery but remained part of the Union anyway—to join the Confederacy.

Black leaders and white abolitionists in the North were outraged at the policies and prejudices that prevented black men from fighting in the Civil War. Free black men from the North had tried to enlist from the earliest days of the conflict. They wanted to help the Union forces put an end to slavery. They also believed that proving their patriotism and courage on the field of battle would help improve their position in American society. Many Northern blacks signed petitions asking the Federal government to change its rules, but the government refused. In the meantime, thousands of blacks—both freemen and escaped or liberated slaves—provided unofficial help for the cause by serving as cooks, carpenters, laborers, nurses, scouts, and servants for the Union troops.

Shaw and some of his fellow officers believed that allowing black men to become soldiers could only help the Union war effort. "Isn't it extraordinary that the Government won't make use of the instrument that would finish the war sooner than anything else—the slaves?" Shaw wrote. "What a lick it would be to [the Confederates] to call on all the blacks in the country to come and enlist in our army! They would probably make a fine army after a little drill, and could certainly be kept under better discipline than our independent Yankees [Northerners]!"

In September 1862, Shaw's regiment joined a large Union force under General **George B. McClellan** (1826–1885; see entry) along Antietam Creek in Maryland. On September 17, they fought a vicious day-long battle against Confederate forces under General **Robert E. Lee** (1807–1870; see entry). The Battle of Antietam killed or wounded more than twenty-three thousand Union and Confederate soldiers, making it the single bloodiest day in Civil War history. Although the fighting ended without a clear winner, Lincoln used it as an excuse to issue his Emancipation Proclamation. This document stated his intention to free all the slaves in Confederate territory on January 1, 1863. In addition, it declared that black men would officially be allowed to serve in the Union Army.

Takes command of the all-black Fifty-Fourth Massachusetts

In January 1863, the United States government authorized Governor John Andrew (1818–1867) of Massachusetts to put together a regiment of black soldiers from his state. Since there were not enough black men living in Massachusetts at that time, Andrew called upon prominent abolitionists and black leaders to recruit men from all over the North to form the Fifty-Fourth Massachusetts Regiment. The Fifty-Fourth Massachusetts would be the first all-black regiment to represent a state in battle during the Civil War.

Many white people in the North were opposed to allowing black soldiers to fight for the Union Army, so Governor Andrew and his recruiters had a lot to lose if the regiment failed. "Andrew wanted to prove that black men would fight—which would in turn prove that they were men and thus entitled to be free citizens," Russell Duncan wrote in his introduction to *Blue-Eyed Child of Fortune: The Civil War Letters of Colonel Robert Gould Shaw*. "Andrew understood the importance of making the venture a success, and he staked his reputation and career upon his conviction [belief] that blacks would fight and fight well."

Since black men were not allowed to become officers in the Union Army, the governor selected several white men to lead the Fifty-Fourth Massachusetts. Andrew knew that the regiment would receive a great deal of publicity, so he chose these officers carefully. In February, he wrote a letter asking Shaw to become colonel of the regiment. "I am about to raise a Colored Regiment in Massachusetts. This I cannot but regard as the most important corps [military unit] to be organized during the whole war," the governor wrote. "I am desirous to have for its officers . . . young men of military experience, of firm Anti-Slavery principles, ambitious, superior to vulgar contempt of color [about common prejudices about blacks], and having faith in the capacity of Colored men for military service."

Shaw's father delivered the message to him personally. The young soldier agonized over the decision. At first, Shaw questioned whether he could handle the responsibility. He knew that leading the first all-black regiment from the North would be a difficult job, and that many people would criticize his efforts and hope that he would fail. In addition, Shaw felt very close to his current regiment. Facing battle together had created a bond of trust that he was reluctant to break. After considering all these factors, Shaw informed his father that he would refuse Governor Andrew's offer. But then his mother wrote him a letter saying that she was bitterly disappointed in him, and his commanding officer expressed faith in his abilities as a leader. As a result, Shaw decided it was his duty to lead the Fifty-Fourth Massachusetts Regiment. He wrote to Andrew a few days later and accepted the job.

Gains respect for his black soldiers

When Shaw arrived in Boston to begin training the recruits for the Fifty-Fourth Massachusetts, he had never been around black men before. At first, he tended to believe some of the stereotypes (a generalized, oversimplified view of an ethnic group's behavior) he had heard about black people. But as he got to know more of his soldiers personally, he gained a great deal of respect and affection for them. "Never before around African Americans, Shaw changed through contact with them. He still held himself above blacks and formally addressed them, but he began to respect their abilities," Duncan noted. "Soon, Shaw became attached to his men and defended them strongly against outside abuse. He had been forced by their actions to question, then conquer, his own misconceptions. They proved their intelligence, commitment to order, pluck [courage], and adaptability to military life. As Shaw changed, he won the respect of his men."

On May 2, 1863, Shaw married Anna Kneeland Haggerty. A few weeks later, she was on hand to watch the Fifty-Fourth Massachusetts take part in a ceremony to mark the end of their training. Many prominent abolitionists and military leaders were in the crowd. At the end of the ceremony, Governor Andrew handed Shaw a flag and said, "Wherever its folds shall be unfurled, it will mark the path of glory." Immediately afterward, the Fifty-Fourth Massachusetts shipped out to Hilton Head, an island off the coast of South Carolina.

For the first month, Shaw's regiment took part in several raids along the Southern coast. On one of these raids, they accompanied a regiment made up of former slaves under the command of Colonel James Montgomery. The two regiments entered the town of Darien, Georgia, and took all the food and supplies they could find. Afterward, Montgomery ordered his troops to burn the town. Shaw protested the order, but Montgomery's troops destroyed the town anyway. Southern newspapers picked up the story and criticized the black regiments, calling them "vandals" and "thieves." Even though Shaw had not participated in the destruction, he ended up sharing the blame.

By early July, Shaw was eager to take his troops into battle and prove what they could do. "I want to get my men along side of white troops, and into a good fight, if there is to be one," he stated. Around this time, the Union military leaders decided to concentrate on capturing the port city of Charleston, South Carolina. General George Strong asked

Shaw to bring his regiment up the coast to help implement the plan. On the way, the Fifty-Fourth Massachusetts stopped on James Island and saw their first real action. In a coordinated effort with white soldiers, they helped beat back a Confederate attack.

Leads Union assault on Fort Wagner

The Fifty-Fourth Massachusetts finally arrived at Charleston Harbor on July 18, 1863. The regiment was chosen to lead an assault on Fort Wagner, a Confederate stronghold that guarded the entrance to the harbor. The soldiers had marched all of the previous day and night, along beaches and through swamps, in terrible heat and humidity. But even though they were tired and hungry by the time they reached Charleston, they still proudly took their positions at the head of the assault.

As evening came, Shaw led the Fifty-Fourth Massachusetts in a charge toward the fort. They were immediately hit with heavy artillery and musket fire from the Confederate troops inside the fort. Shaw was killed in the fighting, along with nearly half of his six hundred officers and men. But the remaining troops kept moving forward, crossed the moat (deep ditch sometimes filled with water) surrounding the fort, and climbed up the stone wall. They were eventually forced to retreat when reinforcements did not appear in time, but by then they had inflicted heavy losses on the enemy.

The next day, Confederate troops dug a mass grave and buried Shaw's body along with his fallen black soldiers, despite the fact that the bodies of high-ranking officers were usually returned by both sides. The Confederates intended this action to be an insult, since they believed that whites were superior to blacks and thus deserved a better burial. Several weeks later, when Union forces finally captured Fort Wagner, a Union officer offered to search for the grave and recover Shaw's body. But Shaw's father refused the offer. "We hold that a soldier's most appropriate burial-place is on the field where he has fallen," he wrote.

Even though the Fifty-Fourth Massachusetts did not succeed in capturing Fort Wagner, their brave performance in

William H. Carney, the First Black Soldier Awarded the Congressional Medal of Honor

William H. Carney was born a slave in Norfolk, Virginia, in 1840. When his owner died in 1854, he and his family received their freedom. They soon moved to New Bedford, Massachusetts, because they felt that black people were not safe in the South. When the call went out for black men to join the Union Army, he was among the first to enlist. He joined the Fifty-Fourth Massachusetts Regiment in February 1863 for a three-year term. He quickly impressed Colonel Shaw and the other officers with his bravery and strength.

Carney played a leading role in the assault on Fort Wagner in July 1863. As the Fifty-Fourth Massachusetts moved forward, artillery and gunfire exploded all around them. Many of his fellow soldiers were killed. At one point, Carney found the American flag lying on the ground. The man who had been carrying it was dead. He picked up the flag and continued his charge across the moat and up the wall of the fort. He caught up with Shaw just as his commanding officer was fatally shot. He then stuck the flagpole he was carrying into the ground and crouched on the top of the wall, firing repeatedly at Confederates inside the fort. He kept on fighting even though he received serious wounds to his chest, arms, and legs.

As the Union troops began to fall back from the assault, Carney limped back to his regiment. He tried to raise their spirits

William H. Carney. *(Reproduced with permission of Fisk University Library.)*

and convince them to return to the fort. But after seeing his wounds, the officer in charge told him he had done enough already. Carney replied: "I have only done my duty, the old flag never touched the ground." He then handed the flag over to the officer and stumbled alone to the field hospital.

After recovering from his wounds, Carney received a discharge from the Union Army. He lived in the Boston area with his wife, Susanna Williams, after the war. He worked for the city as the superintendent of street lighting and as a mail carrier. In May 1900, Carney received the Congressional Medal of Honor for his bravery at Fort Wagner. He thus became the first African American to win the nation's highest military honor. Carney died in 1908 following an elevator accident that crushed his leg.

battle was considered a triumph. Newspapers throughout the North carried the story, even those that had opposed the enlistment of blacks in the Union Army. People were forced to admit that black men were just as capable as whites of fighting and dying for the Union and freedom. By the end of 1863, sixty new black regiments were being formed across the North. The success of the Fifty-Fourth Massachusetts and other black regiments not only helped the North win the Civil War, but also led to greater acceptance of blacks in American society.

Shortly after Shaw's death, Governor Andrew began organizing a memorial to him and his fallen soldiers in Boston. He hired the famous sculptor Augustus Saint-Gaudens (1848–1907) to design the memorial. The artist finally unveiled his work in 1897, at a ceremony attended by many black Civil War veterans. It shows Shaw on horseback, surrounded by his black troops, as they march southward to fight for freedom and equality for people of all races. "There they march, warm-blooded champions of a better day for man," philosopher William James (1842–1910) said at the dedication. "There on horseback, among them . . . sits the blue-eyed child of fortune, upon whose happy youth every divinity had smiled. Onward they move together, a single resolution kindled in their eyes."

Where to Learn More

Burchard, Peter. *We'll Stand by the Union: Robert Gould Shaw and the Black 54th Massachusetts Regiment.* New York: Facts on File, 1993.

Duncan, Russell, ed. *Blue-Eyed Child of Fortune: The Civil War Letters of Colonel Robert Gould Shaw.* Athens: University of Georgia Press, 1992.

Duncan, Russell. *Where Death and Glory Meet: Colonel Robert Gould Shaw and the 54th Massachusetts Infantry.* Athens: University of Georgia Press, 1999.

National Gallery of Art. *Augustus Saint-Gaudens' Memorial to Robert Gould Shaw and the Massachusetts Fifty-fourth Regiment.* [Online] http://www.nga.gov/feature/shaw/home.htm (accessed on October 16, 1999).

Smith, Marion W. *Beacon's Hill Colonel Robert Gould Shaw.* New York: Carlton Press, 1986.

Smith, Marion W. *Colonel Robert Gould Shaw: A Pictorial Companion.* New York: Carlton Press, 1990.

Trudeau, Noah Andre. *Like Men of War: Black Troops in the Civil War.* Boston: Little, Brown, 1998.

Philip H. Sheridan

Born March 6, 1831
Albany, New York
Died August 5, 1888
Nosquitt, Massachusetts

Union cavalry general
Led successful Shenandoah Campaign in 1864 and won Battle of Five Forks in April 1865, which ultimately resulted in General Lee's surrender at Appomattox

P hilip Sheridan was one of the Union Army's finest military leaders during the second half of the Civil War. His steady direction was vital in improving the performance of the Army of the Potomac's cavalry corps in 1863. A year later, his successful invasion of Virginia's Shenandoah Valley pushed the Confederacy one step closer to surrender. Finally, his victory at Five Forks in April 1865 forced General **Robert E. Lee** (1807–1870; see entry) to abandon his defense of Richmond (the capital city of the Confederacy) and helped bring the war to a close. In recognition of these accomplishments, Union commander **Ulysses S. Grant** (1822–1885; see entry) stated, "I believe General Sheridan has no superior as a general, either living or dead, and perhaps not an equal."

Aiming for a military career

Philip Henry Sheridan was born in Albany, New York, in 1831. After attending school in Albany, he was accepted into the U.S. Military Academy at West Point in July 1848. During his time at West Point, however, he got in a quarrel

"I believe General Sheridan has no superior as a general, either living or dead, and perhaps not an equal."

Ulysses S. Grant

Philip H. Sheridan. *(Courtesy of U.S. Army Photographers.)*

with a fellow cadet (military student). Sheridan was suspended for the incident, but he eventually was allowed to return to the academy.

After graduating from West Point in July 1853, Sheridan was assigned to a variety of military posts in Kentucky, Texas, and Oregon. These military assignments in the West often took him to outposts that were hundreds of miles from the population centers of the United States. But no matter where he was stationed, Sheridan followed the growing tensions between America's Northern and Southern regions with great interest.

By the 1850s, the North and South had become deadlocked over several emotional issues, including slavery and the concept of states' rights. Many Northerners believed that slavery was wrong and wanted to abolish (eliminate) it. They also contended that the federal government had the authority to pass laws that applied to all citizens of the United States. But a large part of the South's economy and culture had been built on slavery, and Southerners resented Northern efforts to halt or contain the practice. In addition, they argued that the federal government did not have the constitutional power to institute national laws on slavery or other issues. Instead, white Southerners argued that each state should decide for itself whether to allow slavery. Finally, America's westward expansion made the situation even worse, since both sides wanted to spread their way of life—and their political ideas—into the new territories and states.

In early 1861, several Southern states became so fed up with the situation that they seceded from (left) the United States to form a new country that allowed slavery, called the Confederate States of America. The U.S. government, though, declared that those states had no right to secede and that it was willing to use force to make them return to the Union. In the spring of 1861, these bitter differences finally erupted into war.

Sheridan makes his mark in battle

As a native New Yorker who had pledged to serve the U.S. Army, there was no doubt that Sheridan would fight for the Union in the Civil War. During the first months of the war, he served as a staff officer for higher-ranking officers in the army, helping with strategy sessions and administrative duties. In May 1862, though, Sheridan was promoted to colonel and given command of the Second Michigan Cavalry.

During the remainder of 1862, Sheridan distinguished himself in several different battles in the Civil War's western theater (the region of the South between the Mississippi River and the Appalachian Mountains). First, he led a successful raid on Booneville, Mississippi, in July. Then, Sheridan and his troops helped the North take hard-fought victories at the Battle of Perryville in Kentucky and the Battle of Stones River in Murfreesboro, Tennessee. In recognition of his impressive military performance, Sheridan was promoted to the rank of major-general at the beginning of 1863. During the next sixteen months, he remained in the West as an infantry commander in the Union's Army of the Cumberland.

Service in the Army of the Cumberland

The Army of the Cumberland spent much of the summer of 1863 in the state of Tennessee. Their main opponent in that state was the Confederate Army of Tennessee, led by General **Braxton Bragg** (1817–1876; see entry). By late September 1863, Army of the Cumberland maneuvers masterminded by Union general William S. Rosecrans (1819–1898) convinced Bragg to abandon the city of Chattanooga and clear out of Tennessee. But when Rosecrans continued his pursuit of Bragg into northern Georgia, the Confederate general counterattacked. This battle—known as the Battle of Chickamauga—ended in disaster for the North, as Union divisions under the command of Sheridan and other Union officers broke into chaotic flight.

Bragg's army chased the retreating Union soldiers all the way back to Chattanooga, then surrounded the city. For a short time it appeared that the Army of the Cumberland was in danger of being destroyed. But Union reinforcements soon arrived, and General **George H. Thomas** (1816–1870; see entry) organized a successful counterattack in late November. Sheridan's division played an important part in this counterattack. Their capture of the strategically important position known as Missionary Ridge triggered a complete Confederate retreat back into Georgia.

Sheridan joins Grant

In February 1864, General Grant assumed command of all Union armies. Leaving General **William T. Sherman** (1820–1891; see entry) in charge of the Union Army in the West, Grant moved east to take personal control of the Army of the Potomac. The Army of the Potomac was the primary Union army in the war's eastern theater, and Grant wanted to guide its activities himself. (General **George Meade** [1815–1872; see entry] remained the official head of the Army of the Potomac, but Grant exercised ultimate control over its actions.)

Upon taking over the Army of the Potomac, Grant decided to make Sheridan its new cavalry commander. The reassignment delighted Sheridan, and he immediately requested greater freedom to use his cavalry without waiting for orders all the time. He believed that if he were given an independent command, he could go out and track down **Jeb Stuart** (1833–1864; see entry), the leading Confederate cavalryman in Virginia. Grant liked the idea, and he quickly approved the plan.

The Battle at Yellow Tavern

In the spring of 1864, Sheridan advanced on Richmond with a force of twelve thousand cavalry. As he hoped, his march on the rebel capital convinced the Confederates to send Stuart and his cavalry to stop him. Stuart managed to halt the Union advance at a small village called Yellow Tavern, located a few miles outside of Richmond. But Stuart had only about forty thousand horsemen under his command, which gave Sheridan a big advantage in battle.

The two cavalry forces clashed together on May 11, 1864. Fighting desperately to defend their capital, Stuart's troops halted Sheridan's advance and eventually forced him to retreat. But Stuart was mortally wounded in the clash and died a day later. According to Sheridan, Stuart's death made his mission a success. "Under [Stuart], the cavalry of Lee's army had been nurtured but had acquired such prestige that it thought itself well nigh invincible [unconquerable]," Sheridan later stated. "Indeed, in the early years of the war, it had proved to be so. This was now dispelled [eliminated] by the successful march we had made in Lee's rear, and the removal of Stuart at Yellow Tavern had inflicted a blow from which entire recovery was impossible."

The Shenandoah Valley Campaign

Sheridan's performance against Stuart convinced Grant that he should use the steady cavalry commander against other troublesome Confederate cavalry forces. In the summer of 1864, he sent Sheridan into the Shenandoah Valley, an area of northern Virginia that had been a favorite Confederate invasion route and supply source since the war's early days.

Sheridan's main target in the Shenandoah Valley was a fifteen thousand–strong Confederate cavalry force led by Lieutenant General Jubal Early (1816–1894). But Grant also wanted to eliminate the valley as a source of food and supplies for the South. He thus ordered Sheridan not only to drive Jubal Early's cavalry out of the region, but also to destroy the farmlands that had been used to supply Confederates with needed food and supplies. "Carry off stock [livestock or supplies] of all descriptions and negroes so as to prevent further planting," Grant ordered. "If the War is to last another year we want the Shenandoah Valley to remain a barren waste."

Armed with a forty thousand–man force of cavalry and infantry, Sheridan moved through the valley with grim determination. In August, his army—designated the Army of the Shenandoah by Grant—began their assault on the valley's pro-Confederacy farms and villages. They burned barns, destroyed crops, and captured livestock wherever they went, obeying Sheridan's declaration that "the people [of the Shenandoah Valley] must be left nothing but their eyes to weep with over the war." Confederate guerrillas (armed raiders) led by **John Singleton Mosby** (1833–1916; see entry) repeatedly struck against Sheridan's army during this time, but their efforts proved useless in stopping the destructive Union advance.

George Armstrong Custer (1839–1876)

General Sheridan's favorite officer in his command was George Armstrong Custer, a cavalryman who became known for his bravery and daring during the Civil War. But while Custer's Civil War exploits made him a familiar figure to American newspaper readers, he became even more famous in 1876, when Sioux warriors killed him and all 264 soldiers under his command at the Battle of Little Bighorn.

Born in Ohio in 1839, Custer moved to Michigan as a youngster. In 1857, he enrolled at West Point. He graduated in 1861, but ranked last in his class. Three weeks after graduating from the academy, he fought at the First Battle of Bull Run (July 1861) in the cavalry of the Union's Army of the Potomac.

Over the next four years, Custer fought in many of the Civil War's biggest and bloodiest battles. During this time, the young officer built a reputation as a bright strategist and a fearless soldier. In fact, Custer once said that he would "be willing . . . to see a battle every day during my life." Everyone who knew the dashing young soldier knew that such statements accurately represented his feelings about the war. But Custer was not universally loved. Some of the soldiers in his command viewed him as an unnecessarily harsh disciplinarian. Even people who liked Custer admitted that his thirst for publicity and fame sometimes got out of hand.

Nonetheless, Custer's battlefield performances impressed Sheridan. After Sheridan took command of the Army of the Potomac's cavalry in 1863, he quickly promoted Custer through the ranks. Custer eventually became the youngest

By late September, Sheridan's army had smashed much of the valley's farmland and claimed two victories over Early's dwindling cavalry force. But Early was not forced to leave the valley until mid-October, when Sheridan showed the entire country the strength of his military leadership. Confident that his army could maintain control over the valley in his absence, Sheridan and some members of his staff traveled to Washington for a conference. On the morning of October 19, however, Early's cavalry launched a surprise attack on the Army of the Shenandoah's camp at Cedar Creek. The assault shocked the Union soldiers. They fled the camp in a disorganized retreat, leaving behind food, artillery guns (large guns too heavy to carry), and other supplies.

George Custer. *(Courtesy of the Library of Congress.)*

major general in American military history. During Sheridan's Shenandoah Valley campaign of 1864, Custer's cavalry led many of the Union offensives (attacks) on Confederate foes. The performance of Custer's troops made it much easier for Sheridan to seize control of the valley by the end of the year.

After the Civil War ended, Custer stayed in the U.S. military. When federal efforts to seize lands from Native American tribes heated up, Custer transferred to military posts in the West. In 1876, he led the army's Seventh Cavalry in a campaign against Sioux and Cheyenne Indians in southern Montana. But on June 25, Custer stumbled into a large war party led by the legendary chief Sitting Bull (c. 1831–1890) near the Little Bighorn River. Custer and his cavalrymen were wiped out in the resulting battle, which remains the most famous Indian military victory in American history.

Unfortunately for Early, though, Sheridan ran into his fleeing soldiers on his way back from Washington. "There burst upon our view the appalling spectacle of a panic-stricken army," Sheridan recalled. "Hundreds of slightly wounded men, throngs of others unhurt but utterly demoralized, and baggage-wagons by the score [groups of twenty], all pressing to the rear in hopeless confusion."

The sight of Sheridan, however, immediately changed the attitude of his frightened troops. Using a combination of encouragement and verbal abuse, Sheridan stopped the retreat. He then reorganized his troops and led a furious charge back into their Cedar Creek camp. Sheridan's counterattack crushed Early's cavalry. By the time the Confederate cavalry was able to escape, it had been torn to pieces. Sheridan's victory at Cedar Creek established Union control over the Shenandoah Valley for the remainder of the war.

The Battle of Five Forks

After his triumph in the Shenandoah Valley, Sheridan continued to show his value to the Union cause throughout Virginia. In early 1865, he was ordered to rejoin Grant's Army of the Potomac at Petersburg, where Robert E. Lee's Army of Northern Virginia had maintained a months-long defense of that city and neighboring Richmond. As Sheridan's Army of the Shenandoah moved across the Virginia countryside, it launched a series of successful raids against Confederate positions.

Soon after Sheridan reached Petersburg, Grant sent him on an important mission. Grant knew that both Petersburg and Richmond were running short of food and other supplies. He reasoned that if he could seize control of the Confederates' last remaining railroad line, he could force Lee to evacuate his army from the two cities. He thus ordered Sheridan to take twelve thousand cavalry and capture the railroad at an area south of Petersburg known as Five Forks.

On April 1, Sheridan's force successfully seized the rail line at Five Forks. Confederate troops led by George Pickett (1825–1875) tried to protect the area, but Sheridan smashed them with ease. By the evening of April 1, Sheridan had taken more than five thousand rebel prisoners and cut off the last remaining supply line into Petersburg. When Sheridan informed Grant of his victory at Five Forks, Grant ordered a full assault on the Confederate defenses at Petersburg.

Lee evacuated his army from Petersburg on April 3, leaving it and Richmond to the advancing Union forces. The Confederate general mounted a desperate bid to escape the area, but Grant immediately gave chase. For the next week or so, Sheridan's cavalry struck again and again against Lee's flanks, as the remainder of the Union Army followed in close pursuit. On April 7, Sheridan's cavalry successfully cut off the rebels' last remaining escape route, forcing Lee to halt his battered army at an area known as Appomattox. Lee surrendered two days later, ending Confederate hopes of independence once and for all.

After the war

In the months following the end of the Civil War, Sheridan was appointed to lead federal Reconstruction (1865–77) efforts in Texas and Louisiana. (Reconstruction is the name given for the period immediately after the war, when the federal government worked to put the war-torn nation back together again.) But Sheridan had a difficult time implementing Reconstruction policies, which were intended to rebuild the South and protect the rights of blacks. His policies were so harsh that he was removed from this assignment after only six months.

Sheridan then spent several years in the American West, where he took part in cavalry operations against many Indian tribes in what he called "at best an inglorious [dishonorable] war." He also spent a great deal of time working for the creation of Yellowstone National Park. In 1884, he was named general-in-chief of all U.S. forces. He died four years later.

Where to Learn More

Carter, Samuel. *The Last Cavaliers: Confederate and Union Cavalry in the Civil War.* New York: St. Martin's Press, 1979.

Heatwole, John L. *The Burning: Sheridan in the Shenandoah Valley.* Charlottesville, VA: Rockbridge Pub., 1998.

Hutton, Paul Andrew. *Phil Sheridan and His Army.* Lincoln: University of Nebraska Press, 1985. Reprint, Norman: University of Oklahoma Press, 1999.

Longacre, Edward C. *Mounted Raids of the Civil War.* South Brunswick, NJ: A. S. Barnes, 1975. Reprint, Lincoln: University of Nebraska Press, 1994.

Morris, Roy, Jr. *Sheridan: The Life and Wars of General Phil Sheridan.* New York: Crown Publishers, 1992.

Perry County Historical Society. *The Sheridan Monument.* [Online] http://www.netpluscom.com/~pchs/sheridan_monument.htm (accessed on October 15, 1999).

Stackpole, Edward J. *Sheridan in the Shenandoah.* Harrisburg, PA: Stackpole Books, 1961. Reprint, 1992.

William T. Sherman

Born February 8, 1820
Lancaster, Ohio
Died February 14, 1891
New York, New York

Union general
Led the capture of Atlanta, Georgia, then took his forces on the destructive "March to the Sea"

William T. Sherman was one of the most controversial generals of the Civil War. He rose through the military ranks to become commander of the Union forces in the West (the area west of the Appalachian Mountains). In September 1864, his troops captured the important Southern industrial city of Atlanta, Georgia. Sherman ordered all civilians (people who are not part of the army, including women and children) to leave the city and then burned it down. Afterward, the general marched his Union troops across Georgia to the city of Savannah on the Atlantic coast. During this famous "March to the Sea," Sherman's army lived off the countryside, taking whatever food and supplies they could use and destroying everything else.

Southerners were shocked and angered by Sherman's actions. Before this time, the Civil War was mostly fought between armies on battlefields. Sherman was one of the first leaders to attack civilians and their property under a new strategy known as "total war." He felt that defeating the Confederate Army on the battlefield was not enough to ensure a lasting peace. He thought it was also necessary to break the spirit of

"There is many a boy . . . who looks on war as all glory, but boys, war is all hell."

William Sherman.

391

the civilian population that supplied the army and supported the war effort. Sherman believed that by showing ordinary Southerners the destructive power of war, he could make them want to surrender.

Named after an Indian war chief

William Tecumseh Sherman was born on February 8, 1820, in Lancaster, a wilderness outpost in southern Ohio. He was the sixth of eleven children born to Charles R. Sherman and Mary Hoyt Sherman. His father named him Tecumseh after the great Shawnee Indian chief Tecumseh (1768–1813). His family and friends called him "Cump" for short.

Charles Sherman died in 1829, leaving large debts that the family was unable to repay. Knowing that she could not afford to care for the children, Mary Sherman sent them away to live with various friends and relatives. Nine-year-old Cump moved in with Thomas and Eleanor Ewing, who lived just up the road from the Shermans in Lancaster. The Ewings welcomed the young boy into their family and treated him the same as their own children, but never formally adopted him.

Thomas Ewing (1789–1871) was a successful lawyer who later became a U.S. senator from Ohio. Cump admired his foster father and tried hard to gain his approval. In 1830, the Ewings arranged for the boy to be baptized by a Catholic priest. Since Sherman needed a Christian name for the ceremony, his foster father changed his first name to William. From that time on, Sherman signed his name W. T. Sherman or William T. Sherman.

Attends West Point

In 1836, Sherman entered the prestigious U.S. Military Academy at West Point in New York. He was an excellent student, but he was nearly expelled several times for bad behavior. He managed to graduate sixth in his class in 1840, but his lack of discipline kept him from getting a top appointment in the U.S. military. Instead of fighting in the Mexican War (1846–48)—which gained new territory for the United States and launched the careers of many young army officers—Sherman was posted in Florida and in California during the 1840s.

In 1850, Sherman married his foster sister, Ellen Ewing. They eventually had seven children, although only five survived to adulthood. In 1853, Sherman grew frustrated with his military career and decided to leave the army. He drifted from job to job over the next few years. He became a banker in San Francisco, but the bank failed. He then moved to Kansas and started a law and real estate office, which also failed. Although Sherman was a bright and capable young man, he was also insecure and lacked focus. He took his business failures very hard. "I am doomed to be a vagabond [drifter]," he said. "I look upon myself as a dead cock [rooster] in the [cock-fighting] pit not worthy of further notice."

North and South go to war

In 1859, Sherman finally found a job he liked as headmaster of a military school in New Orleans that eventually became Louisiana State University. While there, he developed a deep affection for the South and its people. But this was a time of great political tension in the United States. For years, the North and the South had been arguing over several issues. The most important issue dividing the two sections of the country was slavery. Many Northerners believed that slavery was wrong. Some people wanted to outlaw it, while others wanted to prevent it from spreading beyond the Southern states where it was already allowed. But slavery played a big role in the Southern economy and culture. As a result, many Southerners felt threatened by Northern efforts to contain slavery. They believed that each state should decide for itself whether to allow slavery. They did not want the national government to pass laws that would interfere with their traditional way of life.

By 1861, this ongoing dispute had convinced several Southern states to secede from (leave) the United States and attempt to form a new country that allowed slavery, called the Confederate States of America. But Northern political leaders were determined to keep the Southern states in the Union. Sherman believed in the Union and felt that the Southern states' secession would cause a long and bloody war.

He resigned from his job and moved his family to the North in February 1861.

Suffers breakdown early in the war

Two months later, the North and South entered into the Civil War. Sherman joined the Union Army. He commanded a brigade (military unit consisting of two or more regiments) during the Union's defeat at the First Battle of Bull Run (July 1861), then served in Kentucky. At this time, he became frustrated with the disorganized state of the Union war effort, as well as with his inability to do anything about it. He became convinced that the Confederate Army was much larger and stronger than his poorly trained Union volunteer force. Feelings of helplessness and insecurity gradually overcame him, and he considered suicide. Sherman finally came out of his depression, but his critics would call him mentally unstable and paranoid for the rest of his career.

After recovering his mental health, Sherman took command of the Department of Cairo in Paducah, Kentucky, in February 1862. He fought well at the bloody Battle of Shiloh (April 1862) in Tennessee, which resulted in a narrow Union victory. His performance got the attention of Union general **Ulysses S. Grant** (1822–1885; see entry), who had been his friend at West Point. Sherman then accepted a position under Grant, who was the Union's top commander in the West. Sherman contributed to the Union victories in Vicksburg, Mississippi (1862–63), and Chattanooga, Tennessee, in October and November 1863. Leading men into battle seemed to give Sherman a sense of purpose that had been missing in his life. He was very popular with his troops, and he could often be found smoking cigars and telling stories with enlisted men.

Captures Confederate city of Atlanta, Georgia

In 1864, Sherman took over as commander of Union forces in the West when Grant was promoted to commander of the entire Union Army. His troops spent much of the spring of 1864 chasing a much smaller Confederate force under General **Joseph E. Johnston** (1807–1891; see entry)

through Tennessee and Georgia. By the time summer arrived, Sherman had pushed Johnston's forces to the outskirts of Atlanta—one of the major industrial cities of the Confederacy. At this point, Confederate president **Jefferson Davis** (1808–1889; see entry) grew frustrated with Johnston's series of retreats and replaced him with Lieutenant General **John B. Hood** (1831–1879; see entry), a bold leader known for his aggressive style. Hood went on the offensive against Sherman's larger Union forces in mid-July with disastrous results. By August, Hood and his troops were trapped in the city.

Rather than attacking Atlanta directly, Sherman decided to lay siege to the city. He surrounded it with troops, cut off the Confederate supply lines, and began pounding the enemy forces with artillery fire. Finally, Hood was forced to evacuate his men from the city. The Union Army captured Atlanta on September 2, 1864, after four months of nearly constant fighting. The victory convinced many Northerners to

The ruins of a Confederate engine house in Atlanta, Georgia. *(Reproduced by permission of the National Portrait Gallery.)*

renew their support for the war effort and for President **Abraham Lincoln** (1809–1865; see entry). In fact, many historians claim that Sherman's capture of Atlanta helped assure Lincoln's reelection as president.

Leads "March to the Sea"

The capture of Atlanta made Sherman one of the top military leaders of the Civil War. He used his hero status to convince Lincoln and Grant to adopt a new strategy of "total war." Sherman had spent his lifetime studying and thinking about the tactics of warfare. He had concluded that the Civil War was more than just a battle between armies—it was also a conflict between two different societies and ways of life. He felt that in order to win the war and achieve a lasting peace, the North had to break the spirit of the Southern people and convince them to give up the fight. In order to do this, Sherman planned to march his army through the heart of the Confederacy and attack civilian as well as military targets.

Sherman turned Atlanta into a fortress and forced all civilians to evacuate the city. In November 1864, he ordered his soldiers to set fire to the railroads, factories, and shops in Atlanta that could be used by the Confederates. The fire spread out of control and ended up consuming one-third of the city, including the main business district and thousands of homes. Then Sherman set out toward Savannah with sixty-two thousand soldiers. During their famous "March to the Sea," Sherman's army lived off the land, with no outside supplies or communications. Sherman spread his forces into a line that stretched sixty miles wide, and authorized them to take food and supplies wherever they found them. They cut a wide strip through the heart of the Confederacy, taking whatever they could use and destroying anything that could be used by the Confederate Army. Sherman concluded his historic march by successfully capturing Savannah on December 24, 1864. He sent a telegraph message to Lincoln that offered him "as a Christmas gift the city of Savannah."

In February 1865, Sherman moved his troops northward into South Carolina. They encountered little resistance as they captured the South Carolina cities of Augusta and Columbia, then moved into North Carolina. In April, Confederate general Joseph E. Johnston—who had regained his command from Hood—requested a meeting with Sherman near Raleigh. Sherman had inflicted more punishment on the Southern people than any other Union general, but mainly because he believed that it would bring a quick end to the war. As soon as he saw an opportunity for peace, he grabbed it. Sherman negotiated generous surrender terms with Johnston. But President Lincoln and Secretary of War Edwin Stanton (1814–1869) rejected the treaty. They felt that Sherman had gone beyond his authority in reaching agreements on nonmilitary matters. Sherman and Johnston met again later in the month, and this time their treaty was accepted. A few weeks earlier, Confederate general **Robert E. Lee** (1807–1870; see entry) had surrendered to Grant to mark the end of the Civil War.

"War Is Hell"

Many people think of General William T. Sherman as the man who came up with the expression, "War is hell." Although Sherman certainly shared this feeling, he never actually said it. Some historians believe that the mistaken quotation was taken from a letter the general wrote to the leaders of Atlanta, Georgia, shortly after capturing the city in 1864. In this letter, he defended his order for civilians to evacuate Atlanta by saying that "War is cruelty." But it is more likely that these words came from a speech Sherman made in 1880. Addressing a group of Civil War veterans, Sherman said: "There is many a boy here today who looks on war as all glory, but boys, war is all hell."

Hero or villain?

After the war ended and Grant was elected president of the United States, Sherman became general in chief of all U.S. armies. He remained in that post for thirteen years, until his retirement from the army in 1883. The Republican political party tried to convince him to become their candidate for the presidency in 1872, but he consistently refused to run for office. "If nominated I will not accept; if elected I will not serve," he stated. In 1876, Sherman published a book about his life, *Memoirs of General William T. Sherman*. He died of pneumonia on February 14, 1891, in New York City. Thousands of people lined the streets as his casket passed by in a huge funeral procession. His body was taken by train to St. Louis, Missouri, where he was buried alongside his wife, who had died two years earlier. His son, Father Tom Sherman, conducted the burial service.

Sherman was considered a great hero by the North and a horrible villain by the South. His "March to the Sea" claimed a great deal of food and other supplies that would have gone to support the Confederate Army. But perhaps more importantly, Sherman's march changed public opinion in the South against the war. Many Southerners, particularly in Georgia, came to believe that continuing the fight was not worth the cost Sherman forced them to pay. Even though Sherman's methods were cruel, he believed that they were necessary in order to bring a quicker end to the war.

Where to Learn More

Barrett, John Gilchrist. *Sherman's March Through the Carolinas*. Chapel Hill: University of North Carolina Press, 1956.

Davis, Burke. *Sherman's March*. New York: Random House, 1980. Reprint, New York: Vintage Books, 1988.

Fellman, Michael. *Citizen Sherman: A Life of William Tecumseh Sherman*. New York: Random House, 1995.

Hart, B. H. Liddell. *Sherman: Solider, Realist, American*. New York: Dodd, Mead, & Company, 1929. Reprint, New York: Da Capo Press, 1993.

Hirshson, Stanley P. *The White Tecumseh: A Biography of William T. Sherman*. New York: John Wiley and Sons, 1997.

Lewis, Lloyd. *Sherman: Fighting Prophet*. New York: Harcourt, Brace, 1932. Reprint, Lincoln: University of Nebraska Press, 1993.

Marszalek, John F. *Sherman: A Soldier's Passion for Order*. New York: Free Press, 1993.

Marszalek, John F. *Sherman's Other War: The General and the Civil War Press*. Memphis, TN: Memphis State University Press, 1981. Reprint, Kent, OH: Kent State University Presss, 1999.

Royster, Charles. *The Destructive War: William Tecumseh Sherman, Stonewall Jackson, and the Americans*. New York: Knopf, 1991.

Sherman, William T. *Memoirs of General William T. Sherman*. New York: D. Appleton & Co., 1876. New York: Da Capo Press, 1984.

Vetter, Charles Edmund. *Sherman: Merchant of Terror, Advocate of Peace*. Gretna, LA: Pelican Pub. Co., 1995.

Walters, John Bennett. *Merchant of Terror: General Sherman and Total War*. Indianapolis: Bobbs-Merrill, 1973.

Whitelaw, Nancy. *William Tecumseh Sherman: Defender and Destroyer*. Greensboro, NC: Morgan Reynolds, 1996.

Robert Smalls

Born April 5, 1839
Beaufort, South Carolina
Died February 22, 1915
Beaufort, South Carolina

**Union Navy pilot and one of the
first black U.S. congressmen**

**Made a dramatic escape from slavery
by stealing a Confederate Navy ship**

In 1862, Robert Smalls stole a Confederate supply ship and turned it over to the Union Navy. What made this feat even more remarkable was the fact that Smalls was a slave. His dramatic escape from slavery brought him wide acclaim in the North as a Civil War hero. After the war ended, Smalls became an important black leader during the difficult period of American history known as Reconstruction (1865–77). He overcame discrimination to serve five terms in the U.S. Congress as a representative from South Carolina.

Born into slavery

Robert Smalls was born a slave on April 5, 1839, in Beaufort, South Carolina. Black people were taken from Africa and brought to North America to serve as slaves for white people beginning in the 1600s. The basic belief behind slavery was that black people were inferior to whites. Under slavery, white slaveholders treated black people as property, forced them to perform hard labor, and controlled every aspect of their lives. States in the Northern half of the United States

> Robert Smalls's escape from slavery was "one of the coolest and most gallant naval acts of war."
>
> *Union admiral Samuel DuPont*

Robert Smalls. *(Courtesy of the Library of Congress.)*

began outlawing slavery in the late 1700s. But slavery continued to exist in the Southern half of the country because it played an important role in the South's economy and culture.

Smalls's mother, Lydia, worked as a house servant on a plantation (a large farming estate) in Beaufort. Smalls did not reveal the identity of his father, but it was probably the owner of the plantation, John McKee. Like many slaves, Smalls did not have a last name as a boy. He began using "Small" as his last name because he was short, so people often called him "Small Robert." He later changed his last name to Smalls.

Compared to slaves who worked in the fields growing cotton and rice, Smalls had a relatively easy life as the son of a house servant. He lived in slave quarters near the main house, helped his mother with the cooking and cleaning, and acted as a personal slave and companion for the master's oldest son, Henry McKee. When John McKee died in 1848, Smalls and all of the other slaves became the property of Henry McKee.

Works in Charleston Harbor

In 1851, Henry McKee sent Smalls to work as a laborer in the nearby port city of Charleston, South Carolina. Slaveowners often arranged for their extra slaves to take jobs in the cities. This way, the master avoided the expense of feeding and housing them, and also collected some of the money that the slaves earned in wages. Although he was just twelve years old, Smalls worked as a waiter, lamplighter, and stevedore (a person who loads and unloads cargo from ships). He enjoyed the freedom of living in the city—away from the watchful eye of his master—but also struggled to provide for himself. In the mid-1850s, Smalls became romantically attached to a slave woman named Hannah. They considered themselves married, even though slaves were not legally allowed to marry.

After working on the docks for several years, Smalls joined the crew of a commercial ship in the late 1850s. But this was a time of great political tension in the United States. For years, the North and the South had been arguing over several issues, including slavery. Growing numbers of Northerners believed that slavery was wrong. Some people wanted to outlaw it, while others wanted to prevent it from spreading beyond the Southern states where it was already allowed. But many Southerners felt threatened by Northern efforts to contain slavery. They believed that each state should decide for itself whether to allow slavery. They did not want the national government to pass laws that would interfere with their traditional way of life.

By 1861, this ongoing dispute had convinced several Southern states to secede from (leave) the United States and attempt to form a new country that allowed slavery, called the Confederate States of America. South Carolina was one of the states leading the secession movement. But Northern political leaders were determined to keep the Southern states in the Union. The two sides soon went to war. Many people in the South used their slaves to perform the hard labor needed to prepare the Confederacy for war. In March 1861, Smalls was hired to serve as a pilot on the *Planter*. This steamboat was originally designed to carry cotton shipments, but during the war it was used to move troops and supplies between Confederate forts along the South Carolina coast.

Escapes from slavery on a Confederate ship

The North had a big advantage on the seas during the Civil War. It controlled most of the ships that made up the U.S. Navy fleet, and it had many factories to make more ships. The Union used this superior naval strength to capture Port Royal Sound—a good harbor near Beaufort, only fifty miles south of Charleston—early in the war. Using Port Royal Sound as a base of operations, the Union Navy then set up a blockade of several major port cities along the Atlantic coast in the South, including Charleston. The blockade consisted of a row of warships that prevented Confederate ships from reaching the Southern cities with shipments of food, guns, ammunition, and other supplies.

In the early morning hours of May 13, 1862, the *Planter* left Charleston harbor on what appeared to be a routine supply mission. On deck, a man wearing a captain's hat even saluted to the Confederate forts as he passed by them at the entrance to the harbor. But the *Planter* steamed directly

Captain Robert Small's medical supply boat, the *Planter,* is docked on the Appomattox River in Virginia. *(Courtesy of the Library of Congress.)*

toward the Union ships forming the blockade. The surprised Union ships nearly fired upon the approaching Confederate vessel, but held off at the last minute as the *Planter* raised a white flag of surrender.

When Union sailors boarded the enemy ship, they found sixteen slaves—including eight male crew members, five women, and three children—along with four cannons and some ammunition. The man in the captain's hat introduced himself as Robert Smalls. He explained that the people on board the *Planter* were slaves who had risked their lives to escape and also to deliver the ship and its guns to the Union. When the *Planter*'s white crew members had gone ashore for the night, the black crew members had picked up their families and made a desperate dash for freedom.

Becomes a Union war hero

The story of Smalls's dramatic escape from slavery attracted a great deal of media attention in the North. Many newspapers and magazines published articles about him and called him a war hero. Admiral Samuel DuPont (1803–1865), the commander in charge of the Union naval blockade of Charleston, called Smalls's escape "one of the coolest and most gallant [brave and daring] naval acts of war." Of course, people in the South were not so thrilled by the news. A newspaper in Richmond, Virginia, called the loss of the *Planter* "one of the most shameful events in this or any other war."

Smalls and the other former slaves on board the *Planter* were accepted into the Union as "contrabands" (the Union Army was authorized to seize any Confederate property used in the war effort, including slaves, as "contraband of war"). The U.S. Congress granted Smalls a $1,500 cash reward for delivering the ship, and gave several hundred dollars to each member of his crew. Smalls continued to help the Union Navy by providing valuable information about Confederate defenses in the Charleston area. After all, he had explored many rivers and inlets during his supply missions on the *Planter*.

At that time, black men were not allowed to serve as Union soldiers. Smalls joined a group of prominent black leaders who tried to convince President **Abraham Lincoln** (1809–1865; see entry) to allow black men to join the army. Lincoln eventually allowed an all-black regiment—the First South Carolina Volunteers—to be formed on the South Carolina coastal islands, near Smalls's home. Smalls helped recruit black men to join the war effort both in his home state and in the North. Smalls himself served in the Union Navy. When he was promoted to captain of the *Planter*, he became the first black man ever allowed to command an American warship. He continued to carry supplies along the coast—this time for the Union—and also fought in seventeen naval battles.

Launches political career

By the time the Civil War ended in 1865, Smalls was a well-known and wealthy man. He arranged to buy the plantation in Beaufort where he was born, and he and his wife raised three children there. The United States continued to struggle with important and complicated issues during this time. For example, federal lawmakers had to decide whether to punish the Confederate leaders, what process to use to readmit the Southern states to the Union, and how much assistance to provide in securing equal rights for the freed slaves. This difficult period in American history was called Reconstruction, and it lasted until 1877.

Now that they were free, black people wanted equal rights and opportunities in Southern society. But many white people in the South wanted things to stay the way they were before the war. In many cases, the struggle between the two groups turned violent. As a result, the U.S. Congress took control of the Reconstruction process in 1866 and sent federal troops into the Southern states to enforce their policies.

Under Congressional Reconstruction, black Americans were allowed to vote and to participate in government in the South for the first time. Smalls decided to put his reputation as a war hero to use by running for public office. In order to rejoin the Union, the Southern states were required to hold conventions to rewrite their state constitutions. Smalls was elected as a delegate to South Carolina's constitutional convention. He helped create a new state constitution that outlawed slavery, provided free public education to all children, and guaranteed black people the right to vote and hold office.

In November 1868, Smalls was elected to the South Carolina state legislature representing Beaufort and the surrounding area along the coast. He was one of 82 black men elected to the state legislature, out of a total of 155 representatives. South Carolina was the only state in which black members made up a majority of the state legislature during Reconstruction. In 1874, Smalls was elected to represent South Carolina in the U.S. Congress. He lost his seat in the elections of 1878, but then regained it in 1880. He failed to hold his seat again in 1882, but was reelected in 1884. Although Smalls lost the election in 1886, he reclaimed his seat anyway because his opponent died before taking office. He completed his final term in public office in 1888.

Retires in Beaufort

In 1890, President Benjamin Harrison (1833–1901) appointed Smalls as the customs collector for the Port of Beaufort. He was in charge of collecting fees from international merchants who shipped goods into the United States. Smalls also married schoolteacher Annie Elizabeth Wigg that year (his first wife had died seven years earlier). They had a son together, William.

In 1895, South Carolina held another convention to rewrite the state constitution. This time, however, the idea was to roll back many of the reforms that had taken place during Reconstruction. Only 6 of the 160 delegates to the convention were black. Racist white people had used violence to intimidate black people so that they would not vote or try to hold office. As a result, whites had gradually returned to power throughout the South, and they passed many laws discriminating against blacks. Smalls knew that the proposed changes to South Carolina's constitution would hurt black people. In a speech at the convention, he said: "My race needs no special defenses. For the past history of them in this country proves them to be the equal of any people anywhere. All they need is an equal chance in the battle of life."

Smalls was not successful in his efforts to prevent discrimination from returning to South Carolina. However, he remained in his job as customs collector for twenty years before retiring in 1913. He died on February 22, 1915, at the age of seventy-five. Since he was still a considered a hero in the black community, his funeral was the largest ever to take place in the town of Beaufort.

Where to Learn More

Cooper, Michael L. *From Slave to Civil War Hero: The Life and Times of Robert Smalls*. New York: Lodestar Books, 1994.

Meriwether, Louise. *The Freedom Ship of Robert Smalls*. Englewood Cliffs, NJ: Prentice-Hall, 1971.

Miller, Edward A., Jr. *Gullah Statesman: Robert Smalls from Slavery to Congress*. Columbia: University of South Carolina Press, 1995.

Sterling, Philip. *Four Took Freedom: The Lives of Harriet Tubman, Frederick Douglass, Robert Small, and Blanche K. Bruce*. Garden City, NY: Doubleday, 1967.

Uya, Okon Edet. *From Slavery to Public Service: Robert Smalls, 1839–1915*. Oxford University Press, 1971.

Williamson, Joel. *After Slavery: The Negro in South Carolina during Reconstruction, 1861–1877*. Chapel Hill: University of North Carolina Press, 1965. Reprint, Hanover, NH: University Press of New England, 1990.

Alexander H. Stephens

Born February 11, 1812
Crawfordsville, Georgia
Died March 4, 1883
Atlanta, Georgia

Vice president of the Confederate States of America

Despite his office, he became one of the most vocal critics of Confederate president Jefferson Davis

A s a prominent Georgia politician, Alexander H. Stephens opposed his state's decision to secede (withdraw) from the Union at the beginning of the Civil War. Nevertheless, he actively participated in forming the Confederate government and ended up becoming the vice president of the new Southern nation. Shortly after taking office, however, Stephens began disagreeing with Confederate president **Jefferson Davis** (1808–1889; see entry) over the need to create a strong central government to manage the war effort effectively. Stephens believed that the right of individual states to decide issues within their borders for themselves was more important than the needs of the Confederacy. "He could not understand that if the war were to be won, great powers must be entrusted to those who had the task of waging the nation's war," Rudolph Von Abele explained in *Alexander H. Stephens: A Biography.* As a result, Stephens became one of Davis's most vocal critics at a time when the president needed his assistance the most.

The Confederacy's "foundations are laid, its cornerstone rests, upon the great truth that the negro is not equal to the white man; that slavery, subordination to the superior race, is his natural and moral condition.

Alexander H. Stephens.
(Reproduced with permission of Archive Photos, Inc.)

Overcomes poverty and the death of his parents

Alexander Hamilton Stephens was born on February 11, 1812, in rural Georgia. His father, Andrew Baskins Stephens, struggled to support the family as a store clerk. His mother, Margaret Grier Stephens, died shortly after he was born. His father eventually remarried, but then both his father and stepmother died when Alexander was a young teen. At this point, Stephens and his siblings were sent away to live with relatives. Alexander was taken in by his maternal uncle, Aaron Grier, who helped him get an education.

Stephens attended Franklin College (which later became the University of Georgia) and graduated first in his class in 1832. He taught school for a while, then studied law. He soon became a successful attorney. As his wealth increased, he showed his generosity by helping his poor relatives. He even adopted his half-brother, Linton, and paid for his education. The two men remained extremely close for the rest of their lives.

Stephens also used some of his money to buy slaves. Beginning in the 1600s, black people were taken from Africa and brought to North America to serve as slaves for white people. The basic belief behind slavery was that black people were inferior to whites. Under slavery, white slaveholders treated black people as property, forced them to perform hard labor, and controlled every aspect of their lives. States in the Northern half of the United States began outlawing slavery in the late 1700s. But slavery continued to exist in the Southern half of the country and became an important part of the region's economy and culture.

Growing up in Georgia, Stephens came to believe that slavery offered the best possible life for black people. He felt that blacks were incapable of living on their own, so they needed white people to give them food, clothing, shelter, and religion. He thought that black people in Africa lived as savages, while black slaves in the South were relatively civilized. Compared to many other slaveowners, Stephens treated his slaves well. He never whipped or beat them, and he never sold family members separately.

Enters politics and supports states' rights

Within a short time, Stephens had become a prominent member of his community. He grew interested in politics
and won election to the Georgia state legislature in 1836. He
remained in office until 1840, then was elected to one more
term in 1842. During this time, Stephens earned the respect of
his fellow lawmakers and voters with his intelligence and bit-
ing speeches. The local press gave him the nickname "Little
Ellick" because he was so small, weighing only ninety pounds.

In 1843, Stephens was elected to represent his region
of Georgia in the U.S. House of Representatives. He remained
in office for the next fifteen years. During this time, the
Northern and Southern sections of the country engaged in a
heated debate over slavery and the power of the national, or
federal, government to regulate it. Like many other Southerners, Stephens defended slavery and supported states' rights.
People who supported states' rights wanted to limit the power
of the federal government. They wanted individual states to
have the right to decide important issues for themselves without interference from the national government.

In the eyes of Stephens and other Southern politicians, one of the most important issues that should be decided by the states was slavery. Many Northerners believed that
slavery was wrong, and they urged the federal government to
take steps to limit it. Some people wanted to outlaw slavery altogether, while others just wanted to prevent it from spreading beyond the Southern states where it was already allowed.
But slavery played a big role in the Southern economy and
culture. As a result, Stephens and many other Southerners felt
threatened by Northern efforts to contain slavery. They believed that each state should decide for itself whether to allow
slavery. They did not want the national government to pass
laws that would interfere with their traditional way of life.

By the late 1850s, several Southern states were threatening to secede from the United States because of this ongoing dispute. Unlike many other Southern politicians,
Stephens opposed the idea of secession. He felt that the
Southern states should remain in the Union and continue to
work out their differences with the North. In fact, he tried
unsuccessfully to form a new political party dedicated to the
principles of the Union, along with fellow lawmakers Robert

A. Toombs (1810–1885) and Howell Cobb (1815–1868). Stephens worried that the North would not allow the South to leave without a fight, so the result of secession would be civil war. "Men will be cutting one another's throats in a little while. In less than twelve months we shall be in a war, and that the bloodiest in history," he warned. "There are not virtue [moral goodness] and patriotism and sense enough left in the country to avoid it."

By 1860, it became clear that the issue of secession depended on the outcome of the upcoming presidential election. If Democratic candidate Stephen A. Douglas (1813–1861) won, then the Southern states might remain in the Union. But if Republican candidate **Abraham Lincoln** (1809–1865; see entry) won, the Southern states would almost certainly secede. Lincoln opposed slavery, so many Southerners felt that his government could not possibly represent their views. Despite the fact that Lincoln was an old friend of his, Stephens campaigned for Douglas. But Lincoln won the election. Just as Stephens had feared, the Southern states reacted by seceding from the United States and forming a new country that allowed slavery, called the Confederate States of America. With their enemies in control of the U.S. government, they felt that the only way they could protect their rights as independent states was to leave the Union.

Elected vice president of the Confederacy

In January 1861, Stephens's home state of Georgia held a convention to decide whether it should join the Confederacy. Stephens argued against the idea of Georgia seceding. "In my judgment, the election of no man, constitutionally chosen to that high office [president of the United States], is sufficient cause for any state to separate from the Union," he stated. "Let us not be the ones to commit the aggression." Despite Stephens's pleas, the men at the convention voted to secede. Once the decision had been made, however, Stephens threw his support behind the Confederacy.

In February 1861, representatives from each of the secessionist states met in Montgomery, Alabama, to design the government of their new nation. Stephens acted as a delegate (representative) to the convention and helped establish the

"Slavery Is the Cornerstone of the Confederacy"

Stephens made probably his best-known speech in 1861, shortly after the Confederacy was formed. In this speech, which was published under the title "Slavery Is the Cornerstone of the Confederacy," he explained his view that slavery was the founding principle of the Southern nation and the main cause of the Civil War. Stephens began by discussing the U.S. Constitution, which did not address the issue of slavery directly. The authors of the Constitution believed that slavery was wrong, but most thought the practice would eventually end on its own, without action by the Federal government. Stephens, on the other hand, claimed that slavery was right and natural because the races were not created equal. In fact, he believed that by making slavery the foundation of their society, the founders of the Confederacy were fixing an error that had been made by the founders of the United States. The following is an excerpt from Stephens's speech:

Our new Government is founded upon exactly the opposite ideas [of equality between the races]; its foundations are laid, its cornerstone rests, upon the great truth that the negro is not equal to the white man; that slavery, subordination to the superior race, is his natural and moral condition. This, our new Government, is the first, in the history of the world, based upon this great physical, philosophical, and moral truth. . . .

It is the first Government ever instituted upon principles in strict conformity to nature, and the ordination [commandment] of Providence, in furnishing the materials of human society. Many Governments have been founded upon the principles of certain classes; but the classes thus enslaved, were of the same race, and in violation of the laws of nature. Our system commits no such violation of nature's laws. The negro by nature . . . is fitted for that condition which he occupies in our system. The architect, in the construction of buildings, lays the foundation with the proper material—the granite—then comes the brick or marble. The substratum [underlying support layer] of our society is made of the material fitted by nature for it, and by experience we know that it is best, not only for the superior but for the inferior race, that it should be so. It is, indeed, in conformity [harmony] with the Creator. It is not for us to inquire into the wisdom of His ordinances or to question them. For His own purposes He has made one race to differ from another, as He has made "one star to differ from another in glory."

The great objects of humanity are best attained, when conformed to his laws and degrees, in the formation of Governments as well as in all things else. Our Confederacy is founded upon principles in strict conformity with these laws. This stone which was rejected by the first builders "is become the chief stone of the corner" in our new edifice [building]. . . .

Confederate Constitution. The delegates then selected Jefferson Davis as president and Stephens as vice president of the Confederate States of America. For the next six weeks, Davis and Stephens tried to negotiate a peaceful settlement with the North. They still wanted to avoid a war if possible. One of the issues they hoped to resolve was the presence of Federal troops at Fort Sumter, located in the middle of the harbor at Charleston, South Carolina. They viewed these troops as a symbol of Northern authority and asked Lincoln to remove them. When negotiations failed, Confederate forces opened fire on Fort Sumter on April 12, 1861. The Confederacy gained control of the fort, but the Civil War had begun.

During the first year of the war, Stephens found that he disagreed with President Davis on a number of important issues. For example, Davis wanted to establish a conscription (military draft) program to register Southern men for service in the Confederate Army. He thought that the government should require men to serve in the military. The president also wanted to suspend the legal provision known as habeas corpus, which prevented government officials from imprisoning people without charging them with a crime. Davis knew that some people in the South did not support the war effort, and he wanted the power to put these people in prison to stop them from helping the North.

Stephens and many members of the Confederate Congress opposed these policies. After all, the Southern states had seceded from the Union in order to assert their right to make important decisions for themselves, without interference from the national government. Yet Davis wanted broad new powers for the Confederate government. He felt he needed to create a strong central government for the Confederacy in order to manage the war effectively. The South would have no chance of winning against larger, better organized Union forces if each state insisted on fighting on its own. But Davis's opponents believed that states' rights and individual freedom were more important than the needs of the Confederacy as a whole. "Away with the idea of getting independence first, and looking after liberty afterward," Stephens stated. "Our liberties, once lost, may be lost forever."

By 1862, Stephens had become one of Davis's most vocal critics. He even argued that the president should give up

the war effort and try to negotiate peace with the North. Because of his disagreements with Davis, Stephens eventually moved away from the Confederate capital of Richmond, Virginia, and returned to Georgia. He only accepted two official missions as vice president during this time. Most of his wartime service to the Confederacy consisted of visiting wounded soldiers in hospitals and promoting the exchange of Union prisoners of war for equal numbers of Confederate prisoners.

Remains in politics after the war

The Civil War ended in defeat for the Confederacy in early 1865. But the United States continued to struggle with complicated issues in the period after the war. For example, Union authorities had to decide whether to punish Confederate leaders, what process to use to readmit the Southern states to the Union, and how much help to provide in securing equal rights for the freed slaves. This difficult period in American history came to be known as Reconstruction (1865–77). Immediately after the war ended, Union officials charged Stephens with treason (betraying his country) and put him in prison in Boston, Massachusetts. But they released him after only six months and allowed him to return home to Georgia.

During this time, President **Andrew Johnson** (1808–1875; see entry)—who took office after Lincoln was assassinated in April 1865—controlled the Reconstruction process. He pardoned many Confederate leaders and established lenient (easy) conditions for the Southern states to return to the Union. Many Northerners worried that Johnson's Reconstruction policies would allow Confederate leaders to return to power in the South and continue to discriminate against blacks. Georgia set up a new state government that met the president's conditions. In January 1866, Stephens was elected to represent the state's interests in the U.S. Senate. But many Northerners were outraged by this turn of events. They felt that Stephens should have been punished more severely for his role in causing the Civil War. They pointed to his election to the Senate as proof that the South had not learned anything from its defeat.

At this point, members of the Republican political party in the U.S. Congress decided to take over control of Reconstruction from the president. They established new, stricter conditions for the Southern states to rejoin the Union, and they sent federal troops into the South to enforce their policies. They also refused to allow Stephens or any other Southern representatives to take their seats in the federal government. As a result, Stephens became a vocal opponent of Congress's Reconstruction policies over the next few years.

Denied a chance to serve in the Senate, Stephens resumed his legal practice in Georgia. He finally regained his former seat in the U.S. House of Representatives in 1872 and served for the next ten years. He also wrote a two-volume history of the Civil War called *A Constitutional View of the Late War between the States*. The book became a best-seller, and Southerners adopted "War between the States" as their unofficial name for the conflict. In 1882, Stephens put the finishing touch on his political career by being elected governor of Georgia. He only served one year in office, however, before he died on March 4, 1883.

Where to Learn More

Schott, Thomas Edwin. *Alexander H. Stephens of Georgia: A Biography.* Baton Rouge: Louisiana State University Press, 1988.

Stephens, Alexander Hamilton. *Recollections of Alexander H. Stephens: His Diary Kept When a Prisoner at Fort Warren, Boston Harbour, 1865.* New York: Doubleday, 1910. Reprint, Baton Rouge: Louisiana State University Press, 1998.

Von Abele, Rudolph. *Alexander H. Stephens: A Biography.* New York: Knopf, 1946. Reprint, Westport, CT: Negro Universities Press, 1971.

Thaddeus Stevens

**Born April 4, 1792
Danville, Vermont
Died August 11, 1868
Washington, D.C.**

**Union political leader, head of the Radical
Republicans in the U.S. Congress**

**Led the fight to abolish slavery and secure equal
rights for black Americans during the Civil War
and Reconstruction**

T haddeus Stevens was a highly influential—and also controversial—politician during and immediately after the
Civil War. People in the North who opposed slavery hailed
him as one of the bravest leaders in American history. No one
did more to promote the principles of freedom and equality
laid out in the U.S. Constitution. "Every man, no matter what
his race or color, has an equal right to justice, honesty, and
fair play with every other man; and the law should secure
him those rights," Stevens once said. "Such is the law of God
and such ought to be the law of man."

But white people in the South hated Stevens. They believed that his radical proposals to free their slaves, take away
their land, and put black people in charge of their government would destroy Southern society. Some people in the
North also felt that Stevens went too far. They worried that
his harsh policies toward the South would prevent the two
halves of the country from reconciling their differences after
the Civil War. Stevens was a complex man who held strong
beliefs and fought for them until the end. "Perhaps if Stevens
had been more forgiving, his ideas might have had a better

> "Every man, no matter
> what his race or color,
> has an equal right to
> justice, honesty, and fair
> play with every other
> man; and the law should
> secure him those rights."

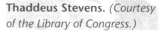

Thaddeus Stevens. *(Courtesy
of the Library of Congress.)*

chance in his lifetime," Joy Hakim wrote in *Reconstruction and Reform*. "Or maybe he was just ahead of his time."

Uses education to escape from poverty

Thaddeus Stevens was born into a poor farming family in Caledonia County, Vermont, on April 4, 1792. His father, Joshua Stevens, was an alcoholic who deserted the family when Thad was five years old. His mother, Sarah Stevens, raised him and his three brothers alone. She encouraged her boys to work hard and get an education. She taught them to read at a young age, using the Bible as a textbook.

Thad was born with a deformed foot and lower leg—known as a clubfoot—that caused him to walk with a limp his whole life. Other children sometimes called him names or imitated the way he walked. But he got back at them with his keen intelligence and wit. Although young Thad could not run and play ball games with other kids, he excelled at swimming and horseback riding.

When a private school opened in nearby Peacham, Vermont, Sarah Stevens sold the farm so that Thad could attend. He was an eager student, although his teachers also called him "headstrong." At the age of nineteen, Stevens continued his education at Dartmouth College in New Hampshire. With his quick mind and excellent speaking ability, he showed great skill in debate.

Becomes a prominent lawyer

After graduating from college in 1814, Stevens moved to the small town of Gettysburg, Pennsylvania, and began to practice law. In one of his early cases, he claimed that his client should not be executed for murder because the client was insane. This marked the first time that a lawyer had attempted to use insanity as a defense in a murder case. Stevens lost the case, but he gained a reputation as a tough, innovative lawyer.

Surprisingly, Stevens represented a slaveowner in his first case before the Pennsylvania Supreme Court in 1821. The slaveowner was a woman from Maryland (a slave state) who spent each summer in the mountains of Pennsylvania (a free state), along with her slaves. Pennsylvania law said that any slave who lived in the state for six months would be free. One of the woman's slaves carefully counted the days she spent in Pennsylvania until they added up to six months, then refused to return to Maryland and sued for her freedom. Stevens won the case by arguing that the law required a slave to live in Pennsylvania for six continuous months, rather than a total of six months over a longer period of time. The slave was forced to return to Maryland. It is not clear why Stevens took the case or how he felt about the outcome. Within a few years, however, he began speaking out against slavery. In his law practice, he became known for defending runaway slaves to prevent them from being forced to return to their masters.

Over time, Stevens's success as a lawyer made him a wealthy man. He bought land in the area around Gettysburg and started an iron forging business. As his wealth grew, so did his reputation for helping others in need. For example, one time he happened to be riding past a farm that was being sold at auction. He found out that the farm belonged to a widow who was unable to pay off a bank loan, and that the loss of the farm would leave her homeless. He bought the farm himself, gave it back to the widow, then quickly rode away. Stevens also helped others to get an education. He opened his extensive private library to the public, and he allowed many young men to study law in his offices.

Begins his political career

In 1833, Stevens was elected to the Pennsylvania state legislature. He immediately began fighting to establish free public schools for all children. Until this time, most schools were private and only children from wealthy families attended. Poor children had to work from a young age to help support their families, and rarely even learned to read and write. But creating free public schools was not a popular idea. Many people resented having to pay taxes to support the schools. Some wealthy people wanted to keep the advantages of education for themselves. Stevens made several speeches that helped convince the legislature and voters to support the idea. The number of schools in Pennsylvania increased from

800 to 3,400 over the next three years, while the number of students enrolled in school went from 32,000 to 150,000.

In 1842, Stevens left politics to deal with his personal affairs. Financial troubles convinced him to move his law practice to Lancaster, Pennsylvania, during this time. In 1848, Stevens was elected to the U.S. Congress. This was a time of great political tension in the United States. For years, the North and the South had been arguing over several issues, including slavery. Growing numbers of Northerners, like Stevens, believed that slavery was wrong. Some people wanted to outlaw it, while others wanted to prevent it from spreading beyond the Southern states where it was already allowed. But slavery played a big role in the Southern economy and culture. As a result, many Southerners felt threatened by Northern efforts to contain slavery. They believed that each state should decide for itself whether to allow slavery. They did not want the national government to pass laws that would interfere with their traditional way of life.

Stevens made his position clear in his very first speech before Congress. He said that slavery was wrong, and that political leaders from the North had an obligation to stand up to the South on the issue. Some Southern legislators claimed that black people were inferior to white people, and said that they were actually better off as slaves than they would be trying to care for themselves. They argued that slaves were well fed and happy, while free blacks in the North were hungry and desperate. But Stevens refused to accept this argument. "If slavery is such a moral, political, and personal blessing, let us give all a chance to enjoy this blessing," he replied. "Let the slaves, who choose, go free, and the free, who choose, become slaves. If these gentlemen believe there is a word of truth in what they preach, the slaveholder need be under no apprehension [fear] that he will ever lack bondsmen [slaves]."

Helps make the Civil War a fight against slavery

By 1861, the ongoing dispute between the two sections of the country convinced several Southern states to secede from (leave) the United States and attempt to form a new country that allowed slavery, called the Confederate

States of America. But Northern political leaders were determined to keep the Southern states in the Union. The two sides soon went to war. Stevens became even more powerful in the U.S. Congress at this time. He served as chairman of the House Ways and Means Committee during the Civil War. This meant that he controlled the collection and spending of tax money that allowed the Union to fight the war.

Stevens also understood the personal cost of the war. Confederate troops destroyed his iron factories during the Battle of Gettysburg. He lost $90,000, or the equivalent of his life savings. But he claimed that he was willing to pay any price for victory. "We must all expect to suffer by this wicked war. I have not felt a moment's trouble over my share of it," he stated. "If, finally, the government shall be reestablished over our whole territory, and not a vestige [trace] of slavery left, I shall deem [believe] it a cheap purchase."

Stevens became very critical of President **Abraham Lincoln** (1809–1865; see entry) during the war years. Lincoln was against slavery, but he wanted to end it gradually. He was also hesitant to grant full civil and political equality to black people. In contrast, Stevens wanted to abolish (put an end to) slavery immediately and completely. And he believed that if black people were free, they should be treated the same as white people.

People like Stevens were considered extreme or radical, while people like Lincoln were considered more cautious or moderate. Stevens and other radicals criticized the president for moving too slowly toward ending slavery and for being too lenient (easy) in his policies toward the South. They kept pushing Lincoln to take dramatic steps toward freeing the slaves and changing the structure of Southern society. But even though Stevens and Lincoln had their political differences, they actually respected and helped each other. As their mutual friend Alexander McClure (1828–1909) described their relationship: "Stevens was ever clearing the underbrush and preparing the soil, while Lincoln followed to sow the seeds that were to ripen in a regenerated Union."

Promotes radical Reconstruction policies

After the Civil War ended in 1865, the United States continued to struggle with important and complicated issues.

For example, Stevens and other federal lawmakers had to decide whether to punish the Confederate leaders, what process to use to readmit the Southern states to the Union, and how much assistance to provide in securing equal rights for the freed slaves. This difficult period in American history was called Reconstruction (1865–77).

President **Andrew Johnson** (1808–1875; see entry)—who took office after Lincoln was assassinated—controlled the earliest Reconstruction efforts. He pardoned (officially forgave) many Confederate leaders and set lenient conditions for the Southern states to return to the Union. But Stevens and other radical Republican members of Congress worried that Johnson's policies would allow the Confederate leaders to return to power and continue to discriminate against black people. They set up a Committee on Reconstruction, with Stevens as its chairman, to study the effects of Johnson's policies. The committee heard numerous stories of discrimination and violence against blacks in the South. As a result, the U.S. Congress took control of the Reconstruction process in 1866 and sent federal troops into the Southern states to enforce their policies.

By this time, Stevens was in his seventies and in poor health. In fact, he sometimes had to be carried into sessions of Congress. His voice was weak, but the other members respected his authority so much that they crowded around his desk to hear him when he spoke. Stevens viewed the North's victory in the war as an opportunity to make fundamental changes in Southern society. He argued that the Southern states should only be readmitted to the Union if they gave black men the right to vote and guaranteed that they would be treated equally under the law. He also wanted to punish the Confederate leaders for their rebellion. Stevens's extreme positions on Reconstruction earned him many enemies in the South. Even in the North, many people did not share his views. Some Northerners worried that his hard line would make it more difficult for the nation to settle its differences and return to normal.

One of Stevens's most controversial proposals involved confiscating (taking away) land that belonged to wealthy planters (plantation owners) who had supported the Confederacy. He wanted to distribute this land to former

slaves and poor white people in forty-acre parcels. Stevens believed that land was the key to making lasting changes in Southern society. Land ownership would allow former slaves to live independently and support themselves and their families. Otherwise, they would be forced to work for wealthy white landowners again. "The whole fabric of southern society must be changed and never can it be done if this opportunity is lost," he said in a speech before Congress in 1865. "No people will ever be republican [where power resides with the voting public and representatives are responsible to that public] in spirit and practice where a few own immense manors and the masses are landless." But Stevens's proposal was rejected by Congress. Many Northerners were hesitant to confiscate property because they feared it could happen to them someday. For example, poor industrial workers might decide to seize factories belonging to wealthy owners. The United States never took meaningful steps to provide land to former slaves.

The U.S. House of Representatives impeachment committee of President Andrew Johnson. Seated from left to right are representatives Benjamin F. Butler (Massachusetts), Thaddeus Stevens (Pennsylvania), Thomas Williams (Pennsylvania), and John A. Bingham (Ohio). Standing are James Wilson (Iowa), George S. Boutwell (Massachusetts), and John A. Logan (Illinois). *(Photograph by Mathew Brady. Reproduced with permission of Corbis.)*

Thaddeus Stevens gives the last speech at the impeachment trial of President Andrew Johnson. *(Reproduced with permission of Corbis.)*

Leads impeachment proceedings against President Johnson

As Stevens and other radical Republican members of Congress implemented their Reconstruction plans, President Johnson fought them every step of the way. He vetoed (rejected) many bills passed by Congress, although Congress was usually able to gather enough votes (two-thirds of its members) to pass the bills over the president's veto. Stevens emerged as the most vocal opponent of Johnson during this time. In 1868, he led a movement to remove the president from office.

The Constitution says that all federal officials can be impeached (brought up on legal charges) and removed from elected office if they are found guilty of "treason, bribery, or other high crimes and misdemeanors." All of the branches of the federal government have roles in an impeachment trial. The House of Representatives brings the charges and acts as prosecutor. The chief justice of the Supreme Court presides over the trial as a judge. The Senate hears the case and votes as a jury. Two-thirds of the senators present must vote to convict in order to remove the impeached official from office.

Most people agreed that the charges against Johnson were not serious enough to remove him from office, but the president was so unpopular that the outcome of the impeachment trial was uncertain. Johnson ended up remaining in office by one vote. Although Stevens had failed in his efforts to impeach the president, he succeeded in passing the Fourteenth Amendment to the Constitution. This amendment made black people citizens of the United States. It also prevented individual states from taking away the civil rights of citizens or denying them equal protection under the law.

Dies fighting for equality

After suffering from poor health for many years, Stevens died on August 11, 1868—just a few weeks after the impeachment trial ended. He had never married or had children. His black housekeeper, Lydia Smith, cared for him in his last days. Some of his political enemies claimed that Stevens and Smith had been lovers, but there was never any proof of a romantic relationship between them. Upon his death, Stevens asked to be buried in a remote cemetery that was open to people of all races. He also prepared a message for his gravestone, which read: "I repose [rest] in this quiet and secluded spot, not from any natural preference for solitude, but finding any other cemeteries limited as to race by charter rules, I have chosen this, that I might illustrate in my death the principles which I advocated through a long life: equality of man before his Creator."

For a few years after Stevens's death, black people were allowed to vote and to participate in government in the South. After the federal troops left the South in 1877, however, black people's civil and political rights were taken away bit by bit through intimidation and violence. But nearly one hundred years later, the civil rights movement of the 1960s built upon the Fourteenth Amendment and other laws that Stevens had put in place.

Where to Learn More

Belcher, Edward. *Thaddeus Stevens: Commoner.* Boston: A. Williams & Co., 1882. Reprint, New York: AMS Press, 1972.

Meltzer, Milton. *Thaddeus Stevens and the Fight for Negro Rights.* New York: Thomas Y. Crowell, 1967.

Hakim, Joy. *Reconstruction and Reform.* New York: Oxford University Press, 1994.

Korngold, Ralph. *Thaddeus Stevens.* New York: Harcourt, Brace, 1955. Reprint, Westport, CT: Greenwood Press, 1974.

Miller, Alphonse B. *Thaddeus Stevens.* New York: Harper, 1939.

Palmer, Beverly Wilson, ed. *The Selected Papers of Thaddeus Stevens.* Pittsburgh: University of Pittsburgh Press, 1997.

Trefousse, Hans L. *The Radical Republicans: Lincoln's Vanguard for Racial Justice.* New York: Knopf, 1969. Reprint, Baton Rouge: University of Louisiana Press, 1975.

Trefousse, Hans L. *Thaddeus Stevens: Nineteenth-Century Egalitarian.* Chapel Hill: University of North Carolina Press, 1997.

Woodley, Thomas Frederick. *Great Leveler: The Life of Thaddeus Stevens.* New York: Stackpole, 1937. Reprint, Freeport, NY: Books for Libraries Press, 1969.

Harriet Beecher Stowe

Born June 14, 1811
Litchfield, Connecticut
Died July 1, 1896
Hartford, Connecticut

Writer and abolitionist
Author of the best-selling antislavery novel *Uncle Tom's Cabin*

H arriet Beecher Stowe brought to life the horrors of slavery for people in the Northern United States through her popular novel *Uncle Tom's Cabin.* Her book was one of the first to portray black characters as real people with the same hopes and dreams as whites. It inspired thousands of people in the North to join the fight against slavery, and also increased the tensions between the North and South. As a result, many historians have claimed that Stowe helped cause the Civil War.

Grows up in a large family

Harriet Beecher Stowe was born on June 14, 1811, in Litchfield, Connecticut. She was the seventh of thirteen children (only eleven of whom survived to adulthood) born to the fiery Puritan minister Lyman Beecher (1775–1863). Her mother, a gentle and well-educated woman named Roxanna Foote Beecher, died of tuberculosis when she was four years old. Harriet—known to her family and friends as Hatty—was a small girl with lots of energy and a playful sense of humor.

"Let the President of the United States proclaim that all men shall hereafter be declared free and equal, and that the [military] service of all shall be accepted, without regard to color."

Harriet Beecher Stowe.
(Courtesy of the National Archives and Records Administration.)

She loved to read and became a very good student. After winning prizes for her essays as a student at Litchfield Academy, she dreamed of becoming a famous writer.

For the most part, Hatty had a happy childhood surrounded by her large family. She was particularly close to her younger brother, Henry Ward Beecher (1813–1887), who would eventually become a famous preacher like their father. Another important influence was her oldest sister, Catherine Beecher, who helped raise her after their mother died. Catherine held progressive views about the role of women that were unusual for that time. Believing that women should have the same educational opportunities as men, she opened a school for girls in Hartford, Connecticut. Hatty attended the school for a time and also taught there during her teen years.

Comes into contact with slavery

Growing up in the Northern United States in the early 1800s, Stowe had little direct contact with black people. But she heard stories about the way black people were treated in the Southern part of the country under the institution of slavery. Black people were taken from Africa and brought to North America to serve as slaves for white people beginning in the 1600s. The basic belief behind slavery was that black people were inferior to whites. Under slavery, white slaveholders treated black people as property, forced them to perform hard labor, and controlled every aspect of their lives. States in the Northern half of the United States began outlawing slavery in the late 1700s. But slavery continued to exist in the Southern half of the country, where it became a dominant part of the region's economy and culture.

One of the stories Stowe heard as a girl helped convince her that slavery was wrong. A few years before Stowe was born, her aunt married a wealthy planter (plantation owner) from the West Indies, a chain of islands in the Caribbean, off the southern coast of North America. She returned to his island plantation with him, only to discover that he had fathered more than a dozen children with his slaves there. He considered the black women his property and saw nothing wrong with breeding new servants the way he might breed livestock. Stowe's aunt was outraged at her husband's attitude and behavior. Overcome with shame, she moved back to Connecticut and died. Whenever Stowe's father told this story, he always concluded by saying that slavery was a sin that would be punished by God.

Stowe received her first real contact with slavery in 1832. At this time, her family moved to Cincinnati, Ohio, so her father could teach at Lane Theological Seminary. Cincinnati was a booming frontier town just across the Ohio River from Kentucky—a state that allowed slavery. As a result, many fugitive slaves passed through Cincinnati on their way to freedom in the North or in Canada. In fact, Cincinnati was a major stop on the Underground Railroad—a secret network of abolitionists (people who fought to end slavery) who helped escaped slaves. The Underground Railroad system consisted of a chain of homes and barns known as "safe houses" or "depots." The people who helped the runaway slaves go from one safe house to the next were known as "conductors."

Since Cincinnati bordered the South, slavery was a subject of great debate there. Some of the students at Lane Theological Seminary formed an antislavery society, and Stowe was exposed to their arguments on the issue. She often saw advertisements offering rewards for the capture of runaway slaves. She spoke with one of her father's colleagues who allowed fugitive slaves to stay in his home. She also visited Kentucky and witnessed plantation life firsthand. But throughout this time, Stowe kept her growing hatred of slavery to herself. She worked as a teacher, joined a literary society, and began publishing articles in magazines. She also wrote her first book, a geography textbook to be used in schools.

Fugitive slave law prompts action

During her time in Cincinnati, Harriet Beecher became close friends with Eliza Stowe, the wife of her father's colleague Calvin Ellis Stowe. When her friend died in 1834, she and Calvin Stowe shared their grief. Eventually their friendship blossomed into love, and they were married on January 6, 1836. In the years following her marriage, Stowe's main responsibility was caring for her growing family. She ended up having seven children (only six survived to adulthood). But she still made time to write articles and stories, mostly because her family needed the money. During this time, her writing focused on domestic and romantic themes and ignored the heated debate over slavery that was taking place across the country.

In 1850, Stowe and her husband moved to Brunswick, Maine. She was very happy to return to New England. But before long an event occurred that made it impossible for her to contain her anger about slavery any longer—Southerners in the U.S. Congress passed the Fugitive Slave Act. This measure granted slaveowners sweeping new powers to capture and reclaim escaped slaves. It also required people in the North to assist the slaveowners in retrieving their property. Many Northerners resented the Fugitive Slave Act. Some people simply disobeyed the act. Others became active in helping escaped slaves to hide or to reach Canada, where slavery was not allowed. The Fugitive Slave Act ended up increasing the antislavery and anti-Southern feelings of many people in the North.

The passage of the Fugitive Slave Act convinced Stowe that she had to do something to help end slavery. Her family encouraged her to write a book on the subject. She began working on a novel at night, when her children were asleep. She hoped that her book would show people the true evil of slavery and inspire them to take action against it. "I feel now that the time is come when even a woman or a child who can speak a word for freedom and humanity is bound to speak," she noted. "My object will be to hold up [slavery] in the most lifelike and graphic manner possible." In order to add realistic details to her novel, Stowe read several books on slavery, including *American Slavery as It Is* by abolitionist **Theodore Dwight Weld** (1803–1895; see entry). She also exchanged letters with former slave and abolition leader **Frederick Douglass** (1818?–1895; see entry).

Uncle Tom's Cabin

Stowe's novel, *Uncle Tom's Cabin,* became the single most important piece of antislavery literature in American history. The story first appeared as a series of short articles in *National Era* magazine in 1851. It proved to be extremely popular with Northern readers, and was published in book form in 1852. *Uncle Tom's Cabin* follows the lives of several black slaves who work for a cruel man named Simon Legree in the South. Through the experiences of Uncle Tom, Eliza, and others, the novel painted a powerful picture of the evils of slavery. It also gave readers a more realistic understanding of slaves. It was one of the first books to portray black characters as human beings with the same desires, dreams, and weaknesses as white people. *Uncle Tom's Cabin* turned out to be a perfect expression of people's guilt, anger, and disgust at seeing slaves being hunted down in the North under the Fugitive Slave Act.

An illustration of the Uncle Tom character from Harriet Beecher Stowe's *Uncle Tom's Cabin*. (Originally published by Coward, McCann & Geoghegan, Inc., 1929.)

Readers all across the North were captivated by *Uncle Tom's Cabin*. The novel sold three hundred thousand copies in the first year following its publication, and went on to sell over two million copies in the next ten years. Stowe's work was so popular that it became the best-selling book ever. More importantly, *Uncle Tom's Cabin* raised people's awareness of the terrible injustice of slavery. It convinced countless Northerners to join the abolitionist movement. Some historians claim that, by making people in the North less willing to compromise on the issue of slavery, it helped cause the Civil War. In fact, President **Abraham Lincoln** (1809–1865; see entry) once called Stowe "the little lady who wrote the book that made this big war."

Of course, reaction in the Southern states was not so positive. Most people in the South were highly critical of the book. They claimed that Stowe distorted the facts of slavery and exaggerated the punishments that blacks received. "There never before was anything so detestable or so monstrous among women as this," wrote a reviewer for the *New Orleans Crescent*. Many states tried to ban the book, but Southerners still wanted to read it. In fact, copies sold so fast that bookstores in Charleston, South Carolina, could not keep up with demand. Still, Stowe was extremely unpopular in the South. She received many obscene or threatening letters, including one that contained a black person's ear.

Continues to write during and after the Civil War

In the years following the publication of *Uncle Tom's Cabin,* Stowe was the most famous writer in the world. She traveled around Europe, where she was entertained by royalty. When she returned to the United States, her home became a center for abolitionist activity. The fees she collected from her book made her wealthy, but all the money and attention did not change the way she lived.

By 1861, the ongoing dispute between North and South over slavery and other issues convinced several Southern states to secede from (leave) the United States and attempt to form a new country that allowed slavery, called the Confederate States of America. But Northern political leaders were determined to keep the Southern states in the Union. The two sides soon went to war. After the Civil War began, Stowe appealed to her friends in England to support the Union. She also argued that President Abraham Lincoln should free all the slaves immediately so they could assist in the North's war effort. "Let the President of the United States proclaim that all men shall hereafter be declared free and equal, and that the [military] service of all shall be accepted, without regard to color," she wrote.

In 1864, Stowe and her husband built an expensive house in Hartford. The following year, the Civil War ended in victory for the North. Stowe was thrilled when the U.S. Congress passed the Thirteenth Amendment outlawing slavery. She continued to write in the years following the war, but she concentrated on less controversial themes. In 1869, she published *Oldtown Folks,* a novel about small-town life in New England in the early nineteenth century. This book is generally considered her most important work besides *Uncle Tom's Cabin.*

By the late 1860s, Stowe and her husband began spending the winter months in Florida, where one of their sons ran a farm. Stowe started a small school there to teach former slaves how to read and write. To her surprise, people in the South treated her kindly. In 1873, she sold the house in Hartford and bought a smaller one next door to fellow writer Samuel Clemens (1835–1910), who later became famous under the pen name Mark Twain. Stowe's husband died in 1886, and her beloved brother Henry Ward Beecher died the following year. In 1889, she helped her son Charles Edward Stowe collect her papers and publish her biography, *The Life of Harriet Beecher Stowe.* Shortly afterward, she suffered a stroke and grew weak. She died on July 1, 1896, at her home in Hartford.

Where to Learn More

Coil, Suzanne M. *Harriet Beecher Stowe.* New York: Franklin Watts, 1993.

Fritz, Jean. *Harriet Beecher Stowe and the Beecher Preachers.* New York: G. P. Putnam's Sons, 1994.

Harriet Beecher Stowe Center. [Online] http://www.hartnet.org/~stowe/ (accessed on October 15, 1999).

Hedrick, Joan D. *Harriet Beecher Stowe: A Life.* New York: Oxford University Press, 1994.

Jakoubek, Robert E. *Harriet Beecher Stowe.* New York: Chelsea House, 1989.

Kirkham, E. Bruce. *The Building of Uncle Tom's Cabin.* Knoxville: University of Tennessee Press, 1977.

Ohio Historical Center. *Stowe House.* [Online] http://www.ohiohistory. org/places/stowe/ (accessed on October 15, 1999).

Stowe, Charles Edward. *The Life of Harriet Beecher Stowe.* Boston: Houghton Mifflin, 1889. Reprint, Detroit: Gale Research, 1967.

Stowe, Harriet Beecher. *Uncle Tom's Cabin.* Originally published in book form in 1852. Various subsequent editions.

Jeb Stuart

Born February 6, 1833
Patrick County, Virginia
Died May 12, 1864
Richmond, Virginia

Legendary general of the cavalry corps of the
Confederate Army of Northern Virginia

Jeb Stuart ranks as one of the great military heroes of the Confederacy. He led the cavalry corps of the South's Army of Northern Virginia in many of the Civil War's greatest campaigns, including First Bull Run (July 1861), Antietam (September 1862), Chancellorsville (May 1863), Gettysburg (July 1863), and the Wilderness (May 1864). The scouting and fighting exploits of his cavalry in these campaigns account for much of Stuart's fame. But he is also well known for leading daring raids on Union positions and supply lines during the war. In fact, Southern newspaper coverage of these raids transformed Stuart into one of the Confederacy's most respected and beloved soldiers.

Trained at West Point

James Ewell Brown "Jeb" Stuart was born in 1833 in Virginia. One of ten children, he was an outgoing boy who was close to both his gentle, poetry-reading mother and his father, who was a prominent lawyer. Stuart enrolled in the U.S. Military Academy at West Point in 1850, where he became one of the school's top students. In 1853, **Robert E. Lee** (1807–1870; see entry) accepted a position at West Point as the school's su-

"The war is going to be a long and terrible one. . . . We've only just begun it and very few of us will see the end. All I ask of fate is that I may be killed leading a cavalry charge."

Jeb Stuart. *(Courtesy of the Library of Congress.)*

perintendent. During the next two years, Stuart established a close relationship with Lee and the rest of his family.

After graduating from West Point in 1854, Stuart was made a second lieutenant in the U.S. Army and assigned to a military post at Fort Leavenworth, Kansas. During his time at Fort Leavenworth he married Flora Cooke, who was the daughter of post commander Colonel Phillip St. George Cooke. Stuart and his wife quickly started a family, producing three children over the next few years.

While stationed in Kansas, Stuart took part in many patrols against Indian raiding parties. He and his fellow soldiers also tried to put a halt to the violence that battered the Kansas Territory in the mid-1850s, when differences between proslavery and antislavery settlers erupted into an epidemic of murder and arson. In 1859, Stuart helped Robert E. Lee capture **John Brown** (1800–1859; see entry) at Harpers Ferry, Virginia, after Brown's violent attempt to start a mass slave uprising failed.

Stuart sides with the Confederacy

In early 1861, tensions between the Northern United States and the Southern United States led Stuart to resign from the U.S. military. For years, the North and the South had been arguing over several issues. The most important issue dividing them was slavery. Many Northerners believed that slavery was wrong. Some people wanted to outlaw it, while others wanted to prevent it from spreading beyond the Southern states where it was already allowed. But slavery played a vital role in the Southern economy and culture, and Southerners resented Northern efforts to halt or contain the practice. They argued that each state should decide for itself whether to allow slavery. By early 1861, this ongoing dispute had convinced several Southern states to secede from (leave) the United States and attempt to form a new country that allowed slavery, called the Confederate States of America. But Northern political leaders refused to stand idly by as the United States was torn in two. They announced that they were willing to go to war to keep the Union together.

In April 1861, the war between the two sides finally began. Thousands of soldiers who had been born and raised in the South resigned from the United States military in order to join the Confederate Army. Many of the soldiers who resigned from the Federal Army left with a heavy heart. After all, they had sworn allegiance to the United States when they joined the army. But these Southerners believed that they owed an even greater allegiance to their home state, where their friends and families lived. In May 1861, Stuart joined the ranks of Southern-born Federal soldiers who decided to serve the Confederacy. He resigned from the U.S. Army and accepted a position as commander of a regiment of cavalry in the Army of Northern Virginia. This army was the largest one in the entire Confederate military.

Stuart's reputation grows

During the first year of the Civil War, Stuart became known to friend and enemy alike as one of the South's top cavalry commanders. Most of the cavalrymen under his command had grown up in rural areas, where they had learned to ride horses and shoot rifles at an early age. But few of them had any military training or background, so Stuart spent a great deal of time training them to operate together as a unit. "I regard it as a foregone [unavoidable] conclusion that we should ultimately whip the Yankees," Stuart stated around this time. "We are bound to believe that anyhow, but the war is going to be a long and terrible one first. We've only just begun it and very few of us will see the end. All I ask of fate is that I may be killed leading a cavalry charge."

By the summer of 1861, Stuart's cavalry was ready for war. In mid-July, large Union and Confederate armies confronted each other outside Manassas, Virginia, in the First Battle of Bull Run. Following the orders of Confederate general **P. G. T. Beauregard** (1818–1893; see entry), Stuart fooled one Union army into staying away from the battlefield. He then rushed his cavalry into the thick of the battle, where they helped push the Union Army into panicked retreat. Stuart's cavalry thus proved vital in delivering a big Confederate victory in the first significant battle of the Civil War.

Over the next several months, the reputation of Stuart and his cavalry continued to grow. They showed that they had a talent for conducting raids on Union railroads and sup-

A cavalry regiment passes the Rappahannock River in Virginia in 1862. *(Reproduced by permission of the National Portrait Gallery.)*

ply centers. In addition, Stuart's cavalrymen proved to be very good spies. They tracked Union Army movements with such great skill that rebel (Confederate) military leaders were able to avoid many surprise attacks from the North. Stuart's reports also helped Confederate leaders plan effective attacks on Union military positions.

Earning Lee's trust

In June 1862, General Robert E. Lee took command of the Army of Northern Virginia. Stuart was delighted to hear about the promotion of his old West Point superintendent, and over the next several months he became one of Lee's most trusted officers. In fact, Stuart proved how valuable he and his cavalry could be almost immediately. In mid-June, Lee sent Stuart and his cavalry on a reconnaissance (exploration and spying) mission into southeastern Virginia, where a large Union force commanded by General **George B. Mc-Clellan** (1826–1885; see entry) had moved. Over the course of four days, Stuart's cavalry gathered a great deal of valuable information about the Union Army's size and movements, while at the same time avoiding all Federal attempts to catch them. One of the many Union commanders who chased Stuart was his father-in-law, General Phillip St. George Cooke. The information that Stuart gathered helped Lee develop a winning strategy to stop the invasion. "History cannot show such another exploit as this of Stuart's!" exclaimed the *Richmond Daily Dispatch*. "The whole country is astonished and applauds. McClellan is disgraced. Stuart and his troopers are now forever in history."

In July 1862, Lee promoted Stuart to major general and placed him in charge of the Army of Northern Virginia's entire calvary corps. Lee's decision was a good one. As historian Gary W. Gallagher noted in *Civil War Journal,* Stuart was "a hard-headed professional soldier who knew exactly what cavalry should do and who was as good at those tasks as anybody on either side. When it came to screening his own army, gathering information about the opposing army, and controlling the middle ground between the two armies, Stuart was unexcelled [unequalled]."

Over the next several months, Stuart's bold raids and clever scouting methods increased his fame throughout the South and his fearsome reputation across the North. During this time, however, he became almost as well known for his colorful taste in clothing as for his military abilities. Unlike other military leaders who preferred to wear regular army uniforms, Stuart wore clothing that reinforced his image as a dashing cavalryman. His garments—which often included a cape lined with red cloth and a fancy hat with a big plume (a large feather) in the band—made him instantly recognizable to Southerners everywhere and contributed to the widespread popularity of the Confederate cavalryman.

Tragedy and triumph

In late 1862 and early 1863, Stuart and his cavalry suffered a number of serious setbacks. First, in November 1862, Stuart learned that one of his young daughters had died of a fever.

Then, in the first months of 1863, several of his most trusted lieutenants were killed in battle. Finally, the improved performance of Union cavalry forces around this time made scouting missions much more dangerous for Stuart and his men.

Nonetheless, Stuart's cavalry forces continued to serve the South with great effectiveness. At the end of 1862, for instance, Stuart led a successful raid deep into Northern territory. And in May 1863, the magnificent performance of Stuart and his cavalry helped the Confederacy win the Battle of Chancellorsville in Virginia. First, Stuart's cavalry tricked a large Union army into stopping in a poor defensive position. Then, Stuart took command of a corps of Confederate infantrymen after their leader, **Thomas "Stonewall" Jackson** (1824–1863; see entry), was wounded in battle. The actions of Stuart and his men helped Lee defeat a much bigger army and secure his greatest victory of the entire war.

Jeb Stuart and the Battle of Gettysburg

After his stunning victory at Chancellorsville, General Lee invaded the North. He hoped to seize badly needed food and supplies and create a surge of antiwar sentiment in the North. Lee knew that President **Abraham Lincoln** (1809–1865; see entry) would not be able to continue the war against the South if he did not have the support of the Northern people.

As Lee's Confederate Army pushed through Virginia's Shenandoah Valley into Northern territory, Stuart's cavalry troops worked to screen their movements from a large Union army in the area. On June 23, Lee ordered Stuart to take his cavalry on a scouting and raiding mission around the Union forces. Over the next several days, Stuart's efforts to maneuver his cavalry past the Union Army undetected were repeatedly delayed by enemy troop movements. Once he reached the lightly defended area behind the advancing Union forces, he captured more than one hundred supply wagons. But his decision to return to Lee with the supply wagons greatly slowed his progress.

In the meantime, Lee struggled to keep track of the approaching Union Army. The general had always relied heavily on Stuart's cavalrymen to scout out enemy locations and movements. Their absence made it difficult for Lee to determine the strength and whereabouts of Union forces in the region. Lee's knowledge of enemy movements grew shakier with each passing day, and the Confederate general became anxious for Stuart's return. He admitted that without Stuart's cavalry reports, "I am in ignorance as to what we have in front of us here."

In the final days of June, Lee suddenly learned that the Union Army, which was led by General **George Meade** (1815–1872; see entry), had drawn dangerously close. The Confederate general hastily gathered his army together at Gettysburg, Pennsylvania, to prepare for battle. A few days later, the famous Battle of Gettysburg began. From July 1 to July 3, Meade's Army of the Potomac and Lee's Army of Northern Virginia fought for control of the Pennsylvania countryside. For the first day and a half of the battle, Lee fought without the use of Stuart's cavalry. Stuart and his men finally returned from their mission on the evening of July 2, but their arrival was not enough to bring victory to the Confederacy. After one final day of warfare, Lee's battered rebel army retreated back to the South in defeat.

Stuart's extended absence from Lee's side has been cited by many historians as a major factor in the Union victory at the Battle of Gettysburg. Some people argue that Stuart's long absence was Lee's fault. They argue that Lee's orders to Stuart were too confusing, and that he never should have ordered his scouts so far away. Many other historians, though, contend that Stuart was far too slow in returning from his mission. In any case, Lee badly missed Stuart's cavalry.

Stuart's death at Yellow Tavern

The controversy over Stuart's performance during the Gettysburg campaign tarnished the cavalryman's previously spotless reputation. But the dashing cavalryman did his best to ignore his critics. Instead, he became even more determined to whip his foes from the North.

In the months following the Confederate defeat at Gettysburg, Stuart and his cavalry continued to strike against Union positions. But by early 1864, Union armies were marching all across the South. One of these armies was a force of ten thousand cavalrymen under the command of General **Philip Sheridan** (1831–1888; see entry). Sheridan wanted to stop Stuart once and for all. He immediately advanced on the Confederate capital of Richmond, Virginia, confident that General Lee would send Stuart's cavalry to stop him.

Sheridan's prediction proved to be accurate. As his Union troops made their way toward Richmond, more than forty thousand Confederate cavalry under the command of Stuart tried to halt their advance. The two cavalry corps met in full battle on May 11, 1864, at Yellow Tavern, only six miles north of Richmond. As the battle wore on, a series of charges led by Union general George A. Custer threatened to collapse Stuart's defensive position. Stuart rode over to help hold the position, only to be shot in the stomach by a Union soldier. Stuart's cavalry quickly retreated from Yellow Tavern and carried their commander into Richmond, where he died the next day.

Stuart's stand at Yellow Tavern had stopped Sheridan's advance on Richmond. But his death was a serious blow to the Confederate Army, as Lee himself admitted. "The commanding general announces to the army with heartfelt sorrow the death of Major General J. E. B. Stuart," proclaimed Lee on May 20. "The mysterious hand of an all-wise God has removed him from the scene of his usefulness and fame. To his comrades in arms, he has left the proud recollection of his deeds and the inspiring influence of his example."

Where to Learn More

Blackford, William Willis. *War Years with Jeb Stuart.* New York: Scribner, 1945. Reprint, Baton Rouge: Louisiana State University Press, 1993.

Carter, Samuel. *The Last Cavaliers: Confederate and Union Cavalry in the Civil War.* New York: St. Martin's Press, 1980.

Davis, Burke. *Jeb Stuart, the Last Cavalier.* New York: Rinehart & Co., 1957. Reprint, New York: Fairfax Press, 1988.

Laurel Hill. *Welcome to Laurel Hill: Birthplace of General J. E. B. Stuart, CSA.* [Online] http://www.jebstuart.org/ (accessed on October 15, 1999).

Longacre, Edward C. *Mounted Raids of the Civil War.* South Brunswick, NJ: A. S. Barnes, 1975. Reprint, Lincoln: University of Nebraska Press, 1994.

McClellan, Henry B. *I Rode with Jeb Stuart: The Life and Campaigns of Major General J.E.B. Stuart.* Bloomington: Indiana University Press, 1958. Reprint, New York: Da Capo Press, 1994.

Nesbitt, Mark. *Saber and Scapegoat: J. E. B. Stuart and the Gettysburg Controversy.* Mechanicsburg, PA: Stackpole Books, 1994.

Pflueger, Lynda. *Jeb Stuart: Confederate Cavalry General.* Springfield, NJ: Enslow, 1998.

Thomas, Emory M. *Bold Dragoon: The Life of J. E. B. Stuart.* New York: Harper & Row, 1986. Reprint, Norman: University of Oklahoma Press, 1999.

Thomason, John W., Jr. *Jeb Stuart.* New York: C. Scribner's Sons, 1930. Reprint, Lincoln: University of Nebraska Press, 1994.

Yates, Bernice-Marie. *Jeb Stuart Speaks: An Interview with Lee's Cavalryman.* Shippensburg, PA: White Mane Pub. Co., 1997.

Charles Sumner

Born January 6, 1811
Boston, Massachusetts
Died March 11, 1874
Washington, D.C.

Republican senator from Massachusetts
Abolitionist and leader in the impeachment trial
of President Andrew Johnson

Charles Sumner was one of America's most prominent political figures during the Civil War era. A dedicated abolitionist, he fought against laws that extended or protected the institution of slavery in any way. Sumner's views made him a hated man in the South, though. In 1856, this hatred became so intense that a Southern congressman viciously attacked him on the floor of the Senate. This physical assault immediately became famous throughout the North as a symbol of Southern wickedness. Sumner spent the following three years recovering from his injuries.

Sumner returned to the Senate, once again establishing himself as one of the nation's most influential politicians. He provided firm support to President **Abraham Lincoln** (1809–1865; see entry) and his wartime policies, and later became a vocal opponent of President **Andrew Johnson** (1808–1875; see entry) and his Reconstruction (1865–77) plans.

"Whatever apologies may be offered for the toleration of slavery in the States, none can be offered for its extension into Territories where it does not exist."

Charles Sumner. *(Reproduced with permission of Archive Photos, Inc.)*

445

Journalist and lawyer

Charles Sumner was born in 1811 in Boston, Massachusetts. His family was wealthy, so young Sumner was able to attend the finest schools in the Boston area. In 1831, he enrolled in the law school at Harvard University. He graduated two years later, and in 1834, passed the state bar exam and became an attorney.

Sumner was both energetic and ambitious, so he spent the mid-1830s engaged in a wide range of activities. In addition to practicing law, he also edited a law review called the *American Jurist,* lectured at Harvard, and worked as a reporter for the U.S. Circuit Court. In 1837, he left America to go to Europe. He traveled through Europe for the next three years, exploring its museums and libraries and establishing friendships with a number of influential European politicians.

Joins abolitionist movement

After returning to the United States in 1840, Sumner became a successful attorney in the Boston area. He became best known, however, for his participation in the growing abolitionist movement (a movement to end slavery in the United States). In fact, Sumner's passionate antislavery speeches soon made him one of Massachusetts's leading abolitionist voices. In the mid-1840s, Sumner's opposition to slavery led him to oppose both America's annexation of Texas (1845) and the Mexican War (1846–48), which forced Mexico to give the United States thousands of square miles of territory in the West. Sumner battled against America's addition of these territories because he feared that the government would allow slavery to expand onto those lands.

In 1851, leaders of the Democratic Party and the antislavery Free-Soil Party selected Sumner to fill the vacated Senate seat of Daniel Webster (1782–1852), who had resigned to become secretary of state. As Massachusetts's newest senator, Sumner quickly established himself as one of the strongest antislavery voices in the entire U.S. Senate. He bitterly denounced the 1850 Fugitive Slave Act, which gave Southern slaveowners sweeping new powers to reclaim runaway slaves in the North. He also opposed the 1854 Kansas-Nebraska Act, which let citizens of western territories decide for themselves whether to permit slavery based on the theory of "popular sovereignty." In fact, Sumner and many other Northern abolitionists viewed the passage of the Kansas-Nebraska Act as a tragedy. After all, the 1854 law explicitly abolished the Missouri Compromise of 1820, which had outlawed slavery in thousands of square miles of American territory for the previous three decades. The passage of the Kansas-Nebraska Act made those territories vulnerable to slavery once again.

Hated in the South

Certain that Southern politicians would soon try to spread slavery into the West, Sumner joined with Ohio senator Salmon P. Chase (1808–1873) and several other antislavery congressmen to issue a document called *The Appeal of the Independent Democrats*. This document criticized the Kansas-Nebraska Act as "part . . . of an atrocious [terrible] plot [to convert the West] into a dreary region of despotism [tyranny], inhabited by masters and slaves. . . . Whatever apologies may be offered for the toleration of slavery in the States, none can be offered for its extension into Territories where it does not exist." Around this same time, Sumner helped organize the national Republican Party, which soon became the leading antislavery political party in the country. Finally, Sumner continued to deliver public speeches in which he harshly criticized the law and the morality (principles of right and wrong conduct) of Southern slaveholders. His fiery words made him a favorite of Northern abolitionists. But in America's slaveholding states, dislike for Sumner grew into outright hatred.

In May 1856, mounting Southern anger over Sumner's harsh criticism of their society and morals finally erupted into a violent incident that became one of the most famous events in U.S. Senate history. On May 19 and 20, 1856, Sumner delivered a speech called "The Crime Against Kansas," in which he condemned Southern leaders for their efforts to expand slavery into Kansas and other territories. During the course of his speech, he criticized a number of Southern politicians by name, including Senator Andrew P. Butler (1796–1857) of South Carolina. At one point, for example, Sumner declared that "[Senator Butler] has chosen a mistress

SOUTHERN CHIVALRY — ARGUMENT versus CLUB'S.

An editorial cartoon pokes fun at Southern chivalry by showing the attack of Massachusetts senator Charles Sumner by South Carolina congressman Preston Brooks. *(Reproduced with permission of Corbis-Bettmann.)*

to whom he has made his vows, and who, though ugly to others, is always lovely to him; though polluted in the sight of the world, is chaste [pure] in his sight. I mean the harlot [prostitute] slavery."

Two days later, South Carolina congressman Preston Brooks, who was Butler's nephew, strode over to where Sumner was seated in the Senate chambers. Without warning, Brooks beat Sumner senseless with his cane. By the time other congressmen intervened to end the assault, Sumner lay bloody and semiconscious on the floor of the Senate.

The attack on Senator Sumner immediately became a symbol of Southern brutality and viciousness across much of the North. "Has it come to this, that we must speak with bated breath [cautiously or quietly] in the presence of our Southern masters?" wrote poet and editor William Cullen Bryant (1794–1878) in the *New York Evening Post.* "Are we to be chastised [punished] as they chastise their slaves? Are we too, slaves, slaves for life, a target for their brutal blows, when we do not comport [behave] ourselves to please them?" Northern outrage over the incident became even greater when the South treated Brooks like a hero. Southerners praised him for defending the region's honor, and South Carolina voters re-elected him to the Senate a few months after the attack. The only punishment that Brooks received for his actions was a $300 fine handed out by a district court. Sumner, meanwhile, spent the next three years recuperating from his injuries.

Sumner and the Civil War

In 1857, the voters of Massachusetts reelected Sumner to the Senate, even though he had not yet recovered from Brooks' attack. In December 1859, he returned to Washington, D.C., and resumed his place in the U.S. Senate. By 1861, when North-South disputes over slavery finally triggered the American Civil War, Sumner had regained his position as a member of the Republican leadership. In fact, he was made chairman of the Senate's important foreign relations committee that year.

Sumner generally supported fellow Republican Abraham Lincoln and his policies during the war's first two years, even though he grew frustrated with the president's refusal to emancipate (free) Southern slaves during this period. In 1863, however, Lincoln issued his Emancipation Proclamation freeing slaves all across the Confederacy. The declaration delighted Sumner, who later introduced a constitutional amendment formally abolishing slavery in America. This amendment—the Thirteenth Amendment—became law in December 1865.

Sumner and Reconstruction

After the Civil War ended in the spring of 1865, Sumner and many other Republican leaders who had led the fight to end slavery wanted to punish the Southern states for their rebellion. Angry about the April assassination of Lincoln and the bloodshed of the war, these Republicans—called "Radical Republicans"—wanted to pass laws that would guarantee black rights, punish Confederate leaders, and change Southern institutions that promoted racism. When their ideas were criticized as unconstitutional, Sumner argued that the Southern states had "committed suicide" by their secession and thus had lost their rights under the Constitution.

Sumner's harsh stance toward the South changed somewhat after he toured the region's devastated farmlands and cities. Stunned by the widespread destruction that he saw, he began to show a greater interest in legislation designed to help the entire region recover from the war. Most of the bills that he personally introduced, however, were designed primarily to help blacks. He introduced a number of civil rights bills, for example. He also helped create the Freedmen's Bureau, an organization charged with helping former slaves build new lives for themselves. In addition, he remained hostile to the South's old political leaders and slaveholders. He held them personally responsible for starting the Civil War.

In the years immediately following the Civil War, President Andrew Johnson and the Republican-led Congress became involved in a bitter dispute about how to rebuild the South and readmit the Confederate states into the Union. For one thing, both sides disagreed about who was responsible for this process, known as Reconstruction, which took place from 1865 to 1877. Congressional leaders, for example, charged that Johnson did not have the authority to shape Reconstruction policies. Johnson, however, argued that he—not Congress—should be primarily responsible for the Reconstruction process.

This disagreement became even more heated when it became clear that Johnson and the Radical Republicans had very different approaches to Reconstruction. Johnson, for instance, pardoned many Confederate leaders and set lenient (easy) conditions for the Southern states to return to the Union. In addition, his Reconstruction plan did not give blacks the right to vote or serve as elected representatives.

Republican members of Congress thought Johnson's Reconstruction policies were too lenient toward the South. They worried that former Confederate leaders would return to power and continue to discriminate against blacks. The Radical Republicans wanted guarantees of increased black rights and other new laws. As a result, the Republican-led U.S. Congress took control of the Reconstruction process in 1866 and sent federal troops into the Southern states to enforce their policies. As Congress began implementing its own Reconstruction program, some members were willing to compromise with President Johnson. But Johnson refused to accept any changes to his policies toward the South. The battle between the two sides continued until 1868, when Sumner and other Republican leaders became so angry that they launched an effort to remove Johnson from office.

Leads impeachment efforts against Johnson

The Constitution notes that all federal officials can be impeached (brought up on legal charges) and removed from elected office if they are found guilty of "treason, bribery, or other high crimes and misdemeanors." All of the branches of the federal government have roles in an impeachment trial. The House of Representatives brings the charges and acts as prosecutor. The chief justice of the Supreme Court presides over the trial as a judge. The Senate hears the case and votes as a jury. Two-thirds of the senators present must vote to convict in order to remove the impeached official from office.

Congress began the process of impeachment on February 22, 1868. It marked the first time in history that an American president had been impeached. The trial lasted for more than two months and captured the attention of the entire country. Finally, the senators voted on the charges on May 16. Johnson was found not guilty by one vote and remained in office. The verdict deeply disappointed Sumner. In fact, Sumner disliked Johnson so much that he unsuccessfully tried to convince his fellow Republicans to impeach the president again.

In 1869, Union war hero **Ulysses S. Grant** (1822–1885; see entry) replaced Johnson as president of the United States. Sumner's relationship with Grant proved to be a difficult one as well, even though they were both Republicans. They clashed over a wide range of issues, and in 1872, Sumner broke with the Republicans and threw his support behind the candidacy of liberal Republican presidential candidate **Horace Greeley** (1811–1872; see entry). On March 10, 1874, Sumner suffered a heart attack in the Senate chamber. He died one day later.

Where to Learn More

Blue, Frederick J. *Charles Sumner and the Conscience of the North.* Arlington Heights, IL: Harlan Davidson, 1994.

Donald, David Herbert. *Charles Sumner.* New York: Da Capo Press, 1996.

Donald, David Herbert. *Charles Sumner and the Coming of the Civil War.* New York: Knopf, 1960. Reprint, Chicago: University of Chicago Press, 1981.

Palmer, Beverly Wilson, ed. *Selected Letters of Charles Sumner.* Boston: Northeastern University Press, 1990.

George Henry Thomas

Born July 31, 1816
Southampton County, Virginia
Died March 28, 1870
San Francisco, California

Union general known as the "Rock of Chickamauga"

Alienated his family and friends by siding with the Union, then became one of the top leaders in the Union Army

Although George Henry Thomas was born into a Southern slaveholding family, he sided with the Union at the start of the Civil War. He went on to become one of the most successful Northern generals. In fact, some historians have ranked him behind only **Ulysses S. Grant** (1822–1885; see entry) and **William T. Sherman** (1820–1891; see entry) among the men they consider most important in securing victory for the Union. Thomas's brave stand during a Union defeat in 1863 earned him the nickname "Rock of Chickamauga." He is also remembered for leading the Army of the Cumberland to an impressive victory at Nashville in 1864. Despite Thomas's successes, some Union leaders questioned his loyalty almost until the end of the war. But the men who served under him loved his cool, steady style and his commitment to always being prepared.

The men who served under George Henry Thomas loved his cool, steady style and his commitment to always being prepared.

George Henry Thomas.
(Courtesy of the Library of Congress.)

Raised on a Virginia plantation

George Henry Thomas was born on July 31, 1816, in Southampton County, Virginia. Like many other Virginia plantation (large farming estate) owners, his parents, John and Mary Thomas, owned slaves. Black people were taken from Africa and brought to North America to serve as slaves for white people beginning in the 1600s. The basic belief behind slavery was that black people were inferior to whites. Under slavery, white slaveholders treated black people as property, forced them to perform hard labor, and controlled every aspect of their lives. States in the Northern half of the United States began outlawing slavery in the late 1700s. But slavery continued to exist in the Southern half of the country because it played an important role in the South's economy and culture.

When Thomas was fourteen years old, his father died. Thomas then became the man of the house, charged with taking care of his family and their farm. In 1831, a slave named Nat Turner (1800–1831) who lived on a nearby plantation started a slave revolt. Turner and a small band of followers murdered the family that owned them, then roamed the countryside, adding dozens of angry slaves to their group along the way. After learning of the revolt, Thomas hid his family in the woods and then rode from house to house to warn others of the danger. The poorly organized rebellion was crushed within two days, and Turner and a number of his followers were eventually executed. But the revolt caused panic in communities throughout the South and fed white fears of a widespread slave rebellion.

Chooses a military career

With the encouragement of his mother, Thomas studied law for awhile as a young man. But in 1836, a local politician helped him obtain an appointment to the U.S. Military Academy at West Point in New York. Thomas was so excited to receive military training at the prestigious school that he showed up several weeks early to prepare for his first term. He studied hard at West Point and finished twelfth in his graduating class of 1840.

After graduating, Thomas joined the army and was posted to an artillery unit. The artillery division of combat forces included heavy weapons like cannons and the men who hauled and operated them. Thomas always enjoyed working with the big guns. Over the next decade, he fought in the Seminole War (1835–42; a clash between the U.S. Army and the Seminole Indian tribe over lands in Florida) and the Mexican War (1846–48; a dispute between the United States and Mexico over territory in the West). He earned two promotions for bravery on the battlefield.

In 1853, Thomas returned to West Point as an artillery instructor. While there, he met and married Frances Kellogg. Two years later, he joined the Second Cavalry in Texas, where the American military was involved in battles over territory with various Indian tribes. In 1860, Thomas was taking part in one of these fights when a Comanche warrior shot him in the chest with an arrow. Thomas removed the arrow himself and then went for medical treatment.

Supports the Union in the Civil War

Thomas was still recovering from his wound when the Civil War began in 1861. By this time, the Northern and Southern sections of the country had been arguing over several issues for many years. The main issue dividing the nation was slavery. Growing numbers of Northerners believed that slavery was wrong. Some people wanted to outlaw it, while others wanted to prevent it from spreading beyond the Southern states where it was already allowed. But many Southerners felt threatened by Northern efforts to contain slavery. They believed that each state should decide for itself whether to allow the practice. They did not want the national government to pass laws that would interfere with their traditional way of life.

America's westward expansion only increased the tension between the North and South. Both sides wanted to spread their political views and way of life into the new states and territories. Finally, the ongoing dispute convinced a group of Southern states to secede (withdraw) from the United States and form a new country that allowed slavery, called the Confederate States of America. Thomas's home state of Virginia was one of those that joined the Confederacy. In March 1861, the governor of Virginia offered him a position of leadership in the state's volunteer military forces.

Thomas faced a difficult decision. After all, he had been raised in Virginia, and his family and friends supported the Confederacy. But he had worn the uniform of the U.S. Army for many years and felt an intense loyalty to his country. He ended up swearing allegiance to the United States and joining the Union Army. Unfortunately, his decision alienated many of the people he cared about. In fact, both of his sisters wrote him letters saying that they did not consider him their brother any longer.

In the early days of the war, Thomas fought in Virginia's Shenandoah Valley. In August 1861, he was promoted to brigadier general and sent to Kentucky. From that point on, he fought in nearly every major battle in the war's western theater (the area west of the Appalachian Mountains). He saw his first major action at Mill Springs, Kentucky, in January 1862. His brigade fended off a surprise Confederate attack and helped open a path for Union forces to move into Tennessee. Thomas also fought in Mississippi at Corinth (October 1862), and in Kentucky at Perryville (October 1862) and Stone's River (also known as Murfreesboro; December 1862–January 1863).

The "Rock of Chickamauga"

Of all the battles in which Thomas fought, he is probably best known for his performance at the Battle of Chickamauga in Georgia. In September 1863, Confederate general **Braxton Bragg** (1817–1876; see entry) sent several of his men into the Union lines claiming to be deserters (soldiers who leave the army illegally before their term of service is completed). The "deserters" told Union leaders that Bragg's forces were retreating. Union general William Rosecrans (1819–1898) believed the story and ordered his army to spread out into a thin line, twenty miles wide, and follow the Confederates.

But Bragg had not really retreated. In fact, he was waiting nearby for the Union troops to spread out, so that he could attack them one section at a time. Thomas soon learned the truth about the Confederate plans. After pulling his troops back into defensive positions, he warned the other Union leaders of the danger. Rosecrans collected his army near Chickamauga Creek, and Bragg launched a full-scale attack on September 19.

It soon became clear that the Confederate forces held an advantage in the battle. One side of the Union line was pushed back almost immediately. But Thomas's brigade held their side of the line for five long hours, and even gained some ground on the Confederates. Finally, Thomas received orders to abandon their position. He organized a fighting retreat that protected the other Union forces. Although the Union had lost the battle, Thomas had saved Rosecrans and his army. Northern newspapers gave him the nickname "Rock of Chickamauga" for his brave performance.

Defender of Nashville, Tennessee

A month later, General Ulysses S. Grant took command of all the Union armies in the West. Grant chose Thomas to command the Army of the Cumberland. By this time, Confederate forces had pushed the Union troops back to Chattanooga, Tennessee, and set up a siege of the city (a blockade intended to prevent the delivery of food and supplies). On November 25, Thomas and his army led an assault on Missionary Ridge—the strong point in the Confederate defenses—that helped break the siege.

In May 1864, Thomas and his army helped Union general William T. Sherman capture the important Southern industrial city of Atlanta, Georgia. That fall, Sherman's army continued moving through Georgia on its destructive "March to the Sea." Meanwhile, Confederate general **John Bell Hood** (1831–1879; see entry) began moving his forces northward toward Tennessee. Thomas and his army of thirty-five thousand men were sent to defend Nashville. If they failed to prevent Hood from taking the city, the Confederates would have a clear path to continue moving north.

Hood reached Nashville in December 1864. Thomas and his men remained behind the city's defenses as the Confederates set up a siege. At this point, Union leaders wondered why Thomas was hesitating and pressured him to attack. Despite his impressive service to the Union, some people questioned his patriotism. In fact, Grant almost removed him from command. But Thomas believed that proper preparation was a key factor in winning battles. He allowed his tired army to recover and regain their strength, then attacked

Union general George Thomas (seated at table) with a group of officers near Ringgold, Georgia, on May 5, 1864. *(Reproduced by permission of the National Portrait Gallery.)*

with great force on December 15. His Army of the Cumberland conquered Hood's troops and forced them to retreat southward all the way to Mississippi.

Thomas's successful defense of Nashville ended up being one of the most decisive Union victories of the Civil War. Afterward, he was promoted to the rank of major general. But Thomas felt he had earned this honor a year earlier. He believed that the promotion had been delayed because he was from the South. "It is better late than never, but it is too late to be appreciated," he stated. "I earned this at Chickamauga." The U.S. Congress later recognized his contributions to the Union cause and gave him their official thanks.

Dies shortly after the war ends

After the war ended in a Union victory in 1865, Thomas remained in the military and took command of the

Department of the Cumberland. For the next few years, he used his troops to help rebuild the city of Nashville. He also helped establish new state governments in Tennessee, Kentucky, Mississippi, Alabama, and Georgia. His fair treatment of his former enemies earned the respect and appreciation of many Southerners. In 1869, Thomas requested a transfer to the West. He took command of the Division of the Pacific in San Francisco, California, that June. But he died of a stroke less than a year later, on March 28, 1870.

Where to Learn More

Cleaves, Freeman. *Rock of Chickamauga*. Norman: University of Oklahoma Press, 1948. Reprint, Westport, CT: Greenwood Press, 1974.

Green, Carl R., and William R. Sanford. *Union Generals of the Civil War.* Springfield, NJ: Enslow, 1998.

Juergensen, Hans. *Major General George Henry Thomas: A Summary in Perspective*. Tampa, FL: American Studies Press, 1980.

Korn, Jerry. *The Fight for Chattanooga: Chickamauga to Missionary Ridge*. Alexandria, VA: Time-Life Books, 1985.

Palumbo, Frank A. *George Henry Thomas, Major General, U.S.A.: The Dependable General, Supreme in Tactics of Strategy and Command*. Dayton, OH: Morningside House, 1983.

Sally L. Tompkins

Born November 9, 1833
Matthews County, Virginia
Died July 25, 1916
Richmond, Virginia

Confederate nurse and hospital administrator
Only woman to hold a position as a commissioned officer in the Confederate Army

Over three thousand American women acted as paid nurses during the Civil War, and thousands more performed nursing duties as volunteers. Sally Tompkins was one of the most successful nurses on either side of the conflict. The private hospital she established for wounded Confederate soldiers in Richmond, Virginia, had the highest survival rate of any Civil War medical facility. Between the time she opened it in July 1861 and the end of the war in 1865, she lost only 73 out of 1,333 patients.

Resident of Richmond at the beginning of the Civil War

Sally Louisa Tompkins was born into a wealthy family on November 9, 1833, at Poplar Grove in Matthews County, Virginia. Her father died when she was five years old, and then her mother moved the family to Richmond, Virginia. She lived there comfortably on her large inheritance until the beginning of the Civil War.

Sally Tompkins overcame traditional attitudes about women and provided much-needed care to Confederate troops.

461

The war resulted from many years of political tension between the Northern and Southern sections of the United States. The two halves of the country mainly disagreed about slavery and the power of the national government to regulate it. Many Northerners believed that slavery was wrong. Some people wanted to outlaw it, while others wanted to prevent it from spreading beyond the Southern states where it was already allowed. But slavery played a big role in the Southern economy and culture. As a result, many Southerners felt threatened by Northern efforts to contain slavery. They believed that each state should decide for itself whether to allow slavery. They did not want the national government to pass laws that would interfere with their traditional way of life.

By 1861, this ongoing dispute had convinced several Southern states to secede from (leave) the United States and form a new country that allowed slavery, called the Confederate States of America. But Northern political leaders were determined to fight to keep the Southern states in the Union. Tompkins's home state of Virginia was one of those that left the Union. Before long, Richmond became the capital of the Confederacy.

First major battle overwhelms Richmond's medical facilities

The first major battle of the Civil War took place in July 1861 near Manassas Junction, Virginia, along the banks of Bull Run Creek. At that time, people on both sides expected the war to end quickly. In fact, Northerners were so confident of victory that thousands of civilians (people who are not part of the army, including women and children) traveled from Washington, D.C., to watch the battle. They brought picnic baskets and champagne, as if they were going to watch a sporting event. But the terrible reality of war soon became clear to both sides. The bloody battle ended in a Union defeat, and the Northern Army and spectators were forced to make a hasty retreat back to Washington.

Even though the South won the First Battle of Manassas (also known as the First Battle of Bull Run), the high number of casualties (killed and wounded soldiers) took the Confederacy by surprise. Injured men soon filled Richmond's hospitals, and hundreds of others still needed medical attention. In desperation, Confederate president **Jefferson Davis** (1808–1889; see entry) asked the people of Richmond to care for wounded soldiers in their homes. Tompkins was one of many people who responded to this call for volunteer nurses. She convinced a local judge, John Robertson, to let her turn his home in downtown Richmond into a hospital. After collecting supplies and recruiting six staff members, she opened the Robertson Hospital on July 31, 1861.

In the early days of the war, both the Union and Confederate armies actively discouraged women from serving as nurses. Many men of that time felt that nursing was not an appropriate activity for women. They did not want "refined ladies" to be subjected to the horrors of war by treating sick, wounded, and dying soldiers in army hospitals. Confederate nurses faced special problems. Since most of the fighting took place in the South, they were often forced to move patients and entire hospitals in order to remain behind the battle lines. In addition, the South suffered from shortages of food, clothing, and medical supplies throughout the war. But Tompkins and other courageous women overcame traditional attitudes and provided much-needed care to Confederate troops.

Made a captain in the Confederate Army

Within a few weeks of asking Richmond residents to care for wounded soldiers in their homes, Confederate officials became concerned that many soldiers were remaining in private hospitals in Richmond rather than returning to active duty with the army. As a result, Davis issued an order that placed private hospitals under the control of military officers. Tompkins met with the Confederate president and requested that he return control of Robertson Hospital to her. On September 9, 1861, Davis made Tompkins a captain in the Confederate Army so that she could run her hospital without violating his earlier order. Tompkins thus became the only female officer in the Confederate Army.

For the next four years, Tompkins and her staff ran the most successful hospital on either side of the Civil War. Even though Robertson Hospital usually treated the most se-

Ella King Newsom, the "Florence Nightingale of the Southern Army"

Ella King Newsom was another wealthy Southern woman who refused to remain on the sidelines during the Civil War. Instead, she established field hospitals, organized the shipment of medical supplies, and trained nurses to help wounded Confederate soldiers. She earned the nickname "Florence Nightingale of the Southern Army" for her efforts.

Newsom was born in June 1838 in Brandon, Mississippi. She married William Frank Newsom, a wealthy doctor and landowner, in 1854. He died a short time later, leaving her a great deal of money. When the Civil War began in 1861, Newsom decided to use the money to provide medical care for wounded Confederate soldiers. She felt that this would be an ideal tribute to her late husband.

After training as a nurse in Memphis, Tennessee, Newsom took over the administration of a hospital in Bowling Green, Kentucky. The South had a shortage of medical facilities and supplies at this time, and Confederate efforts to care for wounded soldiers were not well organized. Newsom directed the movement of hospitalized troops, recruited and trained new nurses, and sent supplies where they were needed. Her organizational skills earned the respect of patients, doctors, and Confederate officials. In the later war years, she took charge of hospitals in Nashville and Chattanooga in Tennessee, as well as in Atlanta, Georgia, and Corinth, Mississippi.

After the war ended in 1865, Newsom wrote a book about her experiences called *Reminiscences of War Time.* She also married a former Confederate officer, William H. Trader. Unfortunately, he managed their finances poorly and left her almost broke when he died in 1885. But Newsom managed to rebuild her life with the help of Southerners in the U.S. government. She moved to Washington, D.C., and worked in the Patent Office, Pension Office, and General Land Office until her retirement in 1916. She died on January 20, 1919.

riously injured men, it had the highest survival rate of any hospital. Out of 1,333 patients who stayed there between the time it opened and the end of the war in 1865, only 73 died. In addition, a higher percentage of the soldiers treated there returned to action than in any other Confederate medical facility. Despite her success, Tompkins refused to accept any salary for her work. Instead, she used her family's money and government rations to supply the hospital.

Continues working for others after the war

After the war ended in 1865, Tompkins continued helping others through her work with veterans' organizations, the Episcopal Church, and various charities. The people of Richmond considered her a hero and affectionately called her "Captain Sally." In 1905, Tompkins retired to the Confederate Women's Home in Richmond. Since she had spent all of her own money caring for soldiers, veterans, and others who needed help, the management allowed her to live there for free for many years. She died on July 25, 1916, and was buried with full military honors in Matthews County, Virginia. Since that time, four chapters of Daughters of the Confederacy have been named in her honor.

Where to Learn More

Chang, I. *A Separate Battle: Women and the Civil War*. New York: Scholastic, 1994.

Hagerman, Keppel. *Dearest of Captains: A Biography of Sally Louisa Tompkins*. White Stone, VA: Brandyland Publishers, 1996.

Massey, Mary Elizabeth. *Women in the Civil War*. Lincoln: University of Nebraska Press, 1966.

Sojourner Truth

Born 1797
Ulster County, New York
Died November 26, 1883
Battle Creek, Michigan

Abolitionist and women's rights activist

Abolitionist Sojourner Truth is one of the most famous women in American history. Born into slavery, she became a leader in the abolitionist movement (the crusade to end slavery in America) and a pioneer in the battle for women's rights during the 1840s and 1850s. Truth also emerged as an energetic advocate (supporter) for blacks during the post–Civil War era known as Reconstruction (1865–77). Today, she is remembered as one of the leading social reformers of her time.

The energetic Sojourner Truth is remembered as one of the leading social reformers of her time.

Born a slave

Sojourner Truth was born as Isabella Baumfree in 1797 in Ulster Country, New York. The daughter of slave parents owned by James and Elizabeth Baumfree, Truth spent her childhood as a slave. As she grew older, she witnessed many of slavery's cruelties firsthand. For example, several of her brothers and sisters were sold and taken away from their family during her childhood.

Sojourner Truth. *(Courtesy of the Library of Congress.)*

Truth was torn away from her family, too. When she was nine years old, her master separated her from her grieving parents by selling her to another planter (plantation owner). By 1810, when Truth was sold to John Dumont, she had been the property of several slaveowners. Her purchase by Dumont, though, brought a measure of stability to her life. She spent the next seventeen years as a slave on the Dumont estate in New Paltz, New York. During this time she married a fellow slave named Thomas, with whom she had five children.

Released from slavery

Truth's life changed dramatically in the late 1820s. In 1827, the state of New York declared slavery illegal within its borders. This meant that Truth and her children were emancipated (freed from slavery). Around this time, however, Dumont illegally sold her youngest child, who was then transported to Alabama. Truth responded by enlisting the aid of Quaker abolitionists, who helped her secure his return. (Quakers were members of a religious group that strongly opposed slavery.) This incident showed Truth's increased willingness to defy America's slavery system.

After gaining their freedom, Truth and her children were taken in by Maria and Isaac Van Wagenen. During her stay with the Van Wagenens, Truth adopted their last name as her own and experienced a profound religious conversion. These new, deeply felt religious beliefs became a guiding force in Truth's life for the rest of her days.

Searching for a home

The next decade was a period of transition for Truth, as she worked to build a life for herself. In 1829, Truth moved to New York City, where she joined a Methodist Church congregation and devoted herself to assisting in the church's worship and social programs.

Truth's increased involvement in religion took place during a period in American history known as the Second Great Awakening. This period, which reached its height during the 1820s and 1830s, was a time in which religion took on greater importance to thousands of people all across the nation. Guided by influential religious leaders, increased numbers of Americans came to believe that they could achieve salvation by leading moral lives and actively opposing sinful practices.

Truth's life was fundamentally changed by her growing religious convictions (beliefs). During the 1830s, she attended dozens of religious gatherings called camp meetings. At these meetings she developed a reputation as a gifted speaker. Truth also became involved in the evangelical activities of Elijah Pierson and Robert Matthews (evangelism is preaching about the teachings and doctrines of Christianity) at various times during this period.

Truth joins abolitionist movement

In 1843, the former Isabella Wagenen changed her name to Sojourner Truth. She later explained that she made the change when God spoke to her and gave her a new name. She also left New York City during this time, in part because she felt depressed about the poverty in which so many of its citizens lived.

After leaving New York City, Truth became a wandering preacher of God's word. Traveling up and down the Connecticut River Valley, she delivered her message about God's love, wisdom, and power to countless rural audiences. During her travels of this period, she also became acquainted with many of the most important members of America's growing abolitionist movement, including **Frederick Douglass** (1817–1895; see entry), William Lloyd Garrison (1805–1879), and George Benson.

Truth's contact with these leaders in the abolitionist cause had a tremendous impact on her. Inspired by their efforts to abolish slavery—and their support for women's rights—Truth added strong statements about these issues to her evangelical message. By the late 1840s, Truth's blunt and fiery speaking style had established her as one of the abolitionist movement's most popular speakers.

Truth speaks out

In 1850, Truth joined with abolitionist Olive Gilbert to write *The Narrative of Sojourner Truth*. Sales of this book, which Truth published herself, became the abolitionist's primary means of supporting herself for the next several years. In 1851, she attended a women's rights conference in Akron, Ohio. Truth had gone to the conference in order to talk with other supporters of women's rights and sell copies of her autobiography. During the conference, however, several male ministers ridiculed female attempts to win the right to vote and gain legal protections that white men took for granted. When none of the white women at the conference rose to defend their cause, Truth boldly stood up and delivered a spirited scolding to the ministers that ended with thunderous applause from her female audience. Her speech, in which she proudly asserted her identity as both a woman and a black person, is remembered today as one of the most significant events in the American women's rights movement.

A painting shows Sojourner Truth's visit with President Abraham Lincoln. *(Courtesy of the Library of Congress.)*

Works on behalf of former slaves

During the mid-1850s, Truth moved to Battle Creek, Michigan, a center of American religious and abolitionist activity. She remained devoted to seeing slavery brought to an end during this time, but also spent a lot of her time on women's rights. As a result, Truth became angry with some male abolitionists who did not seem to realize that the inferior status of women in American society was also an injustice.

During the Civil War, Truth led efforts to provide food, education, and employment opportunities to ex-slave refugees. In 1864, she met personally with President **Abraham Lincoln** (1809–1865; see entry) to discuss the future of those refugees. After the Civil War concluded in 1865, Truth remained a leading advocate for former slaves. She contributed great amounts of time and energy to the Freedmen's Bureau and other relief agencies. In addition, she continued to deliver public lectures in which she championed the cause of equal rights for all. She also submitted a plan to Congress in which government land in the West would be given to former slaves. Congress failed to act on her proposal, but Truth's support for black migration to the West convinced thousands of former slaves to establish homesteads in Kansas.

Truth's activism on behalf of blacks and women ended in the late 1870s, when her health began to decline. She stopped traveling and returned to Battle Creek, where she died in 1883.

Where to Learn More

Bernard, Jacqueline. *Journey Toward Freedom: The Story of Sojourner Truth.* New York: Norton, 1967. Reprint, New York: Feminist Press at the City University of New York, 1990.

Krass, Peter. *Sojourner Truth.* New York: Chelsea House, 1988.

Mabee, Carleton. *Sojourner Truth: Slave, Prophet, Legend.* New York: New York University Press, 1993.

McKissack, Patricia, and Frederick McKissack. *Sojourner Truth: Ain't I a Woman?* New York: Scholastic, 1992.

Painter, Nell Irvin. *Sojourner Truth: A Life, a Symbol.* New York: Norton, 1996.

Sojourner Truth Institute of Battle Creek. *Sojourner Truth Institute.* [Online] http://www.sojournertruth.org/ (accessed on October 15, 1999).

Stetson, Erlene. *Glorying in Tribulation: The Lifework of Sojourner Truth.* East Lansing: Michigan State University Press, 1994.

Truth, Sojourner, and Olive Gilbert. *The Narrative of Sojourner Truth.* 1850.

Whalin, T. *Sojourner Truth: American Abolitionist.* Uhrichsville, OH: Barbour & Co., 1997.

Harriet Tubman

Born 1820 or 1821
Dorchester County, Maryland
Died March 10, 1913
Auburn, New York

Escaped slave who became a leader of the Underground Railroad

Risked her life in order to guide hundreds of slaves to freedom in the North

Harriet Tubman was a fugitive slave who helped other slaves gain their freedom through the Underground Railroad. The Underground Railroad was not actually a railroad. It was a secret network of abolitionists (people who fought to end slavery) who helped slaves escape from their masters and settle in the Northern United States and Canada, where slavery was not allowed. The Underground Railroad system consisted of a chain of homes and barns known as "safe houses" or "depots." The people who guided the runaway slaves from one safe house to the next were known as "conductors." As one of the most successful conductors, Tubman made nineteen dangerous trips into slave territory and helped more than three hundred slaves gain their freedom.

Born into slavery

Harriet Tubman was born on a plantation (a large farming estate) in Dorchester County, Maryland, in either 1820 or 1821. She never knew the exact date of her birth because she was born a slave. Black people were taken from Africa and

"There was one of two things I had a *right* to, liberty, or death; if I could not have one, I would have the other; for no man should take me alive."

Harriet Tubman. *(Reproduced with permission of Archive Photos, Inc.)*

473

brought to North America to serve as slaves for white people beginning in the 1600s. The basic belief behind slavery was that black people were inferior to whites. Under slavery, white slaveholders treated black people as property, forced them to perform hard labor, and controlled every aspect of their lives. States in the Northern half of the United States began outlawing slavery in the late 1700s. But slavery continued to exist in the Southern half of the country because it played an important role in the South's economy and culture.

Most slave owners tried to prevent their slaves from learning much about themselves or the world around them. They believed that educated slaves would be more likely to become dissatisfied with their lives. For this reason, Tubman never knew the details of her birth. However, she did know that she was one of eleven children born to Harriet Greene and Benjamin Ross. Her whole family was the property of Edward Brodas, the white man who owned the plantation where they lived. The name she received when she was born was Araminta. She adopted the name Harriet in 1831.

When Tubman was seven years old, her master hired her out to an impatient and cruel woman named Miss Susan. Many slaveowners loaned their extra slaves to other people in exchange for a fee. Tubman took care of Miss Susan's baby and performed household chores. Miss Susan beat her whenever the house was not clean enough or the baby cried at night. The beatings left scars on her back and neck that would remain visible the rest of her life. Eventually Miss Susan returned Tubman to the Brodas plantation.

From that time on, Tubman worked in the fields and became very strong. She constantly thought about running away from the plantation, but did not know where to go and could not read a map. One day, Tubman noticed a young male slave sneaking away from the fields where they worked. She decided to follow him. Unfortunately, the overseer (a person who watches over field hands and directs their work) chased and caught them. When Tubman refused to help the overseer tie up the male slave, the overseer threw a heavy weight that hit her in the middle of the forehead. She slipped into a coma for several weeks before slowly recovering. This head injury caused her to suffer from blackouts and terrible nightmares for the rest of her life.

Tubman Should Never Have Been a Slave

In 1844, Tubman used some of the money she had earned to hire a lawyer. She wanted someone to research her family's history in order to find out if they were held in slavery legally. Tubman took this unusual step after learning how her new husband had become free. John Tubman had been freed because his former master, who had no children, died without leaving a will.

Then Tubman remembered a story her mother had told about her past. Harriet Greene had once belonged to a woman named Mary Patterson. Patterson died young, had no heirs, and left no will. As a result, Tubman's mother legally should have been freed. But Harriet Greene did not know the law, and no one bothered to tell her. Instead, she remained a slave, and all her children became slaves as well.

After learning that she was being held in slavery illegally, Tubman asked the lawyer what she could do to secure her rights. But the lawyer said that no judge

Harriet Tubman. *(Reproduced with permission of Corbis-Bettmann.)*

would ever consider the case because too much time had passed, and the women had always lived as slaves. Instead of gaining her freedom on legal grounds, Tubman was forced to escape from slavery on the Underground Railroad.

Escapes to the North

Edward Brodas died in 1835, and ownership of Tubman and her family passed to his son. Tubman convinced her new master to let her "hire her time," or find her own jobs outside of the plantation. She still had to pay her master a large chunk of her earnings, but she also got to keep some money for herself. In 1844, she married a free black man named John Tubman and went to live in his cabin. Before long, it became clear that Tubman and her husband had different priorities. She dreamed of escaping from slavery and traveling to the North, but he worried that his freedom would be put in jeopardy if he left Maryland. He threatened to report his wife to her master if she attempted to escape.

In 1849, Brodas's son died. At this point, one of Tubman's worst fears became a reality. She learned that she and her family would be sold in order to pay the plantation's debts. There was little market for slaves in Maryland, so they would likely be taken to the Deep South to pick cotton. Tubman decided that the time had come for her to run away. "I had reasoned this out in my mind," she noted. "There was one of two things I had a *right* to, liberty, or death; if I could not have one, I would have the other; for no man should take me alive."

Late one night, Tubman left the plantation and went to a nearby home that was rumored to be part of the Underground Railroad. The woman who lived there provided directions to the next safe house. For the next few days, Tubman traveled at night with the assistance of strangers who opposed slavery. At one house she pretended to be a servant in order to avoid suspicion. Another time she hid in the back of a vegetable wagon. Sometimes she hiked north along the coast and through swamps and woodlands. She took careful notice of the route so that she could return later to rescue her family. Tubman finally crossed the border into Pennsylvania—where slavery was not allowed—after a one hundred–mile journey. "I looked at my hands to see if I was the same person now that I was free," she recalled. "There was such a glory over everything; the sun came like gold through the trees, and over the fields, and I felt like I was in heaven."

Becomes a conductor on the Underground Railroad

Tubman was finally free, although she knew that she might be captured and returned to slavery at any time. She settled in Philadelphia and took a job washing dishes at a hotel. She saved her money in the hope of returning to Maryland to deliver her family to freedom. She met many prominent abolitionists during this time, including **John Brown** (1800–1859; see entry) and **Frederick Douglass** (1817–1895; see entry). In 1850, Tubman made her first trip to the South as a conductor on the Underground Railroad. She returned to her old plantation in order to rescue her brothers and their families from slavery. Another time, she helped her elderly parents make the trip to the North. She once tried to bring her husband to Pennsylvania, but found that he had remarried and was not interested in leaving Maryland.

Tubman made a total of nineteen trips into slave territory over the next ten years. She guided more than three hundred slaves to freedom. Each time she made the dangerous journey, she risked being captured and returned to her owner, or even killed. As word of her daring rescues spread, white Southerners offered a large reward for her capture. But although she had some close calls, she never ran into serious trouble. "I never ran my train off the track, and I never lost a passenger," she stated. Tubman made her final trip on the Underground Railroad in December 1860. Then it became clear that the issue of slavery would be settled by war.

Serves the Union during the Civil War

The North and the South had been arguing over several issues, including slavery, for many years. Growing numbers of Northerners believed that slavery was wrong. Some people wanted to outlaw it, while others wanted to prevent it from spreading beyond the Southern states where it was already allowed. But slavery played a big role in the Southern economy and culture. As a result, many Southerners felt threatened by Northern efforts to contain slavery. They believed that each state should decide for itself whether to allow slavery. They did not want the national government to pass laws that would interfere with their traditional way of life.

By 1861, this ongoing dispute had convinced several Southern states to secede from (leave) the United States and attempt to form a new country that allowed slavery, called the Confederate States of America. But Northern political leaders were determined to keep the Southern states in the Union. The two sides soon went to war. Once the Civil War began, Tubman began looking for a way to help the Union cause. She ended up volunteering as a cook, nurse, and laundress for Union troops who had taken over Beaufort, South Carolina.

Tubman also served as a spy, conducting several successful raids and scouting missions. In June 1863, she led a group of Union gunboats manned by black soldiers on a raid up the Combahee River in South Carolina. They removed mines from the river, destroyed Confederate supplies, and led 750 slaves to freedom. Nearly all of the male slaves who were freed in this mission later joined the Union Army.

Helps freed slaves after the war

After war ended in a Northern victory in 1865, Tubman expected the U.S. government to pay her for her wartime service. After all, the Union had offered a bounty (reward) to people who recruited new soldiers. Counting the freed slaves Tubman had convinced to sign up after the Combahee River mission, she figured the government owed her $1,800. But the government refused to pay her the money, even when Secretary of State **William Seward** (1801–1872; see entry) made a personal appeal on her behalf.

As a result, Tubman lived in relative poverty after the war. She had a home in Auburn, New York, that she shared with her parents. She earned a living by selling fruits and vegetables from her garden door-to-door. The people in town welcomed her into their homes, bought her goods, and listened to her amazing stories about the Underground Railroad. In 1867, Tubman's friend Sarah Bradford published a book called *Scenes in the Life of Harriet Tubman*. This book discussed Tubman's accomplishments before and during the war and included statements of praise from her important friends, such as Frederick Douglass. Bradford gave the money she earned from sales of the book to Tubman, who used it to build schools to educate freed slaves and facilities to nurse sick and injured blacks.

In 1869, Tubman married Nelson Davis. In the 1870s, she threw her support behind efforts to secure the right to vote for women. In 1897, Tubman received a medal from Queen Victoria (1819–1901) of England. In 1908, she donated land in Auburn to the African Methodist Episcopal Zion Church. The site was to be used for a home for sick and elderly black people. Tubman had several disagreements with the church about how the home should be run, but they eventually settled their differences. As she grew frail, Tubman moved into the home in 1911. She died of pneumonia on March 10,

1913, at the age of ninety-three. A group of Union Army veterans arranged for her to receive a military funeral.

"Harriet Tubman's life story is an inspiration to blacks and women in their ongoing battle for equal rights," Bree Burns wrote in *Harriet Tubman and the Fight against Slavery*. "She is remembered as a hero who was not afraid to fight for her beliefs. Tubman's dedication to justice has become a model for all Americans."

Where to Learn More

Access Indiana Teaching and Learning Center. *Harriet Tubman*. [Online] http://tlc.ai.org/tubman.htm (accessed on October 15, 1999).

AME Zion Church. *The Harriet Tubman Home*. [Online] http://www.ny-history.com/harriettubman/home.htm (accessed on October 15, 1999).

Bentley, Judith. *Harriet Tubman*. New York: Franklin Watts, 1990.

Bradford, Sarah H. *Scenes in the Life of Harriet Tubman*. Auburn, NY: W. J. Moses, 1869. Reprint, Freeport, NY: Books for Libraries Press, 1971.

Burns, Bree. *Harriet Tubman*. New York: Chelsea Juniors, 1992.

Harriet Tubman Historical Society. [Online] http://www.harriettubman.com (accessed on October 15, 1999).

Janney, Rebecca Price. *Harriet Tubman*. Minneapolis: Bethany House, 1999.

McClard, Megan. *Harriet Tubman: Slavery and the Underground Railroad*. Englewood Cliffs, NJ: Silver Burdett Press, 1991.

McMullan, Kate. *The Story of Harriet Tubman: Conductor of the Underground Railroad*. New York: Dell, 1991. Reprint, Milwaukee: Gareth Stevens, 1997.

Sterling, Dorothy. *Freedom Train*. Garden City, NY: Doubleday, 1954.

Taylor, Marian. *Harriet Tubman*. New York: Chelsea House, 1991.

White, Terry Ann. *North to Liberty: The Story of the Underground Railroad*. Champaign, IL: Garrard, 1972.

Clement L. Vallandigham

Born July 29, 1820
New Lisbon, Ohio
Died June 17, 1871
Lebanon, Ohio

Ohio congressman and candidate for governor
Leader of the antiwar "Copperhead" Democrats

As a leader of the antiwar Democrats known as "Copperheads," Clement L. Vallandigham emerged as a bitter critic of President **Abraham Lincoln** (1809–1865; see entry) and his administration during the Civil War. Vallandigham's opposition to Lincoln was based on his belief in the principle of states' rights and his certainty that the Union could never be restored through war. In 1863, however, his criticisms of the war effort became so strong that he was exiled (forced to leave) from the North.

A veteran of Ohio politics

Clement Laird Vallandigham was born in New Lisbon, Ohio, in 1820. The son of a minister, Vallandigham studied at the New Lisbon Academy and Pennsylvania's Jefferson College before opening up a law practice in his hometown in 1842. In the mid-1840s he won election to the state house of representatives, where he became one of Ohio's best known politicians. In 1852 and 1854, however, Vallandigham's campaigns to win a seat in the U.S. Congress ended in defeat.

"Must I shoot a simple-minded soldier boy who deserts, while I must not touch a hair of a wily agitator [Vallandigham] who induces him to desert?" *Abraham Lincoln*

Clement Vallandigham.
(Courtesy of the Library of Congress.)

481

By the mid-1850s, Vallandigham was one of Ohio's leading Democrats. Married to the daughter of a wealthy Maryland planter (plantation owner) and slaveowner, he sided with the South in the growing national debate over slavery. For example, he strongly supported the principle known as "states' rights." This principle was popular among Southerners who feared federal efforts to limit or end slavery. It held that each state has the right to decide how to handle various issues for itself—including slavery—without interference from the national government.

In 1856, Vallandigham ran for a seat in the U.S. House of Representatives once again. At first, it appeared that he had been defeated. He contested the election results, however, and in May 1858, authorities awarded him the seat. After winning reelection in November 1858, he became known across the country for his vocal support of states' rights and active opposition to abolitionism (the movement to end slavery). Vallandigham worried that Northern efforts to end slavery would cause a revolt in the South that might break the Union in two.

During the 1860 presidential campaign, Vallandigham threw his support behind Northern Democratic candidate Stephen A. Douglas (1813–1861), whom he viewed as more moderate on the slavery issue than Republican nominee Abraham Lincoln or Southern Democratic nominee John Breckinridge (1821–1875). Lincoln won the election, though, triggering a wave of secessionist proclamations across the American South. When Southern states declared their intention to secede from (leave) the United States and form their own country, Lincoln ordered the U.S. Army to prepare for war in order to keep them in the Union. By mid-1861 the American Civil War had begun.

Opposes Lincoln and his war policies

During the first months of the Civil War, Vallandigham launched a series of harsh attacks on Lincoln and his war policies. Vallandigham wanted to see the Union restored, but he did not believe that the North could force the South to return. Instead, he thought that the North's best chance to restore the Union was to agree to let slavery continue in the South. "In considering terms of settlement we [should] look only to the welfare, peace, and safety of the white race, without reference to the effect that settlement may have on the African," he stated.

Vallandigham's views and his outspoken nature quickly made him a leader among a group of antiwar Northern Democrats known as "Copperheads." These politicians urged the North to either let the South depart in peace or convince it to return by guaranteeing states' rights.

As the war progressed, Vallandigham actively opposed virtually every aspect of Lincoln's war policies. He voted against conscription (a military draft), criticized Lincoln's efforts to silence unfriendly newspapers, and even encouraged Northern soldiers to desert from the army. Vallandigham's calls for desertion infuriated Lincoln, who viewed the Ohio congressman as a traitor (someone who betrays one's country). "Must I shoot a simple-minded soldier boy who deserts, while I must not touch a hair of a wily agitator [clever troublemaker] who induces [persuades] him to desert?" asked Lincoln. "I think that in such a case to silence the agitator and save the boy is not only constitutional but withal [actually] a great mercy [kindness]."

Vallandigham's actions and statements also made him a target of Lincoln's Republican colleagues. As time passed, they became determined to neutralize the outspoken Ohio legislator. In 1862, they changed the shape of his congressional district to ensure his defeat in that year's elections. They did this through a process called gerrymandering, in which one political party divides a geographic area into voting districts that give an unfair advantage to its party in elections.

Arrested and exiled

After losing his seat in the U.S. House of Representatives, Vallandigham decided to run for governor of Ohio. As he campaigned, he repeatedly denounced Lincoln's policies and leadership. He charged that during Lincoln's presidency, "Money [had been] expended [spent] without limits and blood poured out like water." Vallandigham also suggested that if he was elected governor, he might encourage the state to join the Confederacy. Union military leaders threatened him with arrest for making statements of sympathy for the enemy, but Vallandigham continued to speak out. In fact, the Copperhead leader began to hope for an arrest because he thought that it might energize his fading campaign.

In May 1863, Vallandigham's continued criticisms of Lincoln finally resulted in his arrest by General **Ambrose Burnside** (1824–1881; see entry), the commander of the Department of the Ohio. Charged with treason (betrayal of one's country), Vallandigham was tried by a military court even though he was a civilian. He was found guilty and sentenced to two years in a military prison.

Vallandigham's conviction, though, worried many people in the North, including some members of Lincoln's Republican Party. "The Vallandigham case did indeed raise troubling constitutional questions," wrote James M. McPherson in *Battle Cry of Freedom.* "Could a speech be treason? Could a military court try a civilian? Did a general, or for that matter a president, have the power to impose martial law [temporary military rule over the civilian population] or suspend habeas corpus [a section of the Constitution meant to protect individuals from illegal imprisonment] in an area distant from military operations where the civil courts were functioning?"

As expressions of concern about Vallandigham's conviction increased, President Lincoln decided to commute (end) his jail sentence and banish him (send him away) from Union territory. On May 26, Vallandigham was transported to Confederate territory, where his Union escort released him. Upon arriving in the South, however, he discovered that the Confederate leaders did not trust him. Unwelcome in the Confederacy, Vallandigham moved to Canada. He settled in Ontario, where he began a strange "campaign-in-exile" to win the governorship of Ohio. Despite being forbidden from entering Ohio, he managed to gain the Democratic nomination for governor in June. In October 1863, though, his bid for the governorship ended in a landslide (overwhelming) defeat at the hands of Republican candidate John Brough (1811–1865).

Continues to oppose war

Vallandigham continued to battle Lincoln and his war policies during the final two years of the Civil War. In June 1864, he returned to Ohio in disguise. Resuming his work with the "Copperhead" Democrats, he also became involved with a mysterious antiwar organization known as the Sons of Liberty. Members of this strange organization were dedicated to states' rights, sympathetic to the Confederate cause, and fiercely opposed to the Republican Party. Many Northerners believed that this organization provided dangerous support to the Confederacy through spying and other espionage activities. In reality, however, the group remained small and insignificant throughout the war.

Lincoln learned of Vallandigham's return to the United States almost as soon as it occurred. The president, however, let him resettle in Ohio. Aware that Vallandigham's previous arrest had boosted the Copperhead's popularity, the president decided that it was better to just ignore him. Lincoln's instincts in this situation proved correct. Vallandigham continued to criticize the president and his Republican allies for the war's financial cost and heavy casualties. When Union military forces registered a series of big victories in the summer and fall of 1864, however, Vallandigham's influence diminished quickly.

Postwar career

The North won the Civil War in the spring of 1865, forcing the rebellious Southern states to return to the Union. This development doomed Vallandigham's political career, since he had always insisted that the Union could never be restored by war. He tried to win election to political office in both 1866 and 1867, but both efforts failed miserably.

In the late 1860s, Vallandigham resumed his law practice. He established a partnership with a former judge that became very successful. In June 1871, however, he accidently shot himself during a trial when, using a pistol that he did not realize was loaded, he tried to demonstrate how a murder victim actually might have committed suicide. Vallandigham died one day later from his wound.

Where to Learn More

Klement, Frank L. *Dark Lanterns: Secret Political Societies, Conspiracies, and Treason Trials in the Civil War.* Baton Rouge: Louisiana State University Press, 1984.

Klement, Frank L. *The Limits of Dissent: Clement L. Vallandigham and the Civil War.* Lexington: University of Kentucky Press, 1970. Reprint, New York: Fordham University Press, 1998.

Klement, Frank L. *Lincoln's Critics: The Copperheads of the North.* Shippensburg, PA: White Mane Books, 1999.

Elizabeth Van Lew

Born October 12, 1818
Richmond, Virginia
Died September 25, 1900
Richmond, Virginia

Union spy known as "Crazy Bet"

Escaped detection by pretending to be a harmless eccentric

Elizabeth Van Lew was a wealthy and refined (cultured) lady of Richmond, Virginia—the city that became the Confederate capital during the Civil War. Her neighbors called her "Crazy Bet" and laughed at her strange behavior. But she only pretended to be eccentric (odd or peculiar). In fact, she was a cunning and highly effective spy for the Union. She sent valuable information to the North through the entire course of the war, and she also helped numerous Union soldiers escape from Southern prisons.

Supports the abolition of slavery

Elizabeth Van Lew was born in Richmond in 1818. Her family owned a large farm and several businesses. Their wealth made them part of Richmond's upper class. Like many wealthy Southern families of this time period, Van Lew's family owned slaves. The slaves performed household tasks like cooking and cleaning and also worked on the farm. As a young woman, Van Lew went to the North to complete her

"She risked everything that is dear to man—friends, fortune, comfort, health, life itself, all for the one absorbing desire of her heart—that slavery might be abolished and the Union preserved."

From Elizabeth Van Lew's gravestone

Elizabeth Van Lew.
(Reproduced with permission of the Granger Collection, New York.)

education. During this time, she came into contact with abolitionists (people who worked to end slavery).

The basic belief behind slavery was that black people were inferior to whites. Under slavery, white slaveholders treated black people as property, forced them to perform hard labor, and controlled every aspect of their lives. Thanks to the efforts of the abolitionists, growing numbers of Northerners believed that slavery was wrong. They outlawed slavery in the Northern states and tried to prevent it from spreading beyond the Southern states where it was already allowed. But slavery played a big role in the Southern economy and culture. As a result, many Southerners felt threatened by Northern efforts to contain slavery. They believed that each state should decide for itself whether to allow slavery.

By the time Van Lew returned to the South, she believed that slavery was wrong and felt that black Americans should have the same rights and opportunities as whites. She convinced her family to free all of their slaves and to help them obtain an education in the North. As a result, the freed slaves remained loyal to the family. Most of them stayed with Van Lew throughout the Civil War. In fact, several of her former slaves played important roles in her spy operation.

Decides to help the Union cause

The debate over slavery and other issues caused a great deal of political tension between the North and South. By 1861, the ongoing dispute had convinced several Southern states to secede from (leave) the United States and attempt to form a new country that allowed slavery, called the Confederate States of America. Van Lew's home state of Virginia was among those that seceded. But Northern political leaders were determined to keep the Southern states in the Union. Before long, the two sides went to war.

Since Van Lew strongly opposed slavery, she supported the Northern cause in the war. Shortly after the war started, she decided to help the Union by keeping its military leaders informed of events in the Confederate capital. At first, she simply wrote letters to President **Abraham Lincoln** (1809–1865; see entry). Once Union leaders discovered the value of her information, however, they made her part of the Secret Service—a formal intelligence-gathering network. She then reported to George Sharpe, the main information officer for Union general **Ulysses S. Grant** (1822–1885; see entry).

Many of Van Lew's friends and neighbors realized that she did not support the Confederacy. After all, she spoke out against slavery in Richmond, and she refused to join other local women in sewing shirts for Confederate soldiers. But no one ever suspected that this wealthy, refined lady—who had been born into Richmond's high society—would dream of spying for the Union. Van Lew realized that her image worked in her favor and did her best to keep it up. She often appeared in public with her hair messy and her clothing in disarray, and she did strange things like visiting Union soldiers in prison. She also welcomed Confederate officers into her home, which everyone knew a Union spy would never do. As a result, the people of Richmond viewed Van Lew as a harmless eccentric. They even gave her the nickname "Crazy Bet."

Develops expert spy techniques

Over the course of the war, Van Lew developed excellent spy tactics. For example, she often tore secret messages into pieces and sent each piece with a different courier. That way, any single piece would be meaningless if the messenger was captured. She also invented a special code that she used for many of her messages. Sometimes she wrote them in ink that was invisible until it came into contact with milk. She disguised some secret messages as long, newsy letters from a Miss Eliza Jones of Richmond to her Uncle James Jones in Norfolk, Virginia—behind the Union lines. These people did not actually exist. Instead, the letters went to Union officials, who used milk to read the invisible messages between the lines.

Since Van Lew's family owned a farm outside of Richmond, she managed to obtain passes from the Confederate Army that allowed her and her servants to travel back and forth. This route served as the first leg of the journey to the North for many secret messages. She sometimes carried the messages in baskets with false bottoms. She even hollowed out the inside of eggs to carry some messages.

Elizabeth Van Lew's mansion in Richmond, Virginia.
(Courtesy of the Library of Congress.)

Van Lew often visited Union prisoners held in Richmond jails. These men provided her with information about Confederate troop positions and strategy. She also had a safe room in her house to hide escaped Union prisoners until she could arrange for friends to guide them to freedom in the North. None of the prisoners were ever captured in her home, even though she sometimes had Confederate officers staying with her at the same time. Once, when the Confederates came looking for horses to use in the war effort, Van Lew used her safe room to hide her last horse. She wanted to keep the horse, in case she needed to send a fast message to the North.

One of Van Lew's best sources of information was her former slave, Mary Elizabeth Bowser. Van Lew had sent Bowser to Philadelphia for schooling prior to the war. Once the war started, she arranged for Bowser to become a servant to President **Jefferson Davis** (1808–1889; see entry) in the Confederate White House. Bowser pretended that she could not read, then stole glances at confidential memos and orders while she was cleaning. She also eavesdropped on conversations between Confederate officials while she served dinner. Bowser passed information about troop movements and other Confederate Army plans along to Van Lew, who sent it on to Union officials. Bowser's activities as a Union spy went undetected throughout the war.

Traitor to the South, hero to the North

Van Lew continued spying for the Union until the end of the war and was never arrested. But her friends and neighbors did spread rumors about her, and most people in Richmond eventually came to believe she was guilty. Shortly before the war ended, an angry mob came to her house and threatened to burn it down. Van Lew stopped them by saying that she would send the Union troops to burn the mob members' houses down as soon as they arrived in the city.

When the Union troops captured Richmond in 1865, General Grant assigned a group of soldiers to protect Van Lew and her property. A few years later, when Grant became president of the United States, he rewarded her loyalty by naming her postmistress of Richmond. But the people of Richmond never forgave Van Lew for spying for the Union. She was lonely and isolated in the years after the war. Since she had used her own money to finance her spy operations, she was also poor. In her later years, she was supported by her loyal servants and by donations from some of the Union prisoners she had helped to escape.

Van Lew was considered a traitor in the South, but a hero in the North. "If I am entitled to the name of 'spy' because I was in the Secret Service, I accept it willingly; but it will hereafter have to my mind a high and honorable signification [meaning]," she once wrote. "For my loyalty to my country I have two beautiful names—here I am called 'Traitor,' farther North a 'Spy'—instead of the honored name of 'Faithful.'"

When Van Lew died in 1900, she remained so unpopular in Richmond that no local residents came to her funeral. But a group of admirers in Boston, Massachusetts, bought a granite marker for her grave. The bronze plaque summed up her service to the Union during the Civil War: "She risked everything that is dear to man—friends, fortune, comfort, health, life itself, all for the one absorbing desire of her heart— that slavery might be abolished and the Union preserved."

Where to Learn More

Axelrod, Alan. *The War Between the Spies: A History of Espionage during the American Civil War.* New York: Atlantic Monthly Press, 1992.

Elizabeth Van Lew. [Online] http://pixel.cs.vt.edu./aramsey/civil/van-lew.html (accessed on October 15, 1999).

Hall, Beverly B. *The Secret of the Lion's Head.* Shippensburg, PA: White Mane Pub. Co., 1995.

Kane, Harnett T. *Spies for the Blue and Gray.* Garden City, NY: Hanover House, 1954.

Markle, Donald E. *Spies and Spymasters of the Civil War.* New York: Hippocrene Books, 1994.

Nolan, Jeannette Covert. *Yankee Spy, Elizabeth Van Lew.* New York: J. Messner, 1970.

Ryan, David, ed. *A Yankee Spy in Richmond: The Civil War Diary of "Crazy Bet" Van Lew.* Mechanicsburg, PA: Stackpole Books, 1996.

Zeinert, Karen. *Elizabeth Van Lew: Southern Belle, Union Spy.* New York: Dillon Press, 1995.

Theodore Dwight Weld

Born November 23, 1803
Hampton, Connecticut
Died February 3, 1895
Boston, Massachusetts

Religious leader and abolitionist
Author of the influential book
American Slavery as It Is

Theodore Dwight Weld was a leading abolitionist (person who worked to put an end to slavery) during the years of heated debate over slavery that led to the Civil War. He was one of the most effective opponents of slavery during the 1830s, when the abolitionist movement was just beginning to gain ground in the Northern United States. He converted thousands of people to the cause with his passionate speeches and powerful books. But in the 1840s, long before the issue of slavery was resolved, Weld disappeared from view. Poor health, the loss of his voice, and a series of public defeats caused him to reevaluate his life. He lived quietly from that time on, although he occasionally emerged to comment on a particular social issue.

Brought up in a religious household

Theodore Dwight Weld was born on November 23, 1803, in Hampton, Connecticut. He was the fourth of five children born to the Reverend Ludovicus Weld and his wife, Elizabeth Clark Weld. Both of his parents came from promi-

"The Nation is its citizens, and the Nation's right and duty to protect and defend its citizens, all of them, is absolute and paramount."

Theodore Weld. *(Courtesy of the Library of Congress.)*

493

nent families that had lived in New England for over one hundred years. The Weld house was usually noisy and chaotic during Theodore's childhood. In addition to five active children, it often contained a number of his father's theology students. As a result, Theodore sometimes resorted to practical jokes or wild pranks to get attention.

But the Weld household was also a deeply religious one. The children were expected to live by strict rules of moral conduct. When they made mistakes, they sometimes received harsh punishment. For example, Theodore once cut the casing on a hunk of cheese, causing it to spoil. When his parents asked about it, he lied. In response, they confined him to his bedroom alone for a week and gave him only bread and water. As a boy, Weld respected his minister father but did not feel close to him. He tried to win his father's love by reading the Bible and studying to become a minister.

In 1819, Weld went to the prestigious Andover Academy to further his religious training. But within a year he became ill and suffered an emotional breakdown. One of his teachers suggested that traveling in a warmer climate might help. Since Weld did not have money for a vacation, he took a job as a traveling lecturer on mnemonics—the science of memory. As he visited towns throughout the South, he developed his public speaking and presentation skills. He was also exposed to slavery for the first time.

Joins the abolitionist movement

Black people were taken from Africa and brought to North America to serve as slaves for white people beginning in the 1600s. The basic belief behind slavery was that black people were inferior to whites. Under slavery, white slaveholders treated black people as property, forced them to perform hard labor, and controlled every aspect of their lives. States in the Northern half of the United States began outlawing slavery in the late 1700s. But slavery continued to exist in the Southern half of the country because it played an important role in the South's culture and economy.

For most of his youth, Weld had not thought much about slavery. After all, he lived in the North, a region where slavery was not allowed in most states. In 1826, though, Weld experienced a religious awakening under the guidance of evangelist Charles G. Finney (1792–1875). He began to view slavery as a sin against God. In the early 1830s, he joined a group of young religious leaders who shared his views in forming the American Anti-Slavery Society.

Around this time, Weld began to argue that the best place to wage a war against slavery was in the West. The western United States was still being settled at that time, and much of it remained wilderness. Weld wanted to bring his antislavery message to the West while settlers had not yet formed solid opinions on the subject. He and many other young abolitionists went to Lane Theological Seminary in Cincinnati, Ohio, just across the Ohio River from the slaveholding state of Kentucky.

The head of Lane Seminary (a school that trains for the ministry) was Lyman Beecher (1775–1863), a fiery Puritan minister and father of the writer Harriet Beecher Stowe (1811–1896; see entry). Weld also came into contact with Angelina Grimké (1805–1879) and Sarah Grimké (1792–1873) at Lane. These sisters had been raised in a wealthy slaveholding family in South Carolina, but had adopted the abolitionist cause after converting to the Quaker religion. They were the first American women to speak out against slavery, and eventually became leaders in the fight for women's rights.

Becomes an effective abolitionist speaker and writer

In 1836, a dispute between the students and faculty at Lane caused Weld to leave the school. He then turned his full attention to speaking out against slavery. He traveled to small towns around the country and made passionate speeches about the evils of the institution. Some people called him a fanatic, but many others were forever moved by the experience of hearing him speak. He ended up convincing thousands of people to support the abolitionist cause. For example, he brought six hundred new members to the local antislavery society in Utica, New York, in February 1836. A month later, he converted eight hundred more people in Rochester, New York. In addition, he recruited and taught other talented speakers to spread the antislavery message in other areas across the country.

In his speeches, Weld told his listeners that America had to end slavery in order to relieve itself of sin and follow a path of moral rightness. He argued that the nation was not truly based on principles of liberty if millions of people were denied freedom and basic rights. He supported freeing all the slaves immediately and granting black people equal rights as fellow human beings. "No condition of birth, no shade of color, no mere misfortune of circumstances, can annul [cancel] that birth-right charter [guarantee specified rights], which God has bequeathed [granted] to every being upon whom he has stamped his own image, by making him a free moral agent," Weld stated. "He who robs his fellow man of this tramples upon right, subverts [overthrows] justice, outrages humanity, unsettles the foundations of human safety, and sacrilegiously [in violation of something sacred] assumes the prerogative [special power] of God."

Weld also spread his antislavery message through printed materials during this time. For example, he acted as editor of a magazine called the *Emancipator*. Although he wrote many articles for the magazine, he usually used a different name so that readers would focus their attention on the issue of slavery rather than on him. He also distributed thousands of antislavery pamphlets around the country. In 1839, Weld published an important book called *American Slavery as It Is: Testimony of a Thousand Witnesses*. This book reached a wider audience than any antislavery book ever had before and had a profound effect on its readers. In fact, Harriet Beecher Stowe used it as one of the main sources for her antislavery novel *Uncle Tom's Cabin*.

American Slavery as It Is included a collection of articles and notices from Southern newspapers, as well as letters from people who had had direct personal involvement with slavery. Weld tied all of these materials together with his own analysis. The idea behind the book was to show people the horrors of slavery. At that time, many Southern slaveowners argued that slavery provided the best possible life for black people. They claimed that blacks were not capable of caring for themselves. But Weld's book made an angry and passionate argument against such attitudes. "Suppose I should seize you, rob you of your liberty, drive you into the field, and make you work without pay as long as you live," he wrote. "Would that be justice and kindness, or monstrous injustice and cruelty?"

Disappears from public view

Throughout his career as an abolitionist, Weld experienced periods of intense energy and activity followed by emotional breakdowns. In addition, he had always felt a great need to look inward in an attempt to understand himself and define his relationship with God. Weld suffered his first major public defeat in 1836, when an angry mob prevented him from speaking in Troy, New York. Shortly afterward, he lost his voice from years of shouting to be heard in crowds. By the late 1830s, these factors convinced Weld to step back from the abolitionist movement and reevaluate his life. He gradually came to believe that his efforts were useless in solving America's problems.

In May 1838, Weld married fellow reformer Angelina Grimké. They opened a school in New Jersey in the 1840s and slowly faded from public view. They eventually had two sons and a daughter. When the Civil War began in 1861, Weld came forward to express his support for the Union cause. He even went on a brief speaking tour to encourage public support of the Emancipation Proclamation, an order by President **Abraham Lincoln** (1809–1865; see entry) that freed the slaves living in Confederate territory. He also spoke up during Reconstruction, the period in American history immediately following the Civil War, when the country struggled to settle its differences and bring the Southern states back into the Union.) Weld urged the federal government to send troops into the South to defend the rights of freed slaves. "The Nation is its citizens, and the Nation's right and duty to protect and defend its citizens, all of them, is absolute and paramount [of primary importance]," he stated.

In 1868, Weld and his family found an opportunity to help freed slaves directly. The Grimké sisters discovered that their father had had children with one of his slaves. They suddenly found that they had three half-brothers who had lived in slavery until the end of the Civil War. Weld and his wife accepted these men into their family, paid for their education, and helped them become some of the most prominent black men of their generation. Following the death of his wife in 1879, Weld lived quietly in Boston, Massachusetts. A humble and private man, he refused to allow anyone to write about his life or his activities in the early days of the abolition movement. He died on February 3, 1895.

Where to Learn More

Abzug, Robert H. *Passionate Liberator: Theodore Dwight Weld and the Dilemma of Reform*. New York: Oxford University Press, 1980.

Thomas, Benjamin P. *Theodore Weld: Crusader for Freedom*. New Brunswick, NJ: Rutgers University Press, 1950. Reprint, New York: Octagon Books, 1973.

Weld, Theodore Dwight. *American Slavery As It Is*. New York: American Anti-Slavery Society, 1839. Itasca, IL: F. E. Peacock Publishers, 1972.

Henry Wirz

Born November 1823
Zurich, Switzerland
Died November 10, 1865
Washington, D.C.

Confederate commander of Andersonville Prison

Only Confederate official executed for his actions during the Civil War

Henry Wirz was the commander of Andersonville Prison, a Confederate prisoner-of-war camp that housed more than forty thousand Union soldiers during the Civil War. More than twelve thousand Union prisoners died of disease and hunger at Andersonville, making the prison the most notorious of the many prison camps operated by the Union and Confederate armies. In November 1865, Wirz was hanged by the Federal government for crimes committed at Andersonville. He was the only Confederate official executed for his actions during the Civil War.

Swiss native sides with Confederacy

Heinrich Hartmann Wirz was born in Switzerland in 1823. As a youth he attended schools throughout Europe, including Zurich, Switzerland; Paris, France; and Berlin, Germany. He was interested in studying medicine, but pressure from his father led him to abandon a medical career and go into business. In 1849, Wirz immigrated to America. Changing his first name to Henry, he took a job as a doctor's assis-

"Our feelings cannot be described as we gazed on these poor human beings. . . . Such squalid, filthy wretchedness, hunger, disease, nakedness and cold, I never saw before."

A Union soldier, commenting on his fellow prisoners at Andersonville.

tant in Kentucky. By the time the Civil War started in 1861, Wirz had moved down to Louisiana, where he provided medical services at a plantation.

The Civil War came about because of long-standing disagreements between America's Northern and Southern states. One major area of disagreement was slavery, which was still practiced in the South. Many Northerners believed that slavery was wrong and wanted to abolish (eliminate) it. But the economy of the South had been built on slavery, and Southerners resented Northern efforts to halt or contain the practice. The two regions also disagreed about the appropriate balance between state and Federal authority. The Northern states favored a strong central government, but Southern states supported the concept of states' rights, which held that people in each state could make their own decisions about slavery and other issues. America's westward expansion during this time made these disputes even worse, since both sides wanted to spread their way of life—and their political ideas—into the new territories and states.

In early 1861, these differences became so great that eleven Southern states voted to secede from (leave) the United States and form a new country that allowed slavery, called the Confederate States of America. The North, though, was not willing to let the secessionist states break up the Union without a fight. In the spring of 1861, the two sides finally went to war.

When the Civil War began, Wirz quickly sided with the South, which he had adopted as his homeland. He joined Louisiana's Confederate forces in June 1861 as a private. Over the next fifteen months, he rose through the ranks of the army to the position of captain. His military record during this period, however, was controversial. For example, Wirz claimed that he was wounded in the Battle of Seven Pines in Virginia in 1862. But some historians doubt that he was even present at the battle.

Andersonville Prison

In 1863, Wirz was assigned to a military prison in Tuscaloosa, Alabama. In March of 1864, he was ordered to take command of a prisoner-of-war camp outside of Andersonville, a village in Sumter County, Georgia. The Andersonville prison had opened one month earlier. Located on sixteen acres of open land, it was designed to hold about ten thousand men. For the first two years of the war, the two sides managed to limit the number of prisoners they held by engaging in prisoner exchanges. Each side would exchange a certain number of prisoners for the same number of its own soldiers that had been captured by the enemy. In mid-1863, though, prisoner exchanges between the Federal and rebel (Confederate) armies ground to a halt because the Confederacy refused to turn over black prisoners. In the meantime, newly captured Union soldiers continued to pour into Andersonville, sometimes at the rate of four hundred a day.

By August 1864, Andersonville held more than thirty-three thousand Union soldiers, making it the fifth-largest city in the entire Confederacy. The size of the prison was increased to twenty-six acres, but this did not do much to improve the dreadful living conditions that the prisoners endured. Wirz did not allow them to build shelters, so most of them dug holes in the dirt and used scraps of clothing and blankets to protect themselves from the hot sun. In addition, widespread food shortages across the South meant that inmates at Andersonville received very little to eat. Each inmate's daily ration of food consisted of a teaspoon of salt, three tablespoons of beans, and a small amount of unsifted cornmeal. The water situation at Andersonville was terrible as well. A small stream ran through the camp, but prisoners were forced to use it both as their sole source of drinking water and as a latrine to carry away human waste. After awhile, the stream backed up and flooded large portions of the camp, turning some flooded sections into swampy areas crusted with human waste.

As the summer of 1864 came to an end, an average of more than one hundred Andersonville prisoners died each day from typhoid fever, gangrene, diarrhea, dysentery, and malnutrition. A small number were shot trying to escape or died when their burrows caved in on them, burying them alive. As the conditions worsened with each passing day, the morale of the hungry and feverish soldiers plummeted. Many imprisoned soldiers became hopelessly depressed at the idea of surviving major battles like Gettysburg (July 1863) or Antietam (September 1862), only to die slowly of diarrhea or dysentery.

Civil War Prisons

The Confederate prison in Andersonville, Georgia, is the best known of the many prisoner-of-war camps that operated during the American Civil War. But captured soldiers imprisoned at other camps endured horrible conditions as well. According to mortality (rate of death) statistics, Andersonville was not even the worst prison in the South. That distinction goes to a Confederate prison in Salisbury, North Carolina, where 34 percent of the 10,321 Union soldiers imprisoned died (by comparison, 29 percent of the Union prisoners held at Andersonville died). Meanwhile, at the Belle Isle Prison in Richmond, Virginia, prisoners received so little food that 90 percent of the Union soldiers who survived weighed less than one hundred pounds. "Can these be men?" asked writer Walt Whitman (1819–1892) when he saw several former prisoners at Belle Isle. "Are they not really mummied, dwindled corpses? They lay there, most of them, quite still, but with a horrible look in their eyes and skinny lips (often with not enough flesh to cover their teeth). . . . The dead [at Belle Isle] are not to be pitied as much as some of the living that have come from there . . . many of them are mentally imbecile [suffered mental collapse], and will never recuperate."

Prison conditions at some Union prisons were extremely poor as well, even though the North had far greater supplies of food, medicine, and other supplies. At the prison in Elmira, New York, for instance, approximately one out of four Confederate prisoners of war died. And at the Union prison in Rock Island, Illinois, a smallpox epidemic killed eighteen hundred Southern prisoners in a matter of weeks. Altogether, more than 56,000 Civil War soldiers (25,976 Confederate and 30,218 Union) lost their lives in prisoner-of-war camps. These terrible statistics make it clear that "the treatment of prisoners during the Civil War was something that neither side could be proud of," remarked James M. McPherson in *Battle Cry of Freedom*.

The terrible conditions that existed at many Civil War prison camps developed because the two sides stopped exchanging prisoners in May 1863. This halt came about because the South refused to trade black Union soldiers that it captured. Instead, they forced these black soldiers back into slavery in the South. This policy outraged President **Abraham Lincoln** (1809–1865; see entry) and his administration, which announced that all prisoner ex-

The situation at Andersonville became so bad that when newly captured Union soldiers arrived at the camp, they could hardly believe their eyes. "Hunger, sickness, exposure, and dirt had so transformed them that they more resem-

Prisoners at the Confederate prison in Andersonville, Georgia, await their rations on August 17, 1864. *(Photograph by A.J. Riddle. Courtesy of the National Archives and Records Administration.)*

changes would cease until black Union soldiers were included. This in turn caused the war prisons to become filled far beyond their normal capacity and made it harder for prison officials to provide for all of their inmates' needs.

"The prison camps in the Civil War were inhuman," wrote Bruce Catton in *Reflections on the Civil War*. "[But] with very few exceptions, like perhaps Wirz at Andersonville, the men in charge of the camps did the best they could. . . . The big trouble was that in North and South alike, as far as the authorities were concerned, the prison camps came last. They got what was left over when all of the other needs had been met. They were last on the line for food supplies, for medical supplies, for doctors, for housing, for clothing, for guards, for all of the things that are needed to run a prison camp."

As time passed, the end of prisoner exchanges hurt the South much more than the North, since they began to suffer from a severe shortage of soldiers. Because of this, some people have charged that the North was actually most responsible for ending the prisoner exchanges because it knew that a halt benefited its efforts to break the Confederate Army. But most historians agree that it was the South's refusal to exchange black soldiers that caused the deadlock. In fact, prisoner exchanges did take place from January 1865 forward, after the Confederate government finally agreed to exchange black, as well as white, Union troops.

bled walking skeletons, painted black," recalled one Union soldier who was part of a group of prisoners sent to Andersonville in the fall of 1864. "Our feelings cannot be described as we gazed on these poor human beings. . . . Such squalid [dirty], filthy wretchedness, hunger, disease, nakedness and cold, I never saw before."

Freed prisoners continue to suffer after the war ends

By the time the Civil War finally ended in the spring of 1865, conditions at Andersonville had claimed the lives of an estimated thirteen thousand Union prisoners of war, 29 percent of its total prisoner population of forty-five thousand But many of those who survived felt the effects of their imprisonment for the rest of their lives. Some never fully recovered from the physical stress that they endured, while others struggled to deal with emotional problems that developed as a result of being in the middle of so much death and suffering.

Northerners were horrified when they learned about the prison conditions at Andersonville. Their anger became even greater on April 27, 1865, when the boiler of an overloaded steamship called the *Sultana* blew up on the Mississippi River. An estimated seventeen hundred passengers drowned or burned alive in the accident. Most of the casualties were freed prisoners from Andersonville, on their way home to their families. The *Sultana* disaster remains the worst maritime disaster in American history.

Wirz on trial

In May 1865, Wirz wrote to Union officials asking for permission to return to Switzerland. "The duties I had to perform were arduous [difficult] and unpleasant and I am satisfied that no one can or will justly blame me for things that happened here and which were beyond my power to control," Wirz stated. But he was instead arrested and sent to Washington to be tried for war crimes.

Wirz's trial took place before a special military court that was charged with determining whether Wirz had committed war crimes during his command at Andersonville. Many historians believe that the Confederate officer did not receive a fair trial. For example, some witnesses who were friendly to Wirz were prevented from testifying. Other wit-

nesses claimed that Wirz personally shot or assaulted prisoners on dates when he was actually absent from the prison on medical leave. Prosecutors, though, also presented many other witnesses who testified about Wirz's cruelty and the camp's awful living conditions. After listening to the testimony, the court found Wirz "guilty of murder, in violation of the laws and customs of war," and ordered his execution. Just before he was to be executed, Union officials offered to spare his life if he would testify that Confederate president **Jefferson Davis** (1808–1889; see entry) engaged in a conspiracy to kill Union prisoners. But Wirz refused the offer, saying that "Jefferson Davis had no connection with me as to what was done at Andersonville." Wirz was hanged on November 10, 1865, in Washington's Old Capitol Prison. Wirz thus became the only Confederate official or soldier to be executed for his wartime activities.

Today, historians continue to debate Wirz's responsibility for conditions at Andersonville. Some people believe that the commandant was a cruel and evil man who did not care whether the prison's Union inmates died. Others, though, say that Wirz was only an inefficient administrator who found it impossible to provide for prisoners at a time when the entire Confederacy was crumbling.

Where to Learn More

The Court Martial of Henry Wirz Official Records. [Online] http://www.civilwarhome.com/wirzcourtmartial.htm (accessed on October 15, 1999).

Hesseltine, William B. *Civil War Prisons: A Study in War Psychology.* Columbus: Ohio State University Press, 1930. Reprint, 1998.

Marvel, William. *Andersonville: The Last Depot.* Chapel Hill: University of North Carolina Press, 1994.

Page, James Madison. *The True Story of Andersonville Prison: A Defense of Major Henry Wirz.* New York: Neale, 1908. Reprint, Scituate, MA: Digital Scanning, 1999.

University of Missouri at Kansas City School of Law. *Famous American Trials: The Trial of Captain Henry Wirz.* [Online] http://www.law.umkc.edu/faculty/projects/ftrials/wirz/wirz.htm (accessed on October 15, 1999).

Where to Learn More

The following list of resources focuses on material appropriate for middle school or high school students. Please note that the web site addresses were verified prior to publication, but are subject to change.

Books

Anders, Curt. *Hearts in Conflict: A One-Volume History of the Civil War*. Secaucus, NJ: Carol Pub. Group, 1994.

Anderson, Nancy Scott, and Dwight Anderson. *The Generals—Ulysses S. Grant and Robert E. Lee*. New York: Knopf, 1988.

Aptheker, Herbert. *Abolitionism: A Revolutionary Movement*. Boston: Twayne, 1989.

Basler, Roy P., ed. *The Collected Works of Abraham Lincoln*. New Brunswick, NJ: Rutgers University Press, 1953.

Berlin, Ira, Joseph P. Reidy, and Leslie S. Rowland, eds. *Freedom's Soldiers: The Black Military Experience in the Civil War*. New York: Cambridge University Press, 1998.

Blight, David W. *Frederick Douglass's Civil War: Keeping Faith in Jubilee*. Baton Rouge: Louisiana State University Press, 1989.

Bradford, Ned, ed. *Battles and Leaders of the Civil War*. New York: New American Library, 1984.

Buell, Thomas B. *The Warrior Generals: Combat Leadership in the Civil War.* New York: Crown, 1997.

Carter, Alden R. *The Civil War: American Tragedy.* New York: Franklin Watts, 1992.

Carter, Samuel. *The Last Cavaliers: Confederate and Union Cavalry in the Civil War.* St. Martin's Press, 1980.

Catton, Bruce. *The Centennial History of the Civil War.* 3 vols. Garden City, NY: Doubleday, 1961–65.

Catton, Bruce. *The Civil War.* Boston: Houghton Mifflin, 1960.

Chadwick, Bruce. *The Two American Presidents: A Dual Biography of Abraham Lincoln and Jefferson Davis.* Secaucus, NJ: Carol, 1999.

Chang, Ina. *A Separate Battle: Women and the Civil War.* New York: Scholastic, 1994.

Civil War Generals: An Illustrated Encyclopedia. New York: Gramercy, 1999.

Commager, Henry Steele. *The Blue and the Gray.* Indianapolis: Bobbs-Merrill, 1950.

Davis, William C. *The Commanders of the Civil War.* San Diego: Thunder Bay Press, 1999.

Davis, William C. *Jefferson Davis: The Man and His Hour.* New York: HarperCollins, 1991.

Donald, David Herbert. *Lincoln.* New York: Simon & Schuster, 1995.

Dowdey, Clifford. *Lee's Last Campaign: The Story of Lee and His Men against Grant.* Lincoln: University of Nebraska Press, 1993.

Foote, Shelby. *The Civil War: A Narrative.* 3 vols. New York: Random House, 1958–74.

Freeman, Douglas S. *Lee's Lieutenants.* 3 vols. New York: Scribner's, 1942–44.

Goen, C. C. *Broken Churches, Broken Nation.* Macon, GA: Mercer University Press, 1985.

Grant, Ulysses S. *Personal Memoirs of U. S. Grant.* New York: Library of America, 1990.

Green, Carl R., and William R. Sanford. *Confederate Generals of the Civil War.* Springfield, NJ: Enslow, 1998.

Green, Carl R., and William R. Sanford. *Union Generals of the Civil War.* Springfield, NJ: Enslow, 1998.

Grimsley, Mark. *The Hard Hand of War, Union Military Policy Toward Southern Civilians, 1861–1865.* New York: Cambridge University Press, 1995.

Gutman, Herbert G. *The Black Family in Slavery and Freedom.* New York: Pantheon, 1976.

Hargrove, Hondon B. *Black Union Soldiers in the Civil War.* Jefferson, NC: McFarland, 1988.

Harmon, Dan. *Civil War Generals.* Philadelphia: Chelsea House, 1997.

Harrell, Carolyn L. *When the Bells Tolled for Lincoln*. Macon, GA: Mercer University Press, 1997.

Haskins, J. *The Day Fort Sumter Was Fired On: A Photo History of the Civil War*. New York: Scholastic, 1995.

Hattaway, Herman. *Shades of Blue and Gray: An Introductory Military History of the Civil War*. Columbia: University of Missouri Press, 1997.

Hendrickson, Robert. *The Road to Appomattox*. New York: John Wiley & Sons, 1998.

Hennessey, John. *Return to Bull Run: The Campaign and Battle of Second Manassas*. New York: Simon & Schuster, 1992.

Holt, Michael F. *The Political Crisis of the 1850s*. New York: John Wiley & Sons, 1978.

Kunhardt, Philip B., Jr. *A New Birth of Freedom: Lincoln at Gettysburg*. Boston: Little, Brown, 1983.

Leonard, Elizabeth D. *All the Daring of the Soldier: Women of the Civil War Armies*. New York: W. W. Norton, 1999.

Lincoln, Abraham. *Abraham Lincoln: Speeches and Writings*. 2 vols. New York: Library of America, 1989.

Linderman, Gerald. *Embattled Courage: The Experience of Combat in the American Civil War*. New York: Free Press, 1987.

Litwack, Leon. *Been in the Storm So Long: The Aftermath of Slavery*. New York: Alfred A. Knopf, 1979.

Macdonald, John. *Great Battles of the Civil War*. New York: Macmillan, 1988.

Macmillan Encylopedia of the Confederacy. New York: Macmillan, 1998.

Massey, Mary Elizabeth. *Women in the Civil War*. Lincoln: University of Nebraska Press, 1966.

McFeely, William S. *Grant: A Biography*. New York: Norton, 1981.

McPherson, James M. *Battle Cry of Freedom*. New York: Oxford University Press, 1988.

McPherson, James M. *For Cause and Comrades: Why Men Fought in the Civil War*. New York: Oxford University Press, 1997.

McPherson, James M. *Ordeal by Fire: The Civil War and Reconstruction*. New York: Alfred A. Knopf, 1982.

McPherson, James M., ed. *Encyclopedia of Civil War Biographies*. Armonk, NY: Sharpe Reference, 2000.

Mitchell, Joseph B. *Military Leaders in the Civil War*. New York: Putnam, 1972.

Mitchell, Reid. *Civil War Soldiers: Their Expectations and Their Experiences*. New York: Viking, 1988.

Morris, Roy, Jr. *Sheridan: The Life and Wars of General Phil Sheridan*. New York: Crown, 1992.

Murphy, Jim. *The Long Road to Gettysburg*. New York: Scholastic, 1995.

Nolan, Alan T. *Lee Considered: General Robert E. Lee and Civil War History.* Chapel Hill: University of North Carolina Press, 1991.

Oates, Stephen B. *With Malice Toward None: The Life of Abraham Lincoln.* New York: Harper & Row, 1977.

Paludan, Phillip S. *The Presidency of Abraham Lincoln.* Lawrence: University Press of Kansas, 1994.

Potter, David M. *The Impending Crisis, 1848–1861.* New York: Harper & Row, 1976.

Ritter, Charles F., and Jon L. Wakelyn. *Leaders of the American Civil War.* Westport, CT: Greenwood Press, 1998.

Royster, Charles. *The Destructive War: William Tecumseh Sherman, Stonewall Jackson, and the Americans.* New York: Alfred A. Knopf, 1991.

Sandburg, Carl. *Abraham Lincoln: The War Years.* 4 vols. New York: Harcourt Brace, 1939.

Sifakis, Stewart. *Who Was Who in the Civil War.* New York: Facts on File, 1988.

Stewart, James Brewer. *Holy Warriors: The Abolitionists and American Slavery.* New York: Hill & Wang, 1976.

Stokesbury, James L. *A Short History of the Civil War.* New York: William Morrow, 1995.

Thomas, Emory. *The Confederate Nation, 1861–1865.* New York: Harper & Row, 1979.

Tracey, Patrick Austin. *Military Leaders of the Civil War.* New York: Facts on File, 1993.

Trelease, Allen W. *Reconstruction: The Great Experiment.* New York: Harper & Row, 1971.

Trudeau, Noah Andre. *Like Men of War: Black Troops in the Civil War, 1862–1865.* Boston: Little, Brown, 1998.

Venet, Wendy Hamand. *Neither Ballots Nor Bullets: Women Abolitionists and the Civil War.* Charlottesville: University Press of Virginia, 1991.

Ward, Geoffrey C. *The Civil War: An Illustrated History.* New York: Alfred A. Knopf, 1990.

Woodworth, Steven E. *Jefferson Davis and His Generals.* Lawrence: University Press of Kansas, 1990.

World Wide Web

American Civil War/Conflict Between the States. http://americanhistory.miningco.com/education/history/americanhistory/msub13.htm (accessed on October 20, 1999).

American Civil War Homepage. http://sunsite.utk.edu/civil-war (accessed on October 20, 1999).

American Civil War Resources on the Internet. http://www.janke.washcoll. edu/civilwar/civilwar.htm (accessed on October 20, 1999).

Civil War Music and Poetry and Music of the War Between the States. http://users.erols.com/kfraser/ (accessed on October 20, 1999).

Library of Congress. *Gettysburg Address Exhibit.* www.lcweb.loc.gov/ex-hibits/gadd (accessed on October 20, 1999).

Library of Congress, American Memory. *Selected Civil War Photographs.* lcweb2.loc.gov/ammem/cwphome.html (accessed on October 20, 1999).

Rutgers University Libraries. *Civil War Resources on the Internet.* http:// www.libraries.rutgers.edu/rulib/socsci/hist/civwar-2.html (accessed on October 20, 1999).

Index

Note: *Italic* type indicates volume number; **boldface** indicates main entries and their page numbers; (ill.) indicates photos and illustrations.

D

Daguerre, Louis-Jacques-Mandé, *1:* 42

Daniel, John M., *2:* 342

Davis, Jefferson, *1:* 93–103, 93 (ill.); and assassination of Abraham Lincoln, *1:* 32, and Beauregard, Pierre G. T., *1:* 16, 17, 18; and Bragg, Braxton, *1:* 51, 52, 54; and "Dixie," *1:* 216; and Fort Sumter, *2:* 272; and Hood, John Bell, *1:* 204, 205–6; and Johnston, Joseph E., *1:* 244–45, 246, 247, 248, 249, 250; and Lee, Robert E., *2:* 256, 259; and Pollard, Edward A., *2:* 339, 342, 344; and spies, *1:* 90, 183; and Stephens, Alexander H., *2:* 407, 412–13; and Tompkins, Sally L., *2:* 463; and Van Lew, Elizabeth, *2:* 490–91; and Wirz, Henry, *2:* 505

Davis, Varina, *1:* 83, 101

Delany, Martin R., *1:* 105–12, 105 (ill.)

Democratic Party, *1:* 110–11

"Dixie," *1:* 216

Douglas, Stephen A., *2:* 265, 269–70, 271, 281, 367, 410, 482

Douglass, Frederick, *1:* 57, 107, 113–20, 113 (ill.); *2:* 430, 469, 476

Dred Scott v. Sandford, *2:* 347, 351–52

DuPont, Samuel, *2:* 403

E

Early, Jubal, *2:* 330, 331, 385–87

Edison, Thomas, *1:* 46

Edmonds, Emma, *1:* 121–26, 121 (ill.), 123 (ill.)

Election of 1864, *2:* 314–15, 366–67

Emancipation Proclamation, *1:* 109, 177; *2:* 273–74

Emerson, John, *2:* 348–50

Emmett, Daniel Decatur, *1:* 216

F

Farragut, David G., *1:* 84, 127–34, 127 (ill.)

Fifteenth Amendment, *1:* 179

Fifty-Fourth Massachusetts Regiment, *1:* 109, 118; *2:* 375–80

Finney, Charles G., *2:* 495

First Battle of Bull Run. *See* Bull Run, First Battle of

First South Carolina Volunteers, *2:* 403

Five Forks, Battle of, *2:* 381, 388–89

Floyd, John B., *1:* 153

Forrest, Nathan Bedford, *1:* 135–42, 135 (ill.)

Fort Pillow Massacre, *1:* 139–40

Fort Sumter, *1:* 11, 14–15, 84, 99

Fourteenth Amendment, *1:* 110, 179

Fredericksburg, Battle of, *1:* 63, 67, 75

Freedmen's Bureau, *1:* 110; *2:* 450

Frémont, John C., *1:* 143–50, 143 (ill.)

Fugitive Slave Act, *1:* 57, 213; *2:* 430

G

Gardner, Alexander, *1:* 43, 45, 46

Garfield, James, *1:* 192

Garrison, William Lloyd, *1:* 116; *2:* 469

Gayle, John, *1:* 153

Gettysburg Address, *2:* 274

Gettysburg, Battle of, *1:* 71, 76–78, 187, 190; *2:* 258–59, 285, 289–91, 292, 317, 320–21, 440–41

Gibson, James, *1:* 45

Gorgas, Josiah, *1:* 151–57, 151 (ill.)

Gould, Andrew W., *1:* 139

Grand Army of the Republic, *1:* 126

Grant, Ulysses S., *1:* 159–70, 159 (ill.); *2:* 337 (ill.); and assassination of Abraham Lincoln, *1:* 29; and Battle of Shiloh, *1:* 16, 17, 51; and Battle of the Crater, *1:* 68, 69; and Bragg,

Y